PENGUIN BOOKS

THE PENGUIN BOOK OF
ASHES
ANECDOTES
1882–2005

Gideon Haigh has been writing about sport
and business for more than twenty-two years.
The Penguin Book of Ashes Anecdotes 1882–2005
is the twenty-first book he has either written or
edited. He lives in Melbourne with his cat, Trumper.

THE PENGUIN BOOK OF

ASHES
ANECDOTES

1882–2005

GIDEON HAIGH

foreword by **DAVID FRITH**

PENGUIN BOOKS

PENGUIN BOOKS

Published by the Penguin Group
Penguin Group (Australia)
250 Camberwell Road, Camberwell, Victoria 3124, Australia
(a division of Pearson Australia Group Pty Ltd)
Penguin Group (USA) Inc.
375 Hudson Street, New York, New York 10014, USA
Penguin Group (Canada)
90 Eglinton Avenue East, Suite 700, Toronto ON M4P 2Y3, Canada
(a division of Pearson Penguin Canada Inc.)
Penguin Books Ltd
80 Strand, London WC2R 0RL, England
Penguin Ireland
25 St Stephen's Green, Dublin 2, Ireland
(a division of Penguin Books Ltd)
Penguin Books India Pvt Ltd
11 Community Centre, Panchsheel Park, New Delhi – 110 017, India
Penguin Group (NZ)
67 Apollo Drive, Mairangi Bay, Auckland 1310, New Zealand
(a division of Pearson New Zealand Ltd)
Penguin Books (South Africa) (Pty) Ltd
24 Sturdee Avenue, Rosebank, Johannesburg 2196, South Africa

Penguin Books Ltd, Registered Offices: 80 Strand, London WC2R 0RL, England

First published by Penguin Group (Australia), 2006

10 9 8 7 6 5 4 3 2 1

Cover design by Susannah Low © Penguin Group (Australia)
Text design by George Dale © Penguin Group (Australia)
Cover photographs: The Ashes Cup – Getty Images; Australian cricketers (front left) –
London Stereoscopic Company/Getty Images; Cricket ball (front and back cover)
– Chemistry/Getty Images; Cricket 2005 (front right and spine) – Philip Brown/Corbis
Typeset in Sabon by Midland Typesetters, Australia
Printed and bound in Australia by McPherson's Printing Group, Maryborough, Victoria

National Library of Australia
Cataloguing-in-Publication data:

Haigh, Gideon.
The Penguin book of Ashes anecdotes 1882–2005.
Bibliography.
ISBN-13: 978 0 14300 528 5.
ISBN-10: 0 14 300528 6.
1. Test matches (Cricket) – Australia – History. 2. Test matches (Cricket) –
England – History. 3. Cricket players – Australia – Anecdotes. 4. Cricket players
– England – Anecdotes. I. Title.
796.35865

www.penguin.com.au

CONTENTS

FOREWORD

Ashes cricket – Test matches between Australia and England – arose from the most auspicious of beginnings. The historic match itself – in August 1882 at The Oval, in south London – contained the highest drama, the chief immediate consequence of which was an hilarious spoof announcement. And a few weeks later came a classic romantic sequel. Thus was launched the greatest ongoing sporting contest the modern world has known.

The colonial boys who played under Billy Murdoch's captaincy in that fateful match symbolised an Australian nation that still awaited formal constitutional establishment. During the late nineteenth century, cricket served better than any other pursuit to blend the aspirations of the jealous, squabbling states.

The colonial cricketers, still lacking a recognisable uniform, shocked the Mother Country with that seven-run victory at The Oval, to inspire, among many souvenirs, a latter-day poem by poet laureate John Masefield, re-registering the high drama. More significantly, and more lastingly by far, some English jokers were moved to pen a tongue-in-cheek memorial notice in *The Sporting Times* lamenting (for the first of so many times) the death of English cricket. They could never have guessed the full implications of the final line: 'The body will be cremated and the ashes taken to Australia.'

The romantic element came with the Melbourne society belles' bright creation of the tiny terracotta urn containing the mysterious cinders: a bail . . . a ball . . . a lady's veil? Long may the mystique remain. One of the girls, Florence Morphy, fell in love with the towering gentleman who captained England, the Honourable Ivo Bligh, and their subsequent marriage forged one of the most appealing of Anglo–Australian partnerships. Ivo became Lord Darnley, and after his death in 1927 Florence presented the delicate Ashes urn to Marylebone Cricket Club, who have displayed it at Lord's ever since.

It is way beyond our means to calculate just how many million words have been penned and typed, and how much sweat and blood shed, in the cause of Ashes cricket. Not only the senior Test match series, it is also the richest by far in its tradition and history. It was only a matter of time before somebody came to the conclusion that some of the most interesting writings from the 124 years since Fred Spofforth stunned W.G. Grace and the rest of the Englishmen alongside the Kennington gas-holders should be gathered for our fascination and entertainment.

From the last years of Queen Victoria's reign, through the carefree Edwardian era, across the Charleston years of post-war shock and gay abandon and the 1930s – Bradman, McCabe, Grimmett, O'Reilly, and Hammond, Leyland, Verity – years of swelling global apprehension, the cricket scarred by Bodyline but still free of commercialisation, on and on went the cavalcade. After the Second World War came dramatic Ashes years within living memory of many still alive, the profile changing gradually as society entertained fresh fads. While the fundamentals remained, the trimmings altered. Behaviour on and off the field of play shifted, not always attractively.

While the 1960s were dull in Ashes Test terms, the arrival of Ian Chappell and his 'ugly Australians' livened matters, everything suddenly being turned on its head when the revolutionary World Series Cricket was launched in the wake of cricket's greatest ever birthday party, the Centenary Test match in Melbourne in 1977. From then on money became the driving force – which is not to say that patriotism was in any way diminished. Quite the reverse. It has sometimes become manic.

The modern era has seen an unprecedented grip on the Ashes by Australia, a lopsidedness that seemed for a time to threaten the credibility of the tradition. Michael Vaughan and his Englishmen put that right in 2005 in a series that, after careful consideration, was proclaimed the greatest Test series of all time, Ashes or not.

So, from all this it may easily be deduced that there is a super-abundance of Ashes anecdotage. To those who already know and love their Ashes folklore one would only have to mention some of the more colourful characters who have taken part in these battles over the years: for Australia – Spofforth, George Bonnor, Arthur Coningham, Albert and Harry Trott, Ernie Jones, Warwick Armstrong, H.V. Hordern, Charlie Macartney, Arthur Mailey, Stork Hendry, Bert Ironmonger, Bill O'Reilly, Chuck Fleetwood-Smith, Ernie McCormick, Sid Barnes, Lindsay Hassett, Keith Miller, Sam Loxton, Bill Johnston, Jim Burke, Bill Lawry, Wally Grout, Johnny Gleeson, Kerry O'Keeffe, Terry Jenner, Ian Chappell, Dennis Lillee, Jeff Thomson, Rod Marsh, Max Walker, Ashley Mallett, David Hookes, Rodney Hogg, Greg Ritchie, Dean Jones, Greg Matthews, Merv Hughes, David Boon, Shane Warne . . .

Pause to give the humour glands time for recovery and then reflect on some of the English characters – W.G. Grace, Ted Peate, Billy Barnes, Will Scotton, Bobby Peel, Johnny Briggs, Archie MacLaren, S.F. Barnes, Bernard Bosanquet, Frank Foster, George Gunn, Patsy Hendren, E.R. Wilson, Cec Parkin, Douglas Jardine (no, not many laughs there, but no more interesting character ever played Ashes cricket), the Maurices Tate and Leyland, Tommy Mitchell, Eddie Paynter, Denis Compton, Freddie Brown, Fred Trueman, Tony Lock, Johnny Wardle, Ken Barrington,

Ted Dexter, Colin Milburn, Geoff Boycott, David Lloyd, Tony Greig, Derek Randall, Ian Botham, Jack Russell, Darren Gough, Phil Tufnell, Allan Lamb, 'Freddie' Flintoff, Kevin Pietersen. There's enough talent and fun here to fill the vaudeville halls of both countries for months on end.

Just as central is the role played by the writers who have recorded the cricketers' exploits and their character foibles. We owe an incalculable debt of gratitude to the likes of M.A. Noble, Ray Robinson, Jack Fingleton, A.G. Moyes, Neville Cardus and John Arlott.

Importantly, a word on the compiler of this absorbing compendium of Australia-versus-England anecdotes. Just as Shane Warne came along and rescued wrist-spin bowling when it was on the verge of global extinction because of the obsession with fast bowling, so Gideon Haigh has spared his generation from the serious charge of obliterating history.

History has always been a natural and vital means of enlightenment and entertainment in our lives. In the rudderless, intrusive world of the twenty-first century it has become fashionable to either mock or abandon the study of history. This is an arrogant and tasteless posture, promoted by repressives who have betrayed their responsibilities. And if there is proportionately slightly less in this collection from the modern age, it is because today's lavishly rewarded and feted 'celebrity' Test cricketers (and I expect no forgiveness for saying so) belong to an age that is stereotyped, less relaxed and much narrower in outlook than that of their distant predecessors.

Almost alone among his age group, Gideon Haigh has demonstrated an acute understanding of cricket's precious past, and has already penned some distinguished works of his own. His approach to research and interpretation of times past guarantee that the reader will enjoy page after page to amuse and surprise.

Shame on all the poor souls who assert that today is all that matters. For them, were they only smart enough to know it, their contemporary time must also soon fade into yesteryear. Perhaps then, and only then, will these philistines come to realise that to blank the past is to switch off the most intriguing entertainment known to man. This absorbing collection of Ashes anecdotes is yet another item of proof.

DAVID FRITH
2006

David Frith has written many books on the Ashes theme and with his strong allegiance to both of the old enemies he writes evenhandedly. *Bodyline Autopsy*, his work on the sensational 1932–33 Test series, was an award-winner, and the latest of his Ashes series books, *Battle for the Ashes*, dealt with the never-to-be forgotten 2005 ecounter.

PREFACE

Let me declare myself: I'm an out-and-out, old-fashioned lover of the game played in Heaven, a game noted for its tongue-twisting and often ribaldly referred-to field placings: how could the uninitiated possibly translate 'place your square-leg on the fence and drop your short-leg back, ready for the mis-timed hook'? It's a game that can only be fully understood by those who have donned the *whites* (I'm sorry, but the pyjama game's for bananas or Broadway musicals – *The Pajama Game* made a star of Shirley MacLaine in 1954), and stood on a paddock, an oval or a green sward and day-dreamed of handsomely off-driving a four, or removing that pesky no. 11's off-stump, to clinch the Ashes.

I've been a book publisher for forty-five years, and of the more than 1200 books I've been associated with, a satisfying half-century have been on cricket. John Arlott once observed, 'All the best ideas, it is said, are simple,' and after listening to and watching (often between partially closed fingers) the gripping 2005 Ashes battle, one now generally regarded as the most compelling ever, and then re-living it while editing David Frith's enthralling book on the series, the question came to my mind: was there available a book containing Ashes stories, quotes and gossip, stretching back to 1882? A quick search told me 'no', and an approach to writer, historian and cricket-lover Gideon Haigh to compile one happily received an equally quick 'yes'. And what better choice: as David Frith says in his as-always eloquent and authoritative foreword, 'Gideon has demonstrated an acute understanding of cricket's precious past, and has already penned some distinguished works of his own.' I should also add that my approach to Penguin's ever-perceptive publishing director Bob Sessions received an equally fast 'yes', and so in no time we were underway.

Gideon Haigh's search for material has been extraordinarily wide-ranging, as even a cursory glance at his 252-book bibliography will reveal. And, to use that well-worn cliché 'The more things change the more they stay the same', it is shown to be remarkably true of cricket. On the face of it the 2006 version of the game, with its attendant high-tech, high-profile spotlight on the players, and instant-gratification Twenty20 'matches', is far removed from 1882's colonial days. Then, match reports took weeks to reach the away team's supporters; players commonly wore straw boaters, short neck ties and sported severe centre-head partings in team photographs; and matches were played on treacherous uncovered wickets. Yet as this book reveals, common themes remain: chivalry (yes, even in the 2000s); mutual appreciation of other players' skills, regardless of whose side they represent; competitiveness in every era; boundless wit; and, above all, the sheer joy at being chosen to play in an Ashes Test.

As every cricketer knows, no matter how many memorable innings are played, wickets bagged or catches plucked from the air, there are select moments that stand out. And for me the publishing equivalent is *The Penguin Book of Ashes Anecdotes 1882–2005*. Thank you, Gideon, for compiling such a fine innings, full of neat flicks, full-blooded drives, subtle glances and powerful cuts; some outswing and swerve, sharp turn, a short one or two, and a deadly yorker. The crowd applauds a memorable all-round performance.

RICHARD SMART
2006

INTRODUCTION

America and England were famously described by Oscar Wilde as two nations divided by a common language; Australia and England are two nations divided by a common game. Cricket was imported to Australia more than two centuries ago, but it did not surge in popularity until buoyed by that most deeply embedded of rivalries: between reproving parent and unruly offspring. Almost everything about the relations between the countries has changed since, and the ties now hang loosely indeed. But somehow, cricket hostilities bring forth a flood of feeling, one country's champagne and schadenfreude being the other's beer and brooding.

The Ashes lends itself naturally to the telling of stories. Their inauguration 124 years ago was a jest made real: the mock obituary for English cricket in *The Sporting Times* by Reginald Shirley Brooks turned into a physical artefact by the society belles in the circle of Lady Clarke at Rupertswood. The contents of this book are, likewise, spontaneous acts given permanent form: events that were first thought worth honouring in the memory, and that now form part of the lore and legend of this most enduring rivalry. To quote the

1

Australian historian Greg Dening, 'There is nothing so momentary as a sporting achievement and nothing so lasting as the memory of it.'

In Test cricket, too, stories have the chance to ferment and mature before bottling. The breadth and depth of the game's literature is often chalked up to its steadily unfolding five-day duration, which allows pauses for thought and for documentation. That certainly seems to explain why so few decent yarns concern one-day cricket: everybody's panting too much to deliver the shrewd verdict or the witty riposte. But there may be more to it. The contest is only one dimension of Test cricket: more time is spent in states of anticipation and reflection, which makes for interludes of anxiety and self-control, defiance and resignation, exultation and regret.

Sifted from more than 260 books, newspapers and periodicals, *The Penguin Book of Ashes Anecdotes 1882–2005* attends first to the most exalted players and greatest contests – but it also, like the games themselves, involves a little more. The Ashes fosters competition on whose limits there is not universal agreement: thus, a chronicle of gamesmen, beginning with Dr W.G. Grace, who bent the rules, sometimes to breaking point. The Ashes, similarly, transplants young, sometimes naïve and impressionable men from one country to another, with all that this entails: thus, a chapter of travellers' tales, often demonstrating how small differences can beget big misunderstandings. The Ashes, of course, as any Barmy Army infantryman will tell you, is a theatre in which the audience are very much part of the action: thus, an epidemiological study of that most virulent of contagions, cricket fever. The Ashes, finally, is a world where skill and preparation smack into luck and chance: thus, some stories of the excesses of superstition and the enchantments of selection.

Any cricket history nowadays that emphasises the Ashes courts the displeasure of the game's globalists. The rivalry has never wanted for doomsayers and detractors, and there are neophiliacs now who see a five-day Test as fifteen Twenty20 games forgone. Yet cricket without history and sentiment is a sterile spectacle: even the galacticos gathered by the International Cricket Council could not save the 2005 Super Series in Australia from looking like an ugly trophy in search of a purpose.

That is not to say that the history has been a pageant of unleavened triumph. The Ashes have known their doldrums and *longueurs* – in the 1960s because the gravity and ceremony surrounding Test matches seemed to stifle enterprise and imagination, while in the 1990s the decadence of English cricket rendered the contests hopelessly one-sided.

Yet it is amazing how quickly the whiff of a contest stirs the embers in the fire. When England stormed back from a 0–1 deficit to recapture the trophy in 2005, sixteen years since their dispossession, the scenes at The Oval could have been from 1953, or 1926, or even 1882 – likewise the sense of euphoric unreality among one country's supporters and chagrined disbelief among the other's. One priceless scene unfolded as bad light and rain threatened to interrupt play on the penulti-mate day, at a time when Australia was pressing for victory and England seeking the sanctuary of a draw – the former's fans could be seen removing their shirts and donning sunglasses, while the latter's faithful bran-dished umbrellas and cheered evidence of the use of light meters. Laughter rich and rueful echoed round the ground. The sense was of two countries not merely divided by a common game but united by an ardent rivalry. Long may it continue.

1 | GIANTS OF THE GAME

Great cricketers attract stories as great ships attract barnacles. This chapter collects 260 stories encrusting eight-five outstanding reputations from Australia and England, from Grace to Gilchrist, showing them in action and repose, triumph and adversity. Sir Donald Bradman is chief among them, for everyone who so much as stood next to him at a bus stop has a Bradman story: just as his run-making prowess occasions awe, his moments of fallibility affirm his common humanity. But there are plenty more. Nowadays, the stat enjoys primacy in any reckoning of a player's career. But often a story will do just as well, if not better, in conveying the esteem or otherwise that he enjoyed among contemporary players and public. If it didn't, in fact, cricket would not be the game it is.

DR W.G. GRACE

The best cricketer of all, thought his chief Australian rival, Billy Murdoch . . .

What do I think of W.G.? Why, that I have never seen his like and never shall. I tell you my opinion, which is that W.G. should never be put underground. When he dies his body ought to be embalmed and permanently exhibited in the British Museum as 'the colossal cricketer of all time'.

The Memorial Biography of Dr. W.G. Grace,
Gordon, Hawke and Harris

. . . and certainly among the biggest, observed an Australian in 1891–92.

He is a very big, powerful man, with a bristly black beard nearly to his waist, somewhat slanting eyes, great muscular arms and huge hands. And, Great Scott – such feet! He could get two pounds a week and his 'tucker' merely to walk about in grasshopper districts to kill off the pest.

The Memorial Biography of Dr. W.G. Grace,
Gordon, Hawke and Harris

A fount of cricket wisdom . . .

A promising young batsman invited by W.G. to turn out for his team was asked benevolently where he would prefer to bat in the order. The reply was a slightly boastful, 'It doesn't really matter, Doctor, I've never made a duck in my life.' His gargantuan skipper thundered back, 'Never made a blob, eh? Then it's number eleven for you. Not enough experience.'

Victor Trumper, Sharpham

. . . and onto every trick, even when tossing.
The Australian [Jack Blackham] used a fearfully battered, favourite penny which he had carried for many years. It was apparently so hard to distinguish one side from the other that Grace tossed it up two or three times to see whether it was loaded to come down on a particular side. After careful investigation he seemed satisfied enough to lead his men into the field.

W.G. Down Under: Grace in Australia 1873–74 and 1891–92, Smith and Williams

Recalled by his last opening partner, Charles Fry.
When we were walking out from the pavilion as first pair for England in my first Test the Old Man said to me, 'Now, Charlie, remember that I'm not a sprinter like you.'

Life Worth Living, Fry

Recalled by opponent Monty Noble.
The first time I played against him was at the Crystal Palace in 1899. Just before I went into bat, Hugh Trumble came to me and said, 'Now look here, Monty, when you go in, take care W.G. doesn't talk you out.'

Grace, Hughie explained, had a reputation for getting young players bustled if he could only get them to talk at the wicket.

The Game's the Thing, Noble

FRED SPOFFORTH

Australia's first great Test bowler was a raconteur of whimsical imagination, recalled C.I. Thornton.

Spofforth was at his happiest in country matches where his stories – always told with an air of sincerity – used to amuse people immensely. One special one that never failed to please used to be given in the following circumstances. I would say to him at lunch, 'How did you learn to be such a fine short-slip, Spoff?' And he would reply, 'When I was quite young, I made a boy, when out for a walk, throw stones into a hedge, and as the sparrows flew out I caught 'em.'

Wisden, 1927

It had always taken a strong man to stand up to him and the stories of his being on the wrong end of a joke are very few. One concerned umpire Jim Phillips, an Australian who played for Middlesex before joining the ranks of the judiciary. He once no-balled Spofforth for dragging his foot well over the crease. 'Sorry, Jim. My foot slipped!' explained Spofforth with an evil grin. Next ball, perfectly legitimate, was also called by Phillips, and Spofforth turned upon him and addressed him with a few words chosen at random. 'Sorry, Spoff,' said the umpire blandly. 'My tongue slipped.'

The Fast Men, Frith

BILLY MURDOCH
Recalled by W.G. Grace.

I am not sure, notwithstanding his brilliant batting, that it was not as captain of the Australian XI that he earned his greatest distinction. He was an ideal captain, a born tactician, a genial chief, a firm though gentle ruler, and a man of singular pluck and resource. On one occasion he was captaining an Australian XI against one of our leading counties, and when play had been in progress a little while, Murdoch as captain thought a change of bowling desirable. Addressing one of the bowlers – a well-known cricketer, whose name I need not disclose – he said, 'Mr So-and-so will go on now.' The bowler objected; said he hadn't been given a fair chance. Murdoch said nothing and let him keep on bowling unchanged until the end of the day's play. It is needless to say the bowler never again complained that he was not given a fair chance.

Cricket Reminiscences and Personal Recollections,
Grace

JOHN BLACKHAM

Australia's first great keeper did the job for seventeen years, attaining unprecedented standards.

Once when W.H. Cooper was bowling on the Melbourne ground, George Ulyett jumped out to hit him. He missed the ball and, never looking back, walked straight to the pavilion. On entering the gate, someone said, 'Why didn't you try to get back, he might have missed it?' That 'he' was Jack Blackham. The reply was simply, 'Oi never knowed him to miss one.' Rather a compliment to our prince of wicketkeepers, wasn't it?

The Australasian, 16 January 1909

Cooper recalled an example of Blackham's sportsmanship at Lord's in 1884.

W.G. stepped out to a ball from me and apparently W.G. was six inches out or probably more. He missed the ball and Blackham had the bails off like a shot. W.G. waited for the appeal but none was made. On crossing I asked Blackham why W.G. was not out. He said, 'I did not appeal.' To the question why, he said, 'I was in such hurry to get W.G. out that I took the ball a couple of inches in front of the wicket.'

Wisden Cricket Monthly, June 1983

ARTHUR SHREWSBURY

Shrewsbury, England's best professional batsman of the day, toured Australia four times, learning to put up with the heavy-handed colonial humour in 1886–87.

A local wag sought an introduction to him and gravely stated he had a memento which he begged him to accept. It consisted of a very diminutive pair of specs, and the presenter intimated that they were presented to keep Arthur in mind of his two ducks in the match with New South Wales the previous week, and of his inability to play Turner's bowling. Shrewsbury took the specs so as not to spoil the fun. He had been 'b Turner 0' in each innings in the match in question.

Alfred Shaw: Cricketer, Pullin

TED PEATE

Yorkshire's left-arm spinner Ted Peate drove one (anonymous) Australian opponent to extreme measures.

The Yorkshireman beat him with a clinking leg-break in the first innings. The batsman, determined that such a disaster should not happen again, took a bat into his room at the hotel and began to make strokes at imaginary balls. At one he would play back and mutter, 'That's the way to play you, Peate.' Then he would play forward, remarking, 'Not this time, Peate, my boy.' At last he ventured on a big hit at a leg-ball, and swinging round with a 'How do like that, Peate?' sent the toilet seat which he had forgotten all about in fragments on the floor. Later on in the day, confident that he would make a score, he faced the real Peate – and was bowled first ball.

Cricket of Today, vol. 2, 1902

JOHNNY BRIGGS

Lancashire's Johnny Briggs was admired for his good fellowship as much as his slow bowling.

He was a great peacemaker and his way of settling disputes was, 'Look here, you fellows, if you'd stand each other beer until the floor gets up and hits both your stoopid heads, you'll then know that t'other is champion friend of each.'

Background of Cricket, Gordon

Briggs was baffled by dark-skinned Sam Morris, a Tasmanian of Caribbean ancestry, representing Australia in 1884.

One of our opponents was a 'gentleman of colour' named 'Sammy' Morris, a real good fellow and an excellent cricketer, professional at the time for the Richmond Club. He wore a white shirt with sleeves reaching down to just above the wrist. He was fielding 'out in the country' when Johnny Briggs came in to bat, and on the little Lancastrian seeing him he exclaimed in astonishment, 'Well I'm blest, if there isn't a fellow fielding out there in black kid gloves.'

Alfred Shaw: Cricketer, Pullin

ALICK BANNERMAN

An indispensable member of early Australian XIs, opener Alick Bannerman had no time for levity.

He was always very keen and hardworking; in fact his keenness often developed into outright seriousness. I remember once we had an erratic, lightsome player on our side who, to beguile the tedium of waiting between overs, sang snatches of music-hall ditties. Alick stood it for a while, then went up to our merry friend and – with the seriousness of a judge sentencing a murderer to death – made this speech. 'Do you know, my friend, you are playing cricket? If you want to play cricket, play it, and if you want to sing, go and sing, but for heaven's sake don't sing comic songs in the slips!'

With Bat and Ball, Giffen

His fielding at mid-off was uncommonly aggressive, as shown during a tour game against Yorkshire at Harrogate.

Peate kept dodging a yard or so out of his crease and back again, 'playing the Angora' as George Bonnor in his refined way termed it. Alick noticed this, but did not pretend to throw at the wickets until presently Peate advanced about an extra foot. Then, with surprising dash and rapidity of action, Alick picked up and, letting fly at the stumps, knocked the middle peg out before the astonished Peate could get back.

Never before have I seen a batsman more utterly crestfallen than Peate seemed as he walked to the pavilion amidst the assembled thousands. The only persons who did not laugh were Peate himself and little Alick, whose dander was up to such an extent that his moustache bristled as he said, 'Play the Angora with me, will you?'

The Australasian, 16 October 1897

Bannerman's highest Test score was 91 against England at Sydney in 1891–92, an effort that took seven and a half hours, during which he scored from only five of the 204 balls bowled to him by William Attewell, but which underwrote an Australian victory.

I shall never forget the sight of the field round him as he stonewalled. There was W.G. at point, almost on the point of his bat; Lohmann a couple of yards away at slip; Peel at silly point; Stoddart only a dozen yards away at mid-off; and Briggs at silly mid-on. One gentleman remarked that it reminded him of the famous painting 'Anguish' in which a bevy of crows are swarming round a dead lamb over which the mother is watching. A barracker called out, 'Look out, Alick, or W.G. will have his hand in your pocket!' But Alick stonewalled on, imperturbably blocking the straight ones, sardonically smiling at the off-theory and judiciously tapping a rare loose one to leg. Suddenly he swished at an off ball and cut it past W.G.'s ear to the boundary, and then what a yell rent the air! He was eventually caught by W.G. off Briggs, who had simply tossed balls down slowly with as much twizzle on them as possible in the hope that he might lead Alick into an indiscretion. But the Englishmen had to wait seven and a half hours for that indiscretion! Truly patience is a virtue.

With Bat and Ball, Giffen

GEORGE GIFFEN

A famous fancier of his own abilities, George Giffen got free rein when he was appointed Australia's captain in 1894–95.

The first time he had the say in a Test he bowled 78.2 overs in England's 333 at Melbourne – 23 more overs than anyone else. Other players at last persuaded Hugh Trumble to ask George to take himself off. Giffen, 'Yes, I think I'll go on the other end.' Telling the story against himself years later, Trumble grinned, 'He did – and finished with six wickets.'

On Top Down Under, Robinson

HARRY TROTT

Always confident of his abilities, Harry Trott thought selection for the 1893 team to England a facile business.

H.T. is asked what chance he has of getting into the team for England and he replies, 'Well, that 196 against East Melbourne got me as far as Albany; the

63 in the first innings against NSW got me to Colombo; the 70 not out in the second innings carried me as far as Suez; and being put on to bowl first against SA placed me in the Mediterranean; once there, nothing can keep me back, you know, so I am safe in England.'

The Australasian, 14 January 1893

Trott's easygoing nature and sharp tactical brain made him an ideal captain the next time he toured England.

As befitted one destined to spend his whole working life in the post office as a postman and mail-sorter, he met everyone alike. On one occasion he was introduced to the Prince of Wales, who after a long and convivial conversation conferred on him a royal cigar. Later he was asked what he had done with it: the fashion was for preserving anything of royal provenance as a keepsake. Trott, though, simply looked puzzled. 'I smoked it,' he said.

In his equanimity, Trott was a rarity. Australian teams of the time were notoriously combustible, riven by intercolonial jealousies. Trott's first skipper, Percy McDonnell, survived a 'muffled mutiny' against his leadership because of his over-reliance on New South Welshmen; his second, Jack Blackham, was weak, suggestible, and felt to be the cat's paw of other Victorians; his third, George Giffen, asserted South Australian primacy simply by bowling himself interminably. Discipline was lamentable, with Australia's 1893 tour of England especially unruly. 'It was impossible to keep some of them straight,' complained their manager. 'One of them was altogether useless because of his drinking propensities. Some were in the habit of holding receptions in their rooms and would not go to bed until all hours.'

Appointed to lead Australia's next trip to England in 1896, Harry Trott changed everything. He knew no favourites, was never remembered to quarrel with anyone, and showed a pioneering flair for tactics. Rigid field settings and pre-determined bowling changes were standard operating procedure at the time; Trott set the trend of configuring fielders and employing bowlers with particular batsmen and match situations in mind, and rotating his attack to keep its members fresh. 'His bowlers felt that he understood the gruelling nature of their work,' said *The Referee*, 'and that they had his sympathy in the grimmest of battles.' To some, this sympathy seemed uncanny. Trott's star bowler Hugh Trumble had days, he confessed, when his usual sting and snap were missing; Trott could sense such occasions within a few balls, and would whip him off. Sydney batsman Frank Iredale, meanwhile, was gifted but highly strung, a teetotaller. 'Look here, Noss, what you need is a tonic,' Trott counselled. 'I'll mix you one.' Iredale made more centuries than any other batsman on tour, fortified by what Trott later admitted was brandy and soda. In the end, the Australians were pipped 1–2 in the series, the defeats being narrow, their victory stirring. Opening the bowling on a whim at Manchester, Trott had England's stars W.G. Grace and Drewy Stoddart stumped in his first two overs: a decisive breakthrough. His leadership was then seen to even better advantage when England next visited Australia and was overwhelmed 4–1. 'It didn't seem to matter to Mr Trott whom he put on,' lamented Stoddart, 'for each change ended in a wicket.' *Wisden* thought him 'incomparably the best captain the Australians have ever had'; the Anglo–Indian batting guru Ranjitsinhji concluded that he was 'without a superior today anywhere'.

Game for Anything, Haigh

ERNIE JONES

The fastest bowler of his era was moustached Broken Hill miner Ernie Jones.

It was Jones who in the England v Australia match at Lord's in 1896 bowled the first ball – a very fast and short one – through W.G. Grace's beard for four byes, the champion walking up the wicket and saying, 'What the h— are you doing, Jonah?' To which Jones replied, 'Sorry Doctor, she slipped!'

Long Innings: The autobiography of Sir Pelham Warner, Warner

'Jonah', as he was known throughout the cricket world, snorted if anyone went into rhapsodies about

Larwood's pace in his hearing. 'Fast?' would expostulate Jones, who was once reputed to have bowled a ball through W.G. Grace's beard, the sheer pace beating the Old Man. 'Him fast? Why, s'welp me, he wouldn't knock a dint in a pound of butter on a hot day.'

Cricket Crisis, Fingleton

Even thirty years after his last Test match he was a popular figure at the wharves, one side only of his head having turned grey, welcoming English sides to Australia with stentorian cries of, 'You haven't got a chance!' This was the man who, when asked by King Edward VII if he had attended St Peter's College Adelaide, replied, 'Yes, I drive the dust cart there every week.'

The Fast Men, Frith

ARCHIE MACLAREN
A superlative opening batsman . . .

One wonders if ever a finer batsman played for England than A.C. MacLaren. Certainly there was never a better sportsman. MacLaren's stand at the wickets when batting was peculiar and all his own. First he would place his right foot in position and put his bat very carefully into the block; then he would take up position with legs slightly apart, at the same time up would go his chin, as though he were saying to the bowler, 'Now, bring out your cat.'

The Game's the Thing, Noble

. . . but a strangely pessimistic captain.

I have heard old-timers say he was liable to enter the dressing-room clutching his head and saying, 'Look what they've given me this time.' Or 'Gracious me! Don't tell me you're playing!' Which cannot have been very good for morale.

Batter's Castle, Peebles

PRINCE RANJITSINHJI

The most exotic cricketer of all, a disinherited Indian princeling, Ranji embarked for England with his fortune foretold by the celebrated astrologer Pandit Hareshwar.

Hareshwar was called to a bungalow outside Bombay. Behind the chair of one of them stood a servant waving a fan. 'Tell us,' said one of the men, 'which of us will be a ruler among men?' Hareshwar asked the date of their births and inspected their palms. 'None of you,' he said, 'but I should like to inspect the hand of this servant.' He was allowed to do so. 'This man will be a ruler,' he declared. 'But I also see that he is a ruler in another field – sport, I think.'

Ranjitsinhji, Wild

There was resistance to his selection for the Lord's Test of 1896, but none to his inclusion at Old Trafford, where he scored 62 and 154 not out.

Lord Harris was not, in fact, in favour of playing what he called 'birds of passage', and Ranji, though asked to make himself available, was not chosen for the Lord's Test, an omission that resulted in public and press outcry. The Australians, when Ranji was selected to play in the Second Test at Old Trafford three weeks later, raised no such objections. Ranji, on being invited, insisted that the Australians should be consulted. They were, Trott expressed his delight, and no more was heard of the matter.

Ranji, Ross

Perhaps as a result, Ranji took pity on a bird of passage overcome by the heat in Melbourne in 1898. While Ranji is sitting in the private balcony watching the intercolonial, an unfledged mynah tumbles from the roof into the balcony, and Ranji picks up the callow nestling, puts a finger into its mouth and wishes to have it placed again on the roof. He asks an enthusiastic boy cricketer named Dougall of Boundary Road to climb up the post and put the bird back, but the post is so hot in the terrible heat that young Dougall cannot undertake the climb. The prince, however, was not satisfied until the little squeaker was restored to its nest above.

The Australasian, 1 January 1898

JOE DARLING

With three centuries in the Ashes of 1897–98 Joe Darling set a new record, and convinced his Scottish pastoralist father that he might have a future in the game.

Joe was a great cricketer at school – he made 252 for

his college on Adelaide Oval – but his father, a prominent South Australian politician and in business a keen wheat-buyer, apprenticed him to a farmer in the dry northern areas of South Australia. Joe, however, after about two years of farming, rebelled, returned to Adelaide and started a cricket depot, much to parental disgust. Joe's cricket prowess put him into the SA XI against Stoddart's last team and he thumped their bowling mercilessly, making a century in one innings.

Gradually, the old man relented and he much astonished the family by happening down to cricket matches when the lad was batting. By and by there came a reconciliation. On top of a big score the Hon. John D walked into his son's dressing-room. 'Joe ma boy, I think you're best at cricket. Here's your gold watch and a cheque on ye representing one poun' per run of your score today.'

Joe was speechless. That year the old man followed his offspring to Melbourne, and when he got there said, 'I don't keer about beezness so much noo,' and went from there to Sydney. And now the Hon. John – who five years ago had never seen a cricket match – is always there provided that Joe is there too, and the score of 178 against England on Friday week brought a cheque for £78. The old man only makes it £1 a run over the hundred now. 'One has to be canny wi' Joe, who bats better when the siller is up.'

The Bulletin, 29 January 1898

A hard hitting left-hander . . .

On one tour of Britain, Rhodes was worrying Darling with a ball the Yorkshire left-hander swung with his arm. Instead of natural spin turning into the left-handed batsman, this ball drifted out. When Darling mentioned his difficulty, Victor Trumper promised, 'I'll find his arm ball for you, Paddy.' Before long Trumper described how Rhodes held this ball for delivery. Darling, 'I'll hit him out of the ground next time.' He on-drove it so far out of Old Trafford across Warwick Road that a porter fielded the ball at the railway station.

On Top Down Under, Robinson

. . . and a great sportsman.

Towards the end of the Australians' second innings [at Trent Bridge in 1905], when they were well in the soup, the light became very poor. Charles McLeod, when his partner got out, ran to the pavilion and signalled. The big brown moustache of Joe Darling emerged. There was a consultation at the gate. Joe Darling surveyed the quarters of the sky as a farmer would, then shook his head, slowly indeed, but not without emphasis, turned his broad back and went in. McLeod had wanted to know whether he should appeal against the light. If Joe Darling had allowed the appeal I think it certain the umpires would have stopped play and Australia would have drawn the match. Joe Darling was a sportsman of the best. We had by that time morally won the game and he was not the man to slide out on a side issue. And mark you, McLeod need not have discussed the question: he could have appealed himself, but he, too, felt disinclined to escape when his side was beaten on the play.

Life Worth Living, Fry

CLEM HILL

Twenty-year-old Clem Hill's 188 in five hours out of 323 in the Melbourne Test of 1898 owed a considerable debt to Hugh Trumble, who joined him at 6–58 and they added 165.

It looked as if we would be all out before lunch for less than 100 when in walked, or rather stalked, Hughie Trumble. I strolled across to meet him to give a tip or two about the wicket, when he started on me with, 'Now cut out all this rubbish. You leave that ball outside the stump alone. Do you hear me?' The records tell you that I made 188 and Hughie got 46. They never tell you the real story. Hughie Trumble made every run I got that day.

The Golden Age of Cricket: A memorial book of Hugh Trumble, Trumble

Hill was recalled by team-mate Johnnie Moyes as both player and administrator.

He loved to talk cricket. Who could forget that

mannerism of his – the flick of the fingers that showed how quickly the bowler sent the ball through? And he would vary it by turning his hand as he flicked to indicate the manner in which the bowler turned one back. And sometimes he would gesture with that curved-stem pipe that was his inseparable companion. He was a man born to lead, but by direct methods rather than by finesse. He attacked frontally, never sought to flank. He would go straight through a difficulty. No situation was too difficult to face or solve. Right to the end Clem retained his sense of humour, his direct approach. One day the Board of Control was meeting. There had been no handout for the press. Clem walked out of the room. 'What's the news?' asked a pressman. He grinned and waved a negative reply. 'You never took as long to make a century,' he was told. Quick as a flash came back the answer, 'No, and there was never as much tripe about either.'

A Century of Cricketers, Moyes

No cricketer was more indifferent to records.

When Hobbs passed 60 against Australia in the Leeds Test, 1926, he waved his bat toward a stand where his wife was sitting in front of a group of Australians. One of them, Hill, asked, 'Ada, why is Jack waving his bat like that?' Mrs Hobbs, 'You should know if anyone does, he has beaten your record of most runs in Test matches.'

On Top Down Under, Robinson

MONTY NOBLE

When the gritty Noble batted almost nine hours for
60 not out and 87 in the Old Trafford Test of 1899,
he wasn't allowed to forget it.

During the progress of my innings the crowd sang 'The
Dead March' and, no doubt, I deserved the reproof.
Later one individual, apparently exasperated beyond
endurance, yelled out, 'Put a rope around the bounder's
neck and drag him out.' Perhaps I deserved that, also,
but no rope was forthcoming. After that memorable
match I did receive one token of appreciation from an
anonymous donor – a leather medal about as big as the
top of a jam tin inscribed: 'To M.A. Noble, the greatest Australian cricketer. A thousand runs in a thousand
years.'

The Game's the Thing, Noble

As a captain, Noble was no less a martinet.

A strict disciplinarian on the field, no-one was ever
allowed to forget who was captain. All details were
just as important to him as the big things. I have seen
Noble send a player from the field during a match to
have the spikes in his boots attended to because he
was seen to slip. Sometimes we thought him a little
too severe, but later we found out the benefit of this
severity.

My Cricketing Days, Macartney

VICTOR TRUMPER

A last-minute inclusion on the 1899 tour, Victor Trumper
soon made his presence felt . . .

When he made 300 (not out) against Sussex in 1899,
I asked Joe Darling, who was 70 (not out) when the
innings was closed, 'What do you think of the boy?'

'What do I think of him?' he replied. 'I thought
I could bat.'

The Game's the Thing, Noble

. . . and attracted some noteworthy fans.

Later in the tour, the imposing figure of W.G. suddenly
loomed inside the Australians' dressing-room demand-
ing that Trumper hand over a bat with his autograph
on it. This was done immediately. The great man then,
placing one of his own hallowed blades into the youth's
hand, delivered the following oration in his high voice,
'From today's champion to the champion of tomorrow.' He then turned and strode majestically from the
room.

Victor Trumper, Sharpham

Trumper's 2570 runs with eleven hundreds on the
1902 Ashes tour made him the one team member
his captain considered indispensable.

In those days there were no motor coaches in England,
and the team would be conveyed from its hotel to the
cricket ground by a four-horse-drawn brake, and

the story goes that before the brake moved off Joe Darling would call out, 'Is Vic aboard?' It was only then that the coachman would be given the order to drive off.

Test Tussles On and Off the Field, Darling

Recalled by baggage man Bill Ferguson.

Probably the neatest and most elegant bat in the world at that time, Vic was anything but neat when he was in the dressing-room or at a hotel. He was the despair of his charming wife, and the not-so-charming baggage master, because he simply refused to worry about the condition of his clothes and equipment. Any old bat would do for him, whether there was rubber on the handle or not, and I can still see him now after slaughtering the best bowling in England taking his flannels off in the dressing-room, rolling them into a ball and cramming them into an already overloaded cricket bag, there to remain until they were worn next day.

Mrs Trumper used to say to me, 'Just look at Victor's clothes. Whatever does he do with them?'

Mr Cricket, Ferguson

Warren Bardsley opened the 1909 tour with 63, 76, 63 not out and 219, then he got a lesson in the team ethic from Victor Trumper.

While I was resting on the grass I thought that, being near 200 with almost three hours to go, I might have the luck to go past Warwick Armstrong's 303 and set a new record for an Australian in England. On 219 I pushed a ball into the covers, called Trumper and ran. By the time I noticed Vic was not running I was too far to get back. When Vic came in I asked him why he'd left me stranded when it was my call. Vic said, 'How many more did you want, Curly? Remember, there are others in the side who'd like an innings.'

On Top Down Under, Robinson

While in the grip of poor health, Trumper played what proved his last Tests during the Ashes rubber of 1911–12. But his method and manner left an indelible impression on the young English wicketkeeper 'Tiger' Smith.

I got to know him well on the 1911–12 tour of Australia and I don't think a kinder man ever lived. When I kept to him in Australia he only had three years to live; he was tubercular then and coughing a little when he batted, but he never complained. The off-field incidents in the Australian dressing-room saddened Victor. Stronger men like Warwick Armstrong pressured him into supporting the players' demands to have Frank Laver as their manager on the forthcoming tour of England. So Victor didn't come to England in 1912 and I think he was bewildered by it all. He also heard that some of the Test selectors didn't rate him all that highly, yet he got a beautiful hundred in the First Test and fifty in the last. In that last Test, Victor turned to me at one stage and said, 'Tiger, they think I'm finished.' All I could think of was, 'I wish I could play like you, Victor.'

One example of his sportsmanship on that tour. He was captaining an Australian XI against us and Jack Hearne skied a ball to J.N. Crawford off Roy Minnett. Jack was walking to the pavilion when Victor called him back because someone in the crowd had shouted 'no ball' when Jack was about to play his shot. Can you see a skipper doing something like that today? Like Jack Hobbs, I don't think he had a weakness in his batting apart from his ill-health. A most un-Australian person, he was a champion and one of the most endearing men I've ever met.

'Tiger' Smith of Warwickshire and England,
Smith

Recalled by team-mate Frank Iredale.
Through many years of connection with him, which I am proud to say was never clouded by any misunderstanding, I felt how greatly our country was honoured by his presence as a sportsman in the highest sense. His was one of those natures which called to you and in whose presence you felt it was good to live.

Thirty-three Years of Cricket, Iredale

Recalled by team-mate Charlie Macartney.
One of the greatest tragedies of cricket was the death

of Victor Trumper in June 1915. I have one great satisfaction regarding Victor Trumper – I never saw him get old as a cricketer. I say, without hesitation, that he was the best batsman I ever saw. He excelled on any wicket and against any bowling, but beyond his cricket he was a man, a fighter on the cricket field, and a thorough gentleman at all times.

My Cricketing Days, Macartney

Recalled by team-mate Monty Noble.

The irony of it. He was a teetotaller, a non-smoker; he never gambled and he never kept late hours. Indeed, he was such a clean liver and had such a wholesome mental outlook that one would have expected him to live his full measure of the allotted span. But it was not to be. The last person he would have thought of talking of was himself. No matter how much his friends remonstrated with him, he would only reply, 'Oh I'm all right,' and look around for an opportunity to do someone else a good turn.

The Game's the Thing, Noble

CHARLES FRY

England's captain in 1912 was uncomfortable with the acclamation that followed victory at The Oval.

When the crowd gathered round the pavilion and shouted for me I would not go on the balcony, because I felt that the time for them to cheer me was when I was walking out to bat as captain of my side to try and win the match on a foul wicket. Ranji was in our dressing-room and he said to me, 'Now, Charles, be your noble self.' But I said, 'This is not one of my noble days.'

Life Worth Living, Fry

SYD GREGORY

Fry's rival, forty-year-old Syd Gregory, was one of Australia's finest cover points.

He [Macartney] told me that C.B. Fry and Plum Warner were batting in a Test match at Lord's. Charlie Kelleway bowled to Warner who hit the ball out to the covers and, thinking it was going between the fieldsmen, Warner called Fry and as the batsmen passed each other on the pitch Warner said, 'Two Charles, perhaps three.' Off they went. The Australian captain S.E. Gregory was fielding at cover point, a position where he excelled; he was alert and anticipated the shot, moved across to intercept, which he did and, gathering the ball cleanly, he returned it to the bowler's end on the full. The ball hit the wicket with Warner a yard out of his crease. It was not a case of 'two Charles, perhaps three', but run out on the first. What a reward for anticipation!

The Rattle of the Stumps, Oldfield

JOHNNY DOUGLAS

John William Henry Tyler Douglas, a pace bowling all-rounder, league footballer and Olympic boxer, led

England with tremendous tenacity when they won the Ashes in 1911–12 . . .

His response to the address of welcome at the Town Hall in Melbourne had been one of the shortest but most famous speeches ever made by a captain of MCC: 'I hate speeches. As Bob Fitzsimmons once said, "I ain't no bloomin' orator, but I'll fight any man in this blinkin' country."'

It was in Melbourne, too, in the match against Victoria that an anonymous wag in the crowd had dubbed him 'Johnny Won't Hit Today' when he was in the middle of one of his most dour efforts with the bat. The nickname stuck, and little that Douglas did with the bat over the next seventeen years was calculated to rid him of this title. In truth, he was rather proud of it.

Johnny Won't Hit Today, Lemmon

. . . and nine years later they lost them, not helped by his pig-headedness.

Many commentators noted how Douglas frequently overbowled himself. One of these protracted spells came at the Melbourne Cricket Ground which boasted a scoreboard giving a full breakdown of performances. Douglas was bowling with his back to this and there is a legend that [Cec] Parkin screamed, 'Mr Douglas, if you won't stop bowling, put yourself on at the other end where you can read your analysis!'

Great Characters from Cricket's Golden Age, Mailes

WARWICK ARMSTRONG

Australia's first post-war captain was not a man to take orders, except when once banned from fielding in slips by Joe Darling.

Armstrong knew enough about Joe to keep away from the slips but, after two or three games, when a right- and a left-handed batsman were in and things a bit mixed, he attempted a try on. Tibby Cotter was the bowler and, choosing the right moment, Armstrong sneaked into the slips. For a great wonder this move was unnoticed by Darling, and Cotter, running to the wicket, was just about to deliver the next ball when Hill at mid-off, throwing both arms in the air, yelled 'Hey!' Wondering what on earth was the matter, Cotter stopped abruptly to find Hill pointing at Armstrong but looking straight at Darling and saying, 'He's there again, Joe!'

'Come out of that,' said Joe, and before a big crowd of spectators away went poor Armstrong very sheepishly to another position. Knowing Armstrong as I did, I can imagine he later got even with Clem.

Not Test Cricket, Monfries

Nor was he cowed by grandees like England's Lord Harris.

Armstrong said, 'The umpires are paid little for their services and, as there is a lot of betting on Tests, it would be wise to remove them from temptation.' Lord Harris thought the matter so serious that he suggested holding it over until next day, until inquiries were made. Next day he said, 'I can find no evidence of betting on cricket – people don't bet on cricket.' Armstrong drew deeply on his big bent-stem pipe, then he leaned across and said, 'You don't think so, my Lord? If you'd like £500 on the next Test, I can get it on for you.'

On Top Down Under, Robinson

Recalled by team-mate Charlie Macartney.

On occasions he had streaky periods, and in one match I was associated with him at the wickets he was edging the ball to fine-leg and through the slips with extreme confidence. When I remarked to him that so-and-so was bowling specially well, he said, 'Oh I don't know, I can play him all right with the edge of the bat, just wait till I get the full face onto him!'

The Big Ship, Haigh

Recalled by team-mate Arthur Mailey.

Tremendously tenacious and a relentless fighter, Armstrong bluffed rather than cajoled the opposition out. When he couldn't think of an answer, he smiled blandly and lumbered away. But nobody could deny his courage, his capacity for hard work and his determination. These qualities were more pronounced when he was in conflict with somebody he didn't like. Armstrong had strong dislikes and cast-iron convictions. To him reciprocity was a coward's weapon and he didn't have much time for arbitration unless he himself could act as the arbitrator. He belonged to the older school and appeared to treat newcomers to Test cricket as being beneath his notice.

10 for 66 and All That, Mailey

The post-war Armstrong was on a bigger scale than the pre-war version.

June was at its sunniest when the Australians played Hampshire in 1921 and a Southampton newspaper reported that Armstrong, strolling round the ground while Bardsley and Macartney made centuries, became aware of a little boy dogging his heels. He thought it manifestation of hero worship, but the boy's persistency at last made him say, 'Here, give me your autograph book and I'll sign it.'

The boy: 'I ain't got one.'

Armstrong: 'Then what do you want?'

The boy: 'Please, sir, you're the only decent bit of shade in the place.'

On Top Down Under, Robinson

CHARLIE MACARTNEY

Macartney was known by a deathless nickname.

It was during the English tour of Australia in 1907–8 that I was first dubbed the 'Governor-General'. K.L. Hutchings was responsible for this, and it has stuck to me through all my career. In this connection, my wife relates with glee a conversation overheard by her at a match. One small boy said to another, 'Why do they call Mac the Governor-General?' 'Because he's so cocky, of course,' was the reply.

My Cricketing Days, Macartney

After smashing his way to 99 at Lord's in 1912, Macartney was a victim only of his own impetuosity.

Macartney played the best innings of the tour with 99 at Lord's and the manner of his dismissal typified the man and his outlook on cricket. Most batsmen of the period were wont to creep toward a century like a cat burglar on his objective. Not so Macartney. He tried to hit E.R. Foster into St John's Wood Road.

'I thought I could have hit it for six,' he declared later. 'Should have, too. Full toss. Made a mess of it.'

Masters of Cricket from Trumper to May,
Fingleton

At Lord's fourteen years later, when England declared on the third and last afternoon, Macartney made impetuosity pay.

Woodfull at once was accounted for; Macartney, in first-wicket down, immediately received a really nasty ball from Maurice Tate and crashed it to the off railings, a really bad-tempered stroke. Macartney scored a hundred and pulled Australia through to a draw.

At close of play I asked him about the ball from Tate at his innings' beginning. 'As soon as I saw it,' said Macartney, 'I knew it was either him or me. So it had to be Maurice.'

Barclay's World of Cricket, Swanton (Ed.)

Recalled by opponent Walter Hammond.

Now I had spent all the winter evenings avidly reading up everything I could find about cricket heroes such as Hobbs, Hearne, Bardsley – and particularly Macartney. Perhaps I am prejudiced, but to this day I do not think I have ever seen a better cricketer than 'The Governor-General'.

Cricket My Destiny, Hammond

Recalled by friend Sir Home Gordon.

One of the tales he relates gleefully about himself is that when somebody observed he bowled with his head, a lady enquired how on earth he could do that.

Background of Cricket, Gordon

JACK GREGORY

Australia's star all-rounder after the First World War was magnetic on the field, but acutely shy off it.

Gregory was anything but a limelighter. As Armstrong's Australians crossed the continent to board the England-bound *Osterly* in Fremantle in March 1921, the train had to stop in country South Australia for a civic reception at Quorn. As manager Syd Smith addressed the crowd, a cry went up for a word from Gregory and a posse of locals boarded the train in search of him. The first player they encountered was Gregory himself but, in those days when news was vested in word rather than image, he went unrecognised. Thinking quickly, Gregory confided that the man they sought had slipped off the other side of the train, sending his admirers off in comic pursuit.

Bradman noticed that Gregory could never be drawn to discussing his on-field accomplishments, though unfailingly 'generous-hearted' toward younger teammates. Larwood, so exhilarated by Gregory's bowling, also found him the gentlest of men away from the fray. 'Off the field you could not meet a more friendly and amiable chap.' Leery of the press after once being misquoted, the only interview he granted was a most reluctant one in the year before his death, cricket writer David Frith driving 320 kilometres on the off-chance of catching him in his shack at Narooma on NSW's south coast, and coaxing him into a few quiet reminiscences. There were no visible trophies or mementoes. 'Here,' recalled Frith, 'was a cricketing Garbo.'

Game for Anything, Haigh

TED McDONALD

Australia's finest fast bowler before Lindwall trained on board ship en route to England in 1921.

After leaving Fremantle, McDonald, who knew it was largely due to his captain that he had been selected, took the opportunity to thank him. He then said, 'Is there anything you want me to do, Armstrong?' To which the big fellow replied, 'Yes Mac, I want you to put the "peg" in until we have won the rubber, and this means getting fit.' For the rest of the voyage, Armstrong and McDonald each morning went down to the stokehold of the P&O liner and for two hours worked as firemen. They planned to rid themselves of superfluous fat and became as hard as nails.

Was it all Cricket? Reese

SIR JACK HOBBS

Hobbs' opening partnership with Herbert Sutcliffe was the acme of reliability.

The first time I partnered Jack Hobbs in Test cricket he contented himself with this advice, 'Play your own game.' Four words – they counted for much. They told me all I wanted to know. The master says to the pupil, 'You can do it if you try' and the youngster tries all the harder. It was a source of strength for me to see Hobbs take his stance at the wicket. When I walked out with him I gained confidence and that confidence was increased by almost everything he did.

For England and Yorkshire, Sutcliffe

Sir Robert Menzies delighted to tell that he had only twice taken his wife to watch Test cricket, and each time she saw only two batsmen.

On the first occasion, at Melbourne in 1925, Hobbs and Sutcliffe batted all day. The next time, at Lord's in 1926, when they arrived a few minutes after the start, and as the English opening batsmen walked out, Lady Menzies claimed, 'Well I never, it's those two again' – and when she and her husband had to leave, a few minutes before tea, they were still there.

Jack Hobbs, Arlott

Hobbs doubled as one of the greatest extra cover fieldsmen of all time.

When England came to Australia in 1921 many of the Australian players had never played against Hobbs. When they saw him lazily mooching round the covers they came to the conclusion that a shot in Hobbs' direction meant an easy run. He ran so many batsmen out and gave so many a shock that halfway through the season the Australians held a caucus meeting in the dressing-room and adopted the slogan 'No runs when the ball goes near Jack Hobbs'.

10 for 66 and All That, Mailey

Hobbs was also perhaps the most modest cricketer ever born. After England's Ashes victory in 1926, to which he and Sutcliffe contributed a match-winning opening partnership of 261, he slipped quietly away.

It was hopeless to try to get the crowd to go home. They yelled for us to come out on the pavilion balcony. They were shouting for each of us in turn. We had at last to show ourselves. There were many thousands in the assemblage below us, and yet it struck me as remarkable that in that vast sea of faces I picked out my wife. Next day I heard that it took hours for Sutcliffe to get away from The Oval, but my wife and I slipped off at the Vauxhall entrance where a friend was waiting with a car. Thus we got quietly away from one of the most wonderful scenes that the world of cricket has ever known.

My Life Story, Hobbs

Catching him at Sydney in 1925 gave Bert Oldfield more satisfaction than any other dismissal.

Pitched just outside the leg-stump and with the assistance of the wind it swung well away to the leg-side, aided by the firm glance from Hobbs' bat, but having had those first two deliveries as a guide and seeing that the fourth ball was pitched on the leg-side, I anticipated its course by covering a greater distance, and as soon as I heard the snick I stretched my arms full length while in my stride, probably four or five yards wide of the wicket, and brought off a catch which certainly thrilled me and brought the spectators to their feet.

The roar of the crowd brought home to me the sensation of the catch. There was no describing my delight at the achievement in dismissing such a redoubtable opponent. I can still see Gregory continuing his run down the wicket to greet me with a smile, while Hobbs quietly left the scene no doubt amazed by the suddenness of it all.

Behind the Wicket, Oldfield

HERBERT SUTCLIFFE

His 194 in the Sydney Test of 1932 almost came to a premature end.

When he was 43 a wrong 'un from O'Reilly screwed from the inside edge of the bat. The ball rolled against the stumps hard enough to rebound a foot away, yet fieldsmen and an umpire who inspected the wicket found neither bail disturbed. Sutcliffe seemed the least concerned man on the ground, as if he wondered what all the commotion was about.

Between Wickets, Robinson

Recalled by opponent Bill O'Reilly.

Sutcliffe was the toughest competitor I ever faced in a Test match. He was not unusually gifted, except in his unrelenting purpose to grind a bowler into the grass. I loved bowling to him. It was an exquisite feeling to get one past his defensive bat. His humiliation made the day for me. Whenever he got close to misjudging the position of his off stump in using his left pad to my wrong 'un, I made it a practice to appeal raucously for a leg-before decision. To my great joy this nettled him immensely. In our very first Test encounter – he went on to make 194 – he muttered to me that I must conduct my bowling job much more responsibly if I were to make a name for myself in this game. I got the message that he was really objecting to my loud appeals. Later as I was leaving the field with 'Yorker' Richardson, Herbert came over and said, 'Take no notice of me, Bill. Sometimes I feel I need a good kick in the stern for the things I say out there in the middle.'

'My bloody oath, Herbie, I often feel like giving you one myself,' said Yorker.

'Tiger', O'Reilly

ARTHUR MAILEY

Leg-spinner Arthur Mailey revelled in his battles with Jack Hobbs . . .

On one of those occasions when Hobbs threatened to spend the weekend with us, I entered into a pact with Jack Gregory during the lunch interval. The idea was that my first ball to Jack [Hobbs] in the second over was to be an obvious wrong 'un pitched, if possible, on middle and leg stumps. The moment this ball was bowled, Gregory was to spring round the back of Oldfield and wait at leg-slip for Hobbs to snick an easy catch.

Gregory remembered the plan but I forgot it, and instead of the planned ball being a wrong 'un it was a perfect leg-break on off-stump. When I saw Gregory dashing behind the wicket I realised the blunder I had made. But Gregory, keeping his eye on the ball in flight, saw it spinning the opposite way to what he expected, hurtled back to the slips and was just in time to grab the ball almost off Jack's bat.

Gregory wasn't particularly pleased about the incident. He said I was trying to make a fool of him. That night I asked Jack Hobbs if he knew what had happened. 'Not quite,' he said. 'But I heard a devil of a scramble going on behind the stumps.'

10 for 66 and All That, Mailey

. . . and in self-deprecating stories.

Invited to the Royal Box at Lord's during the 1921 Test, he was seated alongside a princess who was already heavily engaged in conversation. Arthur's presence was overlooked for some time. He had taken six wickets in that Test and hated being ignored. 'I'm a little stiff from bowling,' he remarked to gain the royal attention.

'Oh, is that where you're from?' the princess replied. 'I was wondering.'

Fours Galore, Whitington

When rebuked by the manager of the 1930 Australian team for giving Ian Peebles advice during the Manchester Test, Mailey answered, 'Please understand that slow bowling is an art, Mr Kelly, and art is international.'

10 for 66 and All That, Mailey

BILL PONSFORD

Notoriously camera-shy, Bill Ponsford was also eternally vigilant.

In one picture he was oblivious of the camera which caught him talking out the corner of his mouth to Bradman. It transpired that he was saying, 'What are the beggars up to now?' He had scarcely passed through the gate before he noticed that a couple of English fieldsmen were taking up positions a few yards (or feet) away from where they had been before the luncheon interval.

Between Wickets, Robinson

Too many runs were never enough for Victoria's opener on the 1930 Ashes tour.

In a previous county match Ponsford had scored a double century and had vowed afterwards, 'Never again! Too much like hard work!' At Cambridge before the game against the university he repeated that, and added, 'Today if I get 50, I'll throw my wicket away.' Surely enough he made a chanceless 50, whereon one of our players called to Archie Jackson who was next in the batting list, 'Get your bat, Archie! Ponny will be out any minute now.' But to our surprise, instead of throwing his wicket away, Ponsford took block for his next 50 and by his renowned solid type of batting, went on to score another double century.

The Rattle of the Stumps, Oldfield

While Ponsford's appetite for runs was outsized, it emerged that his eyesight was actually poorer than average.

After all that had been said about Ponsford's wonderful sight, the doctor that examined him when he volunteered for the air force was astonished to find that he was colour blind; he could not distinguish between red and green. A dialogue like this followed:

Doctor: 'What colour did the new ball look to you?'

Ponsford: 'Red.'

Doctor: 'What colour did it look after it became worn?'

Ponsford: 'I never noticed its colour then, only its size.'

Between Wickets, Robinson

ARTHUR GILLIGAN

England's captain in 1924–25, Arthur Gilligan, recalled a day it rained cricket balls.

I recall that, in the Second Test match between England and Australia at Melbourne in 1925 after only 15 runs were on the board – I was bowling at the time – I noticed that a great piece of leather had come off the ball. I immediately showed the ball to umpire Bob Crockett, who consulted his colleague, and a brand new ball was brought out. Before lunch that day we had no fewer than four new balls with the total no more than 87. When we adjourned we discovered that, by mistake, a wrong packet of balls had been delivered to the ground and that we had no. 3 grade cricket balls instead of no. 1. It was agreed between Herby Collins and myself to play out the first innings with both sides using the no. 3 grade variety, and it is interesting now to record that we used eight new balls before the score reached 200, and Australia had seven.

Wisden Cricketers' Almanack, 1939

CLARRIE GRIMMETT

Clarrie Grimmett's 11–82 on Test debut was more than usually extraordinary.

'It must have been my lucky day, because as we left the field some friends called me over to the grandstand dividing fence to congratulate me,' Clarrie recalled. 'As we chatted there was a heavy thud. I looked down and saw a battery box at my feet. It had been accidentally dropped from the balcony above.' As he left the SCG, well satisfied with his bag of five English scalps, a large black limousine pulled up. A man sitting inside waved his hand at Clarrie and called, 'Congratulations, Grimmett.' The car was some distance away before

Clarrie realised that the occupant was Lord Forster, the Australian Governor-General.

Clarrie Grimmett: The Bradman of spin,
Mallett

Grimmett's wrong 'un caused consternation even to the delivery's pioneer, Englishman B.J.T. Bosanquet. During the 1930 tour he [Grimmett] met Bosanquet who asked, 'Am I responsible for you?' Not surprisingly, the spin brethren talked for hours, their scientific discussion at the end of the pier at Hove ending at two in the morning. Grimmett took 28 Test wickets on that tour, a return which, in truth, had as much to do with Australia's success as Bradman's 974 runs.

The Slow Men, Frith

But Grimmett, recalled his partner Bill O'Reilly, was not a man to get carried away. Social life meant little to 'Grum'. Not until late in his career did he discover that it was not a bad idea to relax between matches. In England in 1934 I bought him a beer in the Star Hotel in Worcester to celebrate his first ten wickets of the tour. It took him so long to sink it that I decided to wait for his return gesture till sometime later in the tour. Later he told me, with obvious regret, that on previous tours he had been keeping the wrong company and had never really enjoyed a touring trip. That I thought was sad, but not half as sad as

I felt when, at the zenith of his glorious career, he was tipped out of business altogether. With 'Grum' at the other end, prepared to pick me up and dust me down, I feared no batsman.

Wisden, 1981

PERCY CHAPMAN

Recalled by team-mate Wally Hammond.

Chapman had the right temperament for Australia – sanguine, happy, eager, with plenty of cool strategy; he made friends everywhere, and no-one in our team could resist his cheery good nature and absolute lack of side. As we were walking down the gangway when we landed in Australia, a wharf labourer yelled, 'Good luck to you, Chapman! Have you brought the Ashes with you?'

'We're going to take them back – I'll show them to you when we go!' Percy shouted, grinning.

'I'll have a quid with you on that,' challenged the wharfinger.

'Done!' called Chapman. 'Have the money ready for me when we leave.' He had, too; but Percy just grinned all over and told him to drink our healths with it.

Cricket My Destiny, Hammond

It is not as though, playwright Ben Travers recalled, he got great support from his own country in the 1928–29 Ashes.

On the early morning of 30 November, when the First Test was to begin, I had to share a bath with Percy Chapman. Accustomed as I was to the extravagant practices of the theatre, I expected him to be in receipt of a sheaf of letters and cables from well-wishers in England, but the only communication he had received that morning was a reminder from the British Inland Revenue relating to his income tax. As I told him in the bathroom, England evidently expected that every man that day would pay his duty.

94 Declared, Travers

WALTER HAMMOND

In 1928–29, Walter Hammond was unstoppable.

In the Sydney match he was called upon to bat once and made 251. His subsequent Test scores were: 200 and run out 32; 119 and 177; 38 and 16. After this innings of 251 he showed me his bat. Nowadays in TV close-ups one sees bats festooned with the blobs of impact. Hammond's bat was unmarked except that plumb in the middle of the sweet of the blade there was a per-fectly circular indentation.

94 Declared, Travers

In 1932–33, he was charged with the responsibility of keeping the dangerous Chuck Fleetwood-Smith from Test selection.

He was a bowler with a highly personalised style,

capable on the right wickets of being a match-winner. The selectors were ready to blood him. And England had heard about it. Or rather Douglas Jardine, heart as cold as a fishmonger's slab, had eavesdropped. He told Hammond, 'I want you to murder him. We don't want him ever to play for Australia. Now's the time to destroy him. It's up to you, Wally.' The unscrupulous yet astute order couldn't have been acted on more decisively. Against Victoria, Hammond attacked the raw, unsuspecting bowler with a fury not often to be repeated. Fleetwood-Smith had to be withdrawn from the attack. The English batsman scored 203 that day at Melbourne. As for the disheartened bowler, it took several years before he resurfaced, considered strong and experienced enough to take to England.

Walter Hammond: The reasons why, Foot

Four years later at Adelaide Oval, however, Fleetwood-Smith had his revenge.

Chuck had taken the first two English wickets when Bradman remembered a remark by the wicketkeeper Sammy Carter during Arthur Mailey's 1932 tour of America. Carter had said to Bradman, 'I'd love to play one Test with Fleetwood-Smith. He could win a match for Australia some day.'

Bradman walked over to Fleetwood-Smith and, trying to inspire him, said in a cool voice, 'Chuck, if ever we wanted you to bowl that unplayable ball, now is the time.'

Fleetwood-Smith responded to the challenge, bowling probably the best and certainly the most significant delivery of his career. In the air the heavily spun ball swerved tantalisingly away from Hammond's bat, and pitched on a worn spot outside off-stump. Hammond was drawn defensively forward, but was then caught in no-man's land when the ball spun viciously back between bat and pad, accelerating from the pace it made from the pitch to conclusively bowl him. Fleetwood-Smith, who slumped to his knees in jubilation, turned to Bradman and shouted with a hint of sarcasm, 'Was that what you wanted?'

A Wayward Genius, Growden

Recalled by team-mate Charles Barnett.
'For years I had to play second fiddle to a great batsman, Wally Hammond. I was lucky if I had an average of two balls an over to make my runs. But he never ran me out.'

On Top Down Under, Robinson

SIR DONALD BRADMAN

Twenty-one-year-old Donald Bradman needed precious little time adapting to foreign wickets on his first Ashes tour, scoring 236 at Worcester.
The new ball was taken at 430 and Bradman immediately hit a four, then a single, and was 200. He was given a great ovation as the Cathedral bells were

appropriately chiming 'The Last Rose of Summer'. His score occupied 250 minutes, and it was an Australian's highest individual score against Worcester.

Sydney Sun, 2 May 1930

Australia soon after met the powerful Yorkshire team and its star bowler George Macaulay.

George Macaulay of Yorkshire was my idea of a real bowler with the right spirit. Batsmen did not like him – and in fact, they never do like good bowlers. George had one idea and one only and that was to get each batsman for a duck – if possible, first ball.

Cricketers' School, Hammond

But there would only be one winner in a confrontation with Bradman.

Don Bradman had been batting only a short time and, as usual, looked to be in ominous form. Macaulay, who had been known to quail batsmen with a glare and a mutter, asked for the ball and in a loud voice declared, 'Let me 'ave a go at this booger.' His first over was a maiden to Bradman, but in the next he was hit for five boundaries and a further sixteen runs in his third over. As silently he took his sweater, a voice with the strength of a loudhailer came from the crowd, 'Tha should have kept tha bloody mouth shut, George.'

Fifty Years in Cricket, Hutton and Bannister

At Lord's, he raced to a chanceless 254, an innings he rated his best.

One of the spectators that day, the late Mr H.E. Mathews of New Malden, recalled the impact. 'I well remember when he reached 250 the people round me expressing their amazement and dismay very volubly, when what must have been a cockney retorted, "Blimey, what are you worrying about? It's only a quarter of a thousand."'

Sir Donald Bradman: A biography,
Rosenwater

Not everyone was satisfied by the innings.
The cricket-loving playwright Ben Travers recalled
that Bradman was not, among his team-mates,
a universally popular figure.

On the Sunday of that match I played golf with Tom Webster against Victor Richardson and Alan Kippax. The latter had joined Bradman at the wicket in the late evening with only about half an hour's play still to go. Bradman had by that time made a goodly proportion of his 254 and, being Bradman, had only thoughts for the morrow. Kippax confided to me his utter, bottled-up resentment of Bradman, who had taken care that he, Kippax, the newcomer, had the strike wherever possible. Bradman's Test record on that tour undoubtedly raised jealousy within the Australian camp, Woodfull apart.

94 Declared, Travers

At Leeds he ransacked an unequalled 309 not out
on a single day, barely breaking a sweat.

McCabe joined Bradman about forty-five minutes
before stumps when Don had been batting almost
throughout the day. After they had been together for
less than a half hour Stan, two years younger than Don,
walked down the pitch between overs and exclaimed,
'You'll have to stop running these short singles, Brad-
dles, or you'll have me completely blown out.'

When they returned to the dressing-room at stumps,
Don received congratulations from us all on his superb
batting. He turned to Bill Woodfull and confided, 'That
wasn't a bad bit of practice. I'll be able to have a go at
them tomorrow.'

The Vic Richardson Story,
Richardson and Whitington

Bradman reached 334 next day and, while fielding
later on the leg boundary, was conveyed a telegram
by Woodfull.

It said: 'Kindly convey my congratulations to Bradman. Tell him I wish him to accept £1000 as a token of
my admiration of his wonderful performance. (Signed)
Arthur Whitelaw, Australia House.'

Bradman thought it was another practical joke, but
Woodfull and Kelly assured him it was genuine. A.E.
Whitelaw, an Australian, had settled in England and
become a wealthy soap manufacturer. He said later,

'I thought Bradman's performance merited such recognition . . . we must encourage our cricketers in every way possible since cricket is the greatest of all games. This is not so much a gift as a mark of appreciation on behalf of all Australians.'

Bradman: A biography, Page

All Australians certainly appreciated him.
It was at Northampton that Bradman received a letter addressed simply to: Mr Don Bradman, Champion Cricketer, England.

Sir Donald Bradman: A biography,
Rosenwater

Australia was 3–39 on the evening of the second day of the Fourth Test at Headingley four years later, when Neville Cardus invited Bradman to dinner; Bradman declined.

'Thanks,' he said, 'But I've got to make 200 tomorrow – at least.' Cardus could not resist the reminder that in his last innings at Leeds he had passed 300. 'The law of averages is against your getting anywhere near 200 again.' Firmly enough, Bradman replied, 'I don't believe in the law of averages.'

Sir Donald Bradman: A biography,
Rosenwater

Bradman duly made 304, followed by 244 at The Oval, and became again the cynosure of all eyes, his feats eclipsing even news of King George V's lingering illness. Bill O'Reilly had an intimation of Bradman's thrall when he made up a foursome for dinner with Arthur Mailey, the great journalist Tom Clarke and author Will Dyson at Canterbury.

Tom Clarke, then working with one of the great London morning dailies, was asked what his paper would do with the front page were the King to succumb to his illness that very night. 'Right across the page in banner headlines with a photo and nothing else in sight,' was his immediate response. With that resolved, Dyson asked what would be done if Edward, Prince of Wales, were to depart this world. Clarke said that he would almost certainly be given the whole front page also, if there happened to be no other piece of Empire-shattering news to claim it.

Arthur Mailey then wanted to know how the editor would react if both the Prince of Wales and Don Bradman were to make their exits simultaneously. That query from the puckish Australian furrowed the brows of the pundits ranged round the festive board. It was eventually decided that both would be displayed on the front page. The Prince of Wales would occupy the top left-hand side of the front page, Bradman the top right. Such was the popularity of Bradman in England in 1934.

'Tiger', O'Reilly

As captain of Australia in 1936–37 against Gubby Allen's Englishmen, Bradman had to deal with sensitivities about Bodyline and the possibility of Australian retaliation through its key fast bowler Laurie Nash.

Allen said, 'We don't want a bouncer war but if this starts we will really turn it on.'

Bradman: 'No, that won't happen.'

Allen: 'Why not?'

Bradman: 'Because my bowlers are faster than yours and can bowl nastier bumpers. You know my attitude on this. I have never favoured it and never encouraged it.'

On Top Down Under, Robinson

Bradman the captain was a pragmatist.

In an unthinking moment I allowed myself to go there [to short-leg] for Waite at Birmingham one day and Santall, a massive man of some fifteen stone, gave a short ball all he had. I ducked instinctively as I saw the ball coming for the middle of my forehead and it hit me a glancing blow, shooting up, I believe, tens of feet in the air. As I was lapsing into semi-unconsciousness on the ground I could hear Bradman's piping voice from cover, mixing with bird calls, and calling out, 'Catch it! Catch it!' A practical man, Bradman!

Brown and Company: The tour in Australia,
Fingleton

He was also a disciplinarian.

Always moderate in his habits, Morris was in a group relaxing over a beer after a day's play when Bradman passed through the lounge of the team's hotel and reproved him with, 'That won't bring you any runs.'

Green Sprigs, Robinson

He retained his gifts after the war, as he showed in his 187 in Australia's 721 in a day against Essex in 1948.

The first three balls of one over were pitched on a good length on the off-stump. He smote them all past cover-point to the boundary. 'Can't you hit them anywhere else?' humorously asked the Essex wicket-keeper, F. Rist. Without a word Don picked up the next three, all pitched on the same spot, and pulled them to the mid-wicket boundary. 'How's that?' he enquired turning to Rist at the end of the over.

Flying Stumps, Lindwall

And his popularity was never greater, as England's Alec Bedser found.

The next day being Sunday I went to the beach at Glenelg and while we were lounging contentedly a boy came up to me. He was not, as I first assumed, an autograph hunter, for he said in a hurt voice, 'You've spoilt my weekend. I could hit you. Why did you bowl out Don Bradman for a duck?' I don't think

I have ever seen a youngster bursting with such indignation.

Our Cricket Story, Bedser and Bedser

Bradman's greatness was a subject of endless curiosity and conjecture. Colin McCool had this response for the inquisitive.

Avinish Desai, who turned out for the Cricket Club of India in the mid fifties, also played league cricket in England. He once found himself standing in the loo next to the Australian Colin McCool during the tea-break in McCool's benefit match, both surrounded by several Englishmen. Desai conversationally asked, 'McCool, tell me, how good was this guy Don Bradman?' McCool looked round, gestured to Desai to be quiet and said, 'Ssssh! Not so loud. If any of these Englishmen hear you they'll pee in their pants.'

Willow Tales: The lighter side of Indian cricket,
de Vitre

Bradman's all-conquering personality spilled into all areas of his life, even when he was challenged in his late fifties to a game of royal tennis by Colin Cowdrey.

Directions like 'laying a chase on the hazard side' are beyond most people's comprehension until they have been on a court for several long sessions, but Bradman questioned everything and let nothing pass until he understood it fully. Several times he became quite impatient at my apparent inability to explain all the implications of a certain rule in a single sentence; so penetrating was his mind that by the time we began playing he understood every tactical situation perfectly. What staggered me was his fantastic speed around the court, racing from one corner to the other to retrieve a ball. It was that morning I understood why Bradman was probably the greatest cricketer that ever lived. I was aware not of a man but a machine whirring at my elbow. He was conscious of no mortal thing outside those walls. His concentration and determination were absolute. Here was a man, at an age when most would have been living out their past glories in a rocking chair, aggressively storming a new challenge.

MCC, Cowdrey

Nor did his fame – and correspondence – diminish, as he explained at the opening of the Bradman Museum in 1989.

There was one from a lad who said, 'My name is Terry White and I'm ten years of age and I've admired you ever since I was young.' The next one wasn't quite so pleasant. It said, 'I know this request comes rather late, but I should always regret if it became too late!'

And I also referred to some letters indicating what the future calling of a boy might be. There was a potential insurance agent because the letter said, 'Don't be surprised if you get two letters from me. I posted two in case this one goes astray.'

Then there was the potential PM who finished up, 'PS – Keep this signature, it will be valuable one day.' But somebody must have heard that on air because not so very long afterwards I received a sequel when a chap wrote in similar fashion and said, 'PS – Don't bother to keep this signature, it will never be worth anything.' That has me stumped, I don't know what his occupation is going to be.

Speech at the opening of the Bradman Museum,
14 October 1989, published in
The Cricketer magazine

ARCHIE JACKSON
Bradman's contemporary, who tragically died of tuberculosis at twenty-four, recalled by opponent Wally Hammond.

In his early days in Test cricket, he was still young enough to repeat constantly to himself while batting, 'Don't cut, Archie, don't cut . . .' He had been told again and again at school that he must repress his natural tendency to cut the ball until he had been at the wicket long enough to 'see it big'. Jackson got 164 in his first Test innings at the age of nineteen, and his batting that day is still held up as an example of what perfect batsmanship should be. Critics said he was greater than Bradman, and equal to the nonpareil Victor Trumper.

Unhappily, his health more or less collapsed the same year; he toured England a sick man, and four years after his brilliant entry into Test match cricket, he died. It was a very great loss to the game. I have been told he was murmuring, 'Don't cut, Archie, don't cut . . .' with his last breath.

Cricket My World, Hammond

BILL WOODFULL

No Australian captain was straighter.

Bill was so truthful he could not utter even an off-white lie. More than any predecessor, he showed interest in their personal welfare as well as their on-field performance – all about their families, problems and hopes. From a hundred instances I mention one because Methodism seems to be on the furthest edge of the Christian spectrum from Catholicism. Before bedtime on the Australians' first Saturday outside London the Methodist parson's son quietly told St Joseph's Old Collegian Stan McCabe, 19, the whereabouts of the nearest church for Mass in the morning.

On Top Down Under, Robinson

During the Bodyline series, Jack Fingleton thought he might even have been too straight . . .

Some of the Australian team favoured retaliation and pressed Woodfull accordingly, but he, the peace-loving son of a minister of religion, would have none of it. 'We will play cricket in the manner in which we think it should be played,' was his answer. Then he turned his other cheek. This was a noble and pious sentiment which reflected credit on Woodfull. If any dignity was left to Test cricket at the end of that 1932–33 season it was due entirely to Mr W.M. Woodfull, but Bodyline was a grim and ruthless battle into which a leader of mild gentility came somewhat poorly equipped.

Cricket Crisis, Fingleton

. . . but his players did not cavil.

On one occasion Vic Richardson actually moved into a leg-side fielding position to field to Tim Wall's bowling, inviting the short leg-side delivery that the Englishmen presumably would find just as disconcerting as the Australians. Woodfull simply walked to Richardson and said, 'No thanks, Vic. I'm captain.' Richardson immediately fell into line.

The Captains of the Game, McGilvray

DOUGLAS JARDINE

Woodfull's rival, here recalled by team-mate
Wally Hammond.

Anyone who has ever played in a team with Douglas Jardine has been struck by his imperturbability, his calmness when things go wrong and equally when they go right, his cold determination to win, neither giving nor seeking quarter.

Cricket My Destiny, Hammond

And by opponent Bert Oldfield.

Off the field he could be quite amiable, but changed immediately when he stepped into the cricket arena. He would order his men about with the firmness of a general marshalling his troops.

Behind the Wicket, Oldfield

Jardine's dislike of Australians was formed on his first tour in 1928–29.

The word must have got around that Jardine was a stiff-necked, high-nosed type of cove, as indeed he was. He opened the innings with Sutcliffe and in this, his third innings in Australia, made his third successive century. I was in the dressing-room when he got out and Patsy Hendren was preparing to follow him in. Patsy said, 'They don't seem to like you much here, Mr Jardine.' To which Jardine replied, 'It's — mutual.' The blank was a participle which, however familiar nowadays, was beyond the bounds of refinement then – even in Australia.

94 Declared, Travers

Jardine's fearlessness, however, was legendary.

I remember him during the famous Bodyline tour of

Australia taking one of the hardest blows I ever saw on a cricket field and batting on. It was just after the 'Battle of Adelaide' Test, when objections to Larwood's Body-line bowling came to such a head that scores of police were concentrated behind the pavilion ready to charge the crowds if they tried to interfere with the English players. We went on to play a match with Queensland, and Queensland had a famous bowler, Gilbert, an Aboriginal, said to be, for three or four overs, faster than Larwood himself. Some Australian newspapers frankly called on the Queensland skipper to give Jardine 'a dose of his own Bodyline medicine'. Gilbert was put on with the new ball and I have never seen bowling at such a pace as he achieved in his opening two overs. He was bumping the ball on the leg side, and just about the fastest of those balls leapt up and hit Jardine on the hip bone. Jardine staggered and almost fell, but he waved back assistance as one or two players and the umpire approached him. He stood up, his face very white, and took a fresh guard. We knew he had had a bad knock and felt anxious about him, but he seemed to play with his usual iron composure and steadiness. He scored some boundaries but held up his hand when anything like a short run seemed possible, only running when he had plenty of time. He stuck it out till close of play, more than an hour at the wicket, and then walked stiffly into the dressing-room. 'Shut that door!' he said as he came in – and he fainted onto the massage table.

He opened his eyes almost at once, but he must have been playing in frightful pain, for he had a really damaging blow on the point of the hip bone.

Cricketers' School, Hammond

HAROLD LARWOOD
Recalled by opponent Jack Fingleton.

One could tell his art by his run to the wickets. It was a poem of athletic grace, as each muscle gave over to the other with perfect balance and the utmost power. He began his long run slowly, this splendidly proportioned athlete, like a sprinter unleashed for a hundred-yard dash. His legs and arms pistoned up his speed, and as he neared the wickets he was in truth like the Flying Scotsman thundering through an east coast station. He was full of fire, power and fury – or so he looked at the batting end just before he delivered the ball at you at an estimated ninety mph. The first time I was in with Larwood bowling I was watching, naturally, the batsman at the other end as Larwood ran up. Just as Larwood approached the crease I heard a loud scraping sound and the thought flashed across my mind that Larwood had fallen. He had not. A few yards from the crease he gathered himself up and hurled all his force down onto a stiff right leg which skidded along the ground for some feet. How his muscles and bones stood this terrific test over the years is a mystery to me.

Cricket Crisis, Fingleton

Fingleton had every reason to recall him vividly.

Jack was batting in the Second Test of the Bodyline series at the MCG and after only one ball of the innings he walked down the pitch and patted the turf just three or four yards in front of Larwood. Vic Richardson was sitting with some of the non-playing Englishmen at the time. 'Oooh, Lar won't like that,' he recalled their saying. 'Watch him now!'

From that moment Fingleton took one of the most fearful batterings from a pace bowler in the history of cricket. He was pummelled for two or three overs and finished the day dreadfully bruised. When he arrived at the dressing-room at the end of it, Richardson chided him about his exaggerated protest at the length of Larwood's bowling. 'Well, that'll teach you a lesson, Jack,' Vic said. 'Never kick a tiger when he's quiet.'

The Game is Not the Same . . . McGilvray

HEDLEY VERITY

No bowler has had a more successful day than England's Hedley Verity at Lord's in 1934, recalled Wally Hammond.

Verity came tirelessly up to the wicket at the pavilion end, his long arm came beautifully over putting down a good length turning ball. Bradman, grim-faced, slashed whip-like against the spin with his face set toward the far outfield – but the ball did not go there, it went spinning heaven-high, up and up and up, right over my head. As I moved to take it I heard Les Ames say, 'All right, Wally!' with the sounds of contentment as if all his prayers had been answered, so I stepped aside and watched it come down with a whirr into his big gloves. Don Bradman went walking out, with unlucky 13 on the board against his name. As he passed Woodfull at the other end, his skipper gave him a look so compounded of anger and disappointment and woe that I have never forgotten it. Verity standing at the wicket showed not the slightest expression on his face, though he knew, as we all did, that that ball had won the match. He took 14 wickets that day in about 50 overs.

Cricket My Destiny, Hammond

BILL O'REILLY

Bill O'Reilly's three wickets in an over at Old Trafford in 1934 – three Test captains in Cyril Walters, Bob Wyatt and Walter Hammond – began inauspiciously.

O'Reilly was then coming into the attack. He took the ball, looked at it, and said to Grimmett, 'This ball is out of shape, Grum.' Grimmett replied that he thought so too. The bowler handed it to Woodfull who passed it to the umpire. Another ball was requisitioned. O'Reilly bowled to Walters. It was a 'bosie' and it popped. Walters hit the pitch and at the same time the ball hit high on the blade near the splice to be deflected gently into the air to square-leg. Wyatt appeared and was bowled first ball. Hammond hit a four and then he also was bowled – three wickets in four balls, a sensational piece of bowling which began with a bouncing 'bosie'.

The Changing Face of Cricket, Moyes

No umpire denied O'Reilly lightly . . .

Before entering the field in one Test he said to Hele, Australia's leading umpire, 'How's your sight today, George?' Hele said his eyes were good. 'Hearing all right too?' asked O'Reilly. Hele said there was nothing wrong with his hearing. 'Good,' said O'Reilly. 'You'll need 'em today because I'm going to get among these so-and-sos.'

Between Wickets, Robinson

. . . nor did administrators cross him with impunity, as evidenced when he, McCabe, Leo O'Brien and Chuck Fleetwood-Smith were arraigned before a hearing of the board in 1936 to answer allegations of indiscipline. O'Reilly asked Bradman what was going on. Don said he knew nothing about it, but declined to accompany the four 'miscreants' saying, 'You know what I think of the board.' This was a reference to past troubles Don had experienced in his dealings with the administrators.

It is worth noting that the four were all Catholics of Irish descent. Fingleton, of similar persuasion but a working journalist, was not summonsed. The board members before whom they were paraded included

Roger Hartigan (former Test cricketer), Harry Hodgetts (Bradman's chief in an Adelaide stockbroking firm), Dr Robertson (chairman) and Dr Mailer, a Collins Street medical specialist.

Embarrassment was general on both sides and the preliminaries lacked any noticeable rapport between the two groups. Dr Robertson began reading from a lengthy typewritten screed in which unfitness and insubordination were mentioned, but not applied to any specific people. After a couple of minutes, Bill interrupted and asked if he and the other three were the butt of the allegations. Dr Robertson answered, 'No.' Bill then enquired what they were doing there and, after a few more embarrassing moments, the meeting broke up.

Bill O'Reilly: A cricketing life, McHarg

O'Reilly's 10–122 at Headingley four years later won him praise from home.

In 1938, after Bill O'Reilly had skittled England twice to win the Leeds Test, his students at Sydney Grammar School sent a cable to him in England which read simply: 'Satisfactory – a trier.'

Bill O'Reilly: A cricketing life, McHarg

BILL BROWN

Bill Brown was tired out by the effort of scoring five centuries on his first Ashes tour in 1934.

Because of the ball's repeated jarring of the bat against

his hand, Bill was one of the batsmen who complained of an ache in his right palm near the thumb. O'Reilly told him, 'There's one sure way to get rid of that.'

Brown: 'What is it, Tiger?'

O'Reilly: 'Get out sooner.'

On Top Down Under, Robinson

STAN McCABE

It was while the Australian team was staying in Paris's historic Elysee Palace Hotel en route to England in 1930 that teenager Stan McCabe was delivered of his famous moniker 'Napper' by Vic Richardson and Alan Kippax.

The dawn would sometimes race them to sleep, and one morning Kippax exclaimed, 'All we need now, Vic, is for Napoleon to walk through the door.' As he spoke, the great double doors opened and in came Stan McCabe. At nineteen, his features resembled remarkably those of the first French Emperor, and he still had his hair. 'Well, Kip, there's your Napoleon,' Vic said, and the name stayed.

Fours Galore, Whitington

Stan McCabe carried Australia for much of the 1934 Ashes series, as Bradman rediscovered his touch. McCabe won many friends with his chivalry – here recalled by Herbert Sutcliffe.

When the 1934 Tests began we members of the

England side looked upon McCabe as public enemy number one, and he certainly proved to be a thorn in the side of our attackers in the first three Tests. In my opinion McCabe has never been given credit for the excellence of his work in the last series. Regard for a moment the time when Bradman was batting in a fashion that made us all wonder what had come over him. Then McCabe was reliable, and more than that a fine scoring batsman. In the Fourth and Fifth Tests he had to follow when Bradman and Ponsford had made gigantic stands and I thought in those games he took risks he would not otherwise have done in the attempt to force the pace.

I have a story to tell of the great sportsmanship of McCabe. In the final game of the Australians' tour they played at Scarborough, and there I played a ball from McCabe hard enough, as I thought at the time, for three runs. The shot was to square-leg and it happened that the umpire was in the way. The ball may have swerved towards him; anyway it struck his foot and was deflected to Ebeling who was fielding four or five yards towards mid-wicket. As soon as I hit the ball I called for a run and got three or four yards down the wicket. Then I realised the danger and sent Wyatt, my partner, back. Ebeling had taken the ball easily and just as easily he returned it to McCabe who could have run Wyatt out by several yards, for Wyatt, in answering my call, had advanced quickly up the wicket. McCabe never bothered. He made no show of the fact he was allowing Wyatt to escape. He took the ball and, turning around, walked to the point for the delivery of his next ball.

For England and Yorkshire, Sutcliffe

McCabe provided a scenario for one of O'Reilly's ever-ready one-liners.

When Farnes pitched a ball near the leg stump, McCabe pivoted and effortlessly lifted it over square-leg for six. As the ball was being retrieved Farnes said to McCabe's partner, O'Reilly: 'What can I bowl to him? What can I do next?' O'Reilly: 'Well, you could run down and get his autograph.'

Between Wickets, Robinson

LINDSAY HASSETT

An incurable practical joker, he began young on the 1938 Ashes tour.

The Grindleford hills of Derbyshire have had a strange effect on Hassett. He came to the country inn late one night pulling a wet, muddy and complaining goat, which he later said he had found out in the hills. He particularly insisted that Bradman should see the goat. The next night everybody locked their doors, which was just as well because Hassett found a hedgehog.

Cricket Crisis, Fingleton

Hassett was famous for deadpan, self-deprecating humour, as in a story he told against himself of his maiden Ashes hundred at Brisbane.

It fell on the day that one of my brothers got married. I was at 92 and he was due at the church for the ceremony, but thought he would wait a minute or two for the other eight runs. After ten minutes I got four runs, so he rushed away and duly got married. When he arrived home he turned on the wireless and heard I was at 97. I can assure you, gentlemen, that I got my century before he went on his honeymoon.

The Summer Game, Haigh

The clearest sidelight on his personality was his diverting behaviour on missing (unaccountably) a couple of ballooners during the Manchester Test match, a reverse which might well embitter and nonplus a man. Lindsay merely turned to the policeman behind him and asked if he might borrow his helmet for the next occasion.

Talking of Cricket, Peebles

After victory in the Ashes of 1950–51, Hassett found himself rudely interrupted at a farewell function at Sydney harbour. Eric Hill describes the way Lindsay Hassett discharged his leadership duties.

I was in conversation with Bill [O'Reilly] and Lindsay when a lady, for want of a different word, butted in rudely. She was approaching forty-five, as Groucho once put it, from the wrong side and was dressed outrageously in a bikini and rainbow-coloured half jacket which would have delighted on a slender young gazelle. This person gushed, 'Are you the great Mr Hassett?' The elfin admission came a little sourly but improved as the next question arrived, 'My two little boys would love your autograph.' 'Have you got a pen?' he asked lovingly. All saccharin and treacle she produced the pen, as Hassett invited her to sit alongside him with an interested and growing group gathering round. Timing his moves to absolute perfection, Lindsay signed his autograph twice – on the inside of each fat, sun-burned, overgenerous thigh of that very surprised Australian lady.

Wisden Cricket Monthly, December 1980

He expressed his distrust of Tony Lock's action in the Ashes of 1953 in characteristic fashion.

There were widespread doubts concerning Tony Lock's action – not all the time but particularly when he bowled his faster ball. When facing Lock, Hassett would often call down the pitch, 'Strike 1', 'Strike 2' and so on.

Arthur Morris: An elegant genius, McHarg

SID BARNES

Sid Barnes batted Australia to victory at Trent Bridge in 1948 but missed out on the spoils.

A strange interlude occurred when Barnes glanced a

ball to the leg boundary and imagined he had scored the winning runs. He turned and commandeered the leg stump and made off for the pavilion in haste. Seeing him check out, the English fieldsmen and the umpires began to move towards the stand, but they were greeted with howls of derision from the gallery who realised that there was still one run to be scored before Australia could claim victory. Everyone returned to the wickets; Barnes, who had disappeared into the dressing-room, seemed loath to re-enter the playing field. He finally appeared, preceded by the stump which he hurled out onto the field, and on picking it up he proceeded to the wicket and shaped up with it as he handed his bat to the umpire to place in the ground. With Barnes it was more likely to have been a mathematical inaccuracy than excitement that this incident occurred. It fell to Hassett to make the winning hit and Barnes, running through to make the single, failed to souvenir a stump after all – much to his disgust.

Cricket Conquest, O'Reilly

Fielding at the shortest of short-legs at Old Trafford while tailender Dick Pollard was batting, the irrepressible Barnes was momentarily repressed.

Barnes had no chance of evading the ball and he collapsed writhing in pain as it struck him like a bullet in the ribs. As four policemen carried him off the ground, and an ambulance rushed him to Manchester Royal Infirmary, everyone was convinced he had received a grave internal injury. But on the Saturday morning he got out of his hospital bed and, with typical Barnes bravery, insisted he was going to bat. During a trial at the nets he joked with press photographers, but after a while grew so weak that he had to rest on the running-board of a car. Yet no-one could restrain him from going out to the wicket. After a sympathetic reception from the crowd, and a somewhat theatrical handshake from Dick Pollard, he stayed at the wicket for nearly half an hour, then sank to the ground with a cry of pain. He took no further part in the game.

How's That? Chester

Recalling the incident some months later, Sid said, 'I had some Minties in my pocket when I got hit but I haven't seen them since those policemen carried me off.'

Slasher Opens Up, Mackay

Barnes also revelled in presenting the injury as footage in his own films. When the film showed him writhing on the ground in pain after Pollard's hit injured him, he commented drily, 'It would have killed any ordinary man.'

From the Boundary, Robinson

A tough-talking press man, he momentarily silenced the great English cricket prose stylist Neville Cardus during the Ashes of 1950–51.

'Look here, Neville,' said Sid, 'I've got an idea. What about me slipping a carbon paper into my copy today for you and you can do the same for me tomorrow. We both write the same sort of stuff.' I think it is true to say that that was the only time I have seen Cardus stumped for a word.

Brown and Company: The tour in Australia,
Fingleton

SIR LEONARD HUTTON

BBC broadcaster Howard Harshall calling The Oval Test of 1938 where Hutton passed Bradman's Ashes record of 334.

707 for 5; Hutton 332, and all our hearts are with this young Yorkshireman at this moment. Here's Fleetwood-Smith bowling to him. He bowls, Hutton hits him, drives him, but he won't take a single; it's gone to mid-off, deepish mid-off, no run. Well, it's a great day this for Hutton, and what I admire so much is the character which enables him to carry on like this. Fleetwood-Smith bowls to him. Hutton late cuts this but Hardstaff sends him back as he trots up for a run to third man. Hardstaff quite rightly says, 'No you don't, it's not worth taking a risk now.' Well, this morning Hutton's gone from 300 to 332 in an hour

and a quarter. He's been in for twelve and a quarter hours. It just hardly bears thinking about the amount of strain involved. Here's Fleetwood-Smith to Hutton, Hutton right back and tries to turn it round the corner, doesn't quite get hold of it and drops it down. Quite all right, perfectly safe, but no run. Barnett the wicketkeeper is round there to pick it up. Hutton's total: 332. It sounds like the total of a whole side. The England total 707 for 5. And the gasometer sinking lower and lower and here comes Fleetwood-Smith running up to bowl. He bowls and Hutton gets a short one. Hutton forces it past silly mid-off where Bradman's fielding; yes it is Bradman himself crouching at silly mid-off. Now here's Fleetwood-Smith in again to Hutton. Hutton hits him. Oh, beautiful stroke, there's the record! Well that was the most lovely stroke, a late cut, off Fleetwood-Smith's leg-break, which absolutely flashed to the boundary for four runs to give Hutton the record, beating Bradman's record made at Leeds in 1930 of 334, beating that record with the highest score ever made by an individual in Test matches between England and Australia. They're singing. Terrific reception. The whole crowd's standing up and cheering all around the ground. Thousands of them all standing up. Bradman's rushed over to shake Hutton by the hand. The whole Australian team have congratulated him and now here's everybody cheering. It really is a wonderful scene this; here in this brilliant sunshine, they won't stop cheering.

Len Hutton Remembered, Trelford

Recalled by opponent Chuck Fleetwood-Smith.
When he was 290, I bowled him a half-pitcher. He could have hit it anywhere for four. But he got over it carefully and steered it away for a single. I said to him, 'That was a terrible ball. You could hit it anywhere for four!' 'Aye,' he said. 'But there might have been a trap in that.'

Parson's Pitch, Sheppard

Recalled by rival captain Lindsay Hassett.
I won all five tosses against him in 1953. He was a Yorkshireman and Yorkshiremen are supposed to be a bit tight-fisted. In the Fifth Test he produced a crown piece and I won the toss again; Len picked up the coin and heaved it out into the crowd. I said, 'That couldn't have been yours.' He said, 'No, I borrowed it.'

Len Hutton Remembered, Trelford

His leadership in 1954–55 recalled by his amateur team-mate Colin Cowdrey . . .
As we walked off he said, 'How are you then?' I said, 'It's hard work.' His reply was a classic Huttonism. 'Aye, and what's more you're not getting paid for it.'

MCC, Cowdrey

. . . and by opponent Alan Davidson.

He could 'needle' an opponent. When Richie Benaud came out to bat in this series he said more than once to him, 'Come on, Richie, let's get you over with,' as though it was simply a tedious formality. At Hobart, Benaud, Harvey, Favell and I were having a late coffee in our hotel lounge when Hutton paused at our table. Things had gone badly in the Tests and our confidence was badly dented. Hutton suggested that if we liked to come to the nets in Sydney before the Fifth Test he would give us each an hour's free coaching. I don't think he was joking.

Fifteen Paces, Davidson

Recalled by playwright Harold Pinter.

Pinter, I am told, once wrote a poem on Hutton himself and distributed it among his literary friends. It went like this:

> I saw Hutton in his prime
> Another time.
> Another time . . .

Puzzled by the lack of reaction from his friends, Pinter challenged a cricket-loving fellow playwright, Simon Gray, 'What do you think of my poem?' After a pause Gray replied, 'I'm afraid I haven't finished it yet.'

Len Hutton Remembered, Trelford

KEITH MILLER

Hutton's great rival in many a game was the mighty, mercurial all-rounder Keith Miller.

The worst mistake a batsman could make against him was to hit him for four. He accepted 1s, 2s and 3s but boundaries were an indignity he did not cheerfully tolerate, and invariably the next ball would be an absolute fizzer. At Trent Bridge in 1948, he was trundling away with medium-pace off-breaks when I took two successive boundaries and fourteen in the over. That was too much for Keith, but what else can a batsman do with half-volleys? I knew what to expect, and in eight balls I had five bouncers, one of which left the manufacturer's imprint on my left shoulder. Two others leapt at my throat from just short of a length as if they had been bowled from no more than ten yards away with a tennis ball.

Fifty Years in Cricket, Hutton and Bannister

Miller was also bored easily, as he was by Australia's 721 in a day against Essex.

Bradman, Saggers, Loxton and Brown all made centuries, their distinguishing feature being their rate of progress, which varied from just under a run a minute to a run in a minute and a half. Miller came in to bat when the score was 2–364; he took guard perfunctorily and to the very first ball that was bowled to him he lifted his bat, flung his hair back and was walking back to the pavilion before the bails hit the ground. If ever a situation could be said to epitomise the man, then this was it. Runs were there to be had, the Australians were to score another 357, but the idea had no appeal for him.

Keith Miller: A cricketing biography, Bose

The experience of being bowled by Miller at Melbourne in 1955 devastated Peter May.
I like to think that I used to look no more than ordinarily disconsolate but on this occasion I was half way back on the long walk to the Melbourne pavilion when a surge of depression overcame me. What a birthday, I thought. My head dropped and I gazed miserably at the ground. When I looked up, I had missed the pavilion gate by ten yards. Keith Miller's bowling had its great moments such as this because it fell into no particular pattern. It was unpredictable, especially in its changes of pace. He did not always bowl off the same mark but rather when the mood took him. He was immensely strong and supple as well.

A Game Enjoyed, May

Miller's fighting spirit was contagious, as his young team-mate Neil Harvey found when he played his first Ashes Test at Headingley.
The first three balls I played at and missed. Then Keith Miller, who was batting at the other end, came down

the pitch to have a few words with me and settle me down. But the best encouragement Keith gave me was when English spinner Jim Laker came on. I still hadn't scored at that point. Keith said to me, 'Let me take him for a while.' Next thing I knew Keith played one of his lusty drives and hit Laker straight over my head and over the fence for six runs. Three balls later he did it again – another six. I thought to myself, 'Well this is not such a tough game after all.' Thanks to Keith my nerves vanished.

> *Winning: Face to face with Australian sporting legends,*
> Writer

His confidence, too, was boundless, as Bradman found in discussion before selection of the 1956 Australians. Later at a cocktail party on the night of the Centenary match between NSW and Victoria, I was talking to Arthur Mailey when Bradman came up and said, 'Ah, Nugget, how's your back?'

'Good, Don. How's yours?' I replied.

'When are you going to see the doctor?'

'I'm not going to see any doctor. I'm finished with doctors.'

'When are you going to practise again?'

'I'm not practising. I've finished with cricket this season.'

'But we have to pick the team for England in a couple of days.'

'OK, Don. You pick it on this season's performance. If I remember rightly I was top of the batting and bowling averages.'

Cricket Crossfire, Miller

Nobody epitomised the clubbable touring cricketer more completely than Keith Miller.

Having spent his war years in England he seemed to have friends everywhere, from the highest to the humblest. John Rutherford remembers the day the 1956 Australians arrived in England. 'I looked in a paper when we got to London and saw that there was a performance of Beethoven's Ninth at Festival Hall, so I suggested to Keith that we go. And, as Keith walked in, all these people were coming up and saying, "Hello Keith, it's great to have you back." There must have been fifty or so, but Keith replied to them all by name.'

The Summer Game, Haigh

RAY LINDWALL

When Lindwall took 5–70 in his first Test at Lord's in 1948 his partner-in-pace ensured he had a memento.

As Lindwall left the field, someone threw him the ball to keep as a souvenir. But he gave it up when umpire Davies asked for it. Miller did not think this at all appropriate. He ran up behind the umpire, knocked the ball from his unsuspecting grasp, and pocketed it.

He presented it with due ceremony to Lindwall once they were back in the dressing-room.

Ray Lindwall: Cricket legend, Ringwood

Lindwall's 6–20 at The Oval was climaxed with one of Test cricket's greatest catches, by Don Tallon – here described by Keith Miller.

Lindwall, bowling to Hutton, was delicately turned off in the direction of fine-leg. Everyone on the ground including the fieldsmen peered toward the fine-leg fence expecting to hear the crash of the ball on the wooden fence. Instead there was a raucous, 'Howzat!' Tallon, slithering through the mud and sawdust, had the ball wedged firmly in his left hand. Hutton was out. I was standing in slips and, to this day, I cannot imagine how Tallon moved to take the catch.

Sporting Life, November 1950

When England's young star Peter May faced Lindwall in 1953, there was no diminution of his talents.

We lasted a day and a half and were also beaten by an innings, May contributing 0 and 1. The match began on a grey, murky Oval morning, perfect for bowling. It was obvious from a certain tautness and expectancy in the field as I walked to the wicket in the first innings with the score at 4 for 2 that, as a newcomer to Test cricket since they last played against England, the Australians viewed me as a young man to be put very firmly in his place from the start. I suppose that I should have regarded it as a compliment that I should receive such treatment, but as Ray Lindwall bowled me a bewildering over I saw little cause to feel flattered. He bowled me five late away-swingers which had me groping, followed by an inswinger which went through everything. He was a master of control.

A Game Enjoyed, May

When Lindwall was recalled for the 1958–59 series, his former protégé Alan Davidson found the choice of ends daunting.

In the early days to bowl at the other end to Lindwall, especially uphill and into the wind, was really something. I found probably the hardest thing I ever did, when Ray came into the side in Adelaide in 1959, was to be bowling with the wind and downhill and seeing Ray coming uphill and into the wind. When you have a hero you only see him as a hero. And I always had it in my mind that he was the greatest and it was silly for me to be over him.

Ray Lindwall: Cricket legend, Ringwood

ALEC BEDSER
England's greatest medium pace bowler, Bedser bowled Bradman with a legendary leg-cutter at Adelaide in 1947.

Jim Swanton described this as a red-letter day. He had

received an invitation to dinner at Bradman's home. Along with Jessie Bradman and her son John, he elected to escape the rush by leaving an over before the close. They were beneath the stand when there was a tremendous uproar from above. 'That'll be Dad,' said John happily. And he was right. Bedser had bowled his father for nought.

The Bedsers: Twinning triumphs, Hill

When Bedser dismissed him in four consecutive innings on the 1948 tour, Don Bradman was unconcerned.

As he said, 'You have to get out to someone, and who better than Bedser?' Alec was easily England's best bowler.

Flying Stumps, Lindwall

Lindsay Hassett felt similarly when Bedser bowled him at Trent Bridge five years later for 115, one of fourteen wickets for the match.

Lindsay Hassett had moved so certainly to his hundred that his dismissal by Bedser came as a surprise. It was Alec's leg-cutter, sharply deviating once again to hit Hassett's off-stump. The Australian captain wittily described his downfall, 'I tried to play three shots off one ball and almost made contact the third time.'

The Bedsers: Twinning triumphs, Hill

ARTHUR MORRIS

Arthur Morris always faced the best of Bedser, usually
with masterful control. Ian Johnson recalled opening the
second innings with Morris in the 1948 Manchester Test.

There had been a little rain and the pitch was a bit
responsive. Arthur took strike to Alec Bedser, who
moved the ball both ways in the air and off the pitch.
He hit every ball of the first over in the middle. At
the end of the over he came down the pitch and said,
'It's doing a bit. We'd better stick around or Alec will
run through us.' Johnson was more than happy to
agree with Arthur's suggestion that he (Morris) face
Bedser, as Johnson felt he'd have 'no hope' against him
in his present spell. Morris and he hung on for about an
hour during which time the wicket improved slightly
but, more significantly, Johnson did not face one ball
from Bedser. 'It was fantastic to watch the way Morris
handled everything Alec Bedser could hurl at him from
an extensive repertoire.'

Arthur Morris: An elegant genius, McHarg

In the 1950–51 Ashes series Arthur Morris suffered
a run of outs at Bedser's hands, which finally turned
on a joke.

The turning point came finally when Bedser famously
presented Morris with a present of Lindsay Hassett's
Better Cricket before the Adelaide Test, with batting
passages underlined. Morris was able to return it when,

giving away his wicket rather than sit in for a splash of red ink, he was last out throwing the bat for 206.

One Summer, Every Summer: An Ashes journal, Haigh

In 1953 he even got his own back.

In the Manchester Test, Morris was given an over and bowled Bedser with the only ball he sent along to him. 'Never knew it was so easy,' he remarked as he waddled away.

Green Sprigs, Robinson

DENIS COMPTON

Skipper Wally Hammond recalled Denis Compton's popularity on his first Australian tour, 1946–47.

Denis Compton was by far the most popular man among us with the barrackers; in fact, in my four tours of Australia, I have never seen a newcomer there go down so well with them. The cry, 'Have one with us, Denis!' became almost an embarrassment, as men in the stands overwhelmed him with offers of glasses of beer while he was fielding. Now and again he would accept a glass between the fall of one batsman and another, but I think he limited himself to two a day at most, one in the morning and one in the afternoon.

Cricket My World, Hammond

His finest Ashes hour, at Adelaide in 1955, as his
captain despaired, turned back a magnificent spell
by Keith Miller to win the Ashes for England.

We were 18 for 3 and it was as Colin was out that Len
made his famous remark, 'The so-and-sos have done
us,' he said. It was often very hard to tell when Len was
being serious and I doubt if he genuinely thought that
we were in trouble. The humour of the remark lay in
the fact that it was made in front of Denis Compton,
still one of the world's great batsmen, and sitting there
adjusting his pads preparing to go in. 'Steady on, Len,'
he said, 'There's still me.'

    A Game Enjoyed, May

Recalled by Mark Taylor at a lunch attended by the
1989 Australians.

At the end of his speech the special guest concluded,
'Gentlemen, let us hope that at the end of this forthcoming series that it's not Australia or England who
are winners . . . but that cricket is the winner.' At this
there was loud applause, many 'hear-hears', and the
rapping of cigars and glasses on tables. As it subsided,
I felt a tap on my shoulder. It was Denis. 'What a load
of #$%^&*@ crap!' he said.

    Time to Declare, Taylor

NORMAN YARDLEY

Yorkshire's Norman Yardley saved England at Adelaide in 1947 with 61, 53 not out and 5–117, but the important thing he saved, as far as he was concerned, was a souvenir stump.

As Lindwall ran up to bowl the final ball of the game he waved to me to hit the ball back to him so he could have it to keep; but out of the corner of my eye I could see the Australian wicketkeeper, slips and gully all creeping in a sinister way towards the stumps behind my back. So I just stopped the ball and rapidly spun around and tore up a stump from a lot of greedy, clutching hands – and instantly found myself three feet up in the air between six struggling Australians, forced upwards, in fact, as a bubble is forced upwards . . . but I still held my stump!

Cricket Campaigns, Yardley

FREDDIE BROWN

The invitation to take MCC to Australia in 1950–51 took 39-year-old Freddie Brown by surprise.

The skipper was under a shower when he was first asked the question, 'Can you take the team to Australia?' Freddie, who had recently taken up an appointment with an engineering firm, said with typical candour, 'I'll ask the boss.' And with equal forthrightness the boss replied on the telephone, 'If you don't take the job, you're fired.' Freddie Brown had first toured Australia as a junior member of D.R. Jardine's team in 1932–33, a fact that did not escape leg-pulling Australians. Often they would say, on being introduced, 'I knew your father when he was here eighteen years ago.'

Following On, Bedser and Bedser

Brown was a talented all-round sportsman, a hearty and a martinet, as young all-rounder Brian Close discovered when dismissed on the stroke of lunch at Melbourne.

When I got back to the dressing-room there was a deathly silence. I sat in there through lunch nearly in tears. I was sick with misery. Years later Ian Johnson told me he saw me in the dressing-room and said to Freddie Brown: 'Young Close looks a bit down. Go and have a word with him. He needs a little help.' Evidently my captain replied, 'Let the — stew. He deserves it.'

I Don't Bruise Easily, Close

England's win at Melbourne was their first in thirteen years.

The whole cricket world seemed to be delighted that we had found the winning way again at last. I received 400 cables in Melbourne from friends known and unknown. One of them was a neat twist on the now fairly well-known chant of the Sydney barrow boy, who sought to boost his sales of lettuces with the words 'with hearts as big as Freddie Brown's'. The cable read: 'Well done. Lettuce will go up to eighteen pence.' Another, which came from friends in the East

India and Sports Club, London, read as follows: 'Can you get back in time to play centre at Twickenham next month?'

Cricket Musketeer, Brown

BILL EDRICH

England might have fared better had they not excluded Denis Compton's great comrade Bill Edrich for his indiscretions during the 1950 Old Trafford Test against the West Indies.

Bailey recalled the events of a critical weekend for Edrich at the team's Cheshire headquarters at Alderley Edge. 'I was a little surprised to see Bill in his dinner jacket at breakfast on the Sunday morning. But that was excusable with a rest day ahead. The problem was that he had to be put to bed on Sunday night. The porter undertook this task and Bill was so paralytic that he woke everyone up.' Edrich, in his own version of the episode, said, 'After a personal failure in the first innings, I got involved in a party. I returned to bed in my hotel room in the small hours, and apparently went to bed rather noisily. It wouldn't have mattered had not the chairman of selectors, Bob Wyatt, been occupying the next room. I was arraigned before a high-powered committee at Lord's. 'We've had this report from Bob Wyatt,' said Pelham Warner who presided at the meeting. 'Would you like to withdraw your name from the list of possibles for the tour of Australia?' he asked. According to Edrich the deciding factor was that Freddie Brown, the third-choice captain for the Australian tour, did not want him in the team.

Bill Edrich, Hill

NEIL HARVEY

Neil Harvey was eighteen when he made 69 for Victoria against MCC in February 1947; others could see the man he'd become.

Things went well for me that day and I can still hear Godfrey Evans saying as I reached my 50, 'Well played, son, we'll be seeing you in England next year.'

My World of Cricket, Harvey

Harvey was a famously straight talker.

Once he answered the telephone in a team manager's room in London and heard a knighted Australian representative propose a function for the team to attend. 'How do you think they would like that?' the politician asked. Neil replied candidly, 'I don't think they would like it very much at all.'

Green Sprigs, Robinson

Although Harvey was the favourite to become Australian captain in 1956, he missed out to Ian Craig of New South Wales – just as they were about to meet as captains in a Sheffield Shield match.

I didn't see Ian at the nets that afternoon, but next morning as we went out to toss for choice of innings he sportingly said, 'Bad luck, Nin. I thought you might have got it.'

My World of Cricket, Harvey

Two years later he missed out again, to Richie Benaud. On 25 November 1958, the telephone rang in Neil Harvey's office at John Dynon & Co. It was Richie Benaud. 'Guess who's captain?' he asked.

'You are,' Harvey replied.

'That's right,' said Benaud. 'I'm sorry. I thought you should have got it.'

Harvey was disappointed, but phlegmatic. 'There was no point moaning about it,' he recalls. 'And Richie and I had been mates for years, so it wasn't so hard missing out to him. I was glad to be his vice-captain.'

The Summer Game, Haigh

Harvey's opportunity finally came at Lord's in 1961 when Benaud was injured, and his friend Alan Davidson strove to make it a memorable occasion.

In the Kent match at Canterbury I had damaged my back, and on the day before the Lord's Test I could not even stand erect, much less bowl a ball. I told Richie, 'I definitely cannot play tomorrow. There's no way I could see this Test out.' He replied, 'Alan, you have to play. I am out of the Test now and Neil needs you badly.' My back was not much better next morning but I reluctantly agreed to play, fearful of a complete breakdown. There was no day's respite for we were in the field on the opening morning. I walked across to wish Neil luck and he said he hoped I would pull out something special for him. I bowled that day as hard as I have ever bowled in my life. Once I had warmed to my task I was able to keep going and the sharp bounce of the ridge was always a pick-up for flagging spirits. Before the day was out England had been dismissed for 206 and I had taken 5–42 from 24 overs.

Fifteen Paces, Davidson

GODFREY EVANS
England's irrepressible keeper would give anything a go . . .

Evans is a good gambler, because he will always accept the risk of losing. After England retained the Ashes at Adelaide in 1955, Godfrey, among the popping of champagne corks, was wagered a hundred pounds by a camp follower, Arthur Hughes, that he could not climb a twenty-foot column in the team's hotel and touch the ceiling. Godfrey shot up the pole like a possum. Then, strike me, if he didn't toss Arthur double or quits and lose his hundred pounds.

Cricket from the Grandstand, Miller

. . . and sometimes to his cost.

I will always remember the First Test at Brisbane in 1954 with a slightly guilty conscience. It was in this match that Keith Andrew deputised manfully for Godfrey Evans who was suffering from a fever due partly to heat exhaustion. And hereby hangs a tale! Godfrey Evans was always a stickler for fitness and two days before the Test was due to start he felt below his scintillating best. Unfortunately he prescribed for himself a double dose of the hardest training he could find and promptly demanded my presence as a sparring partner on the squash court. Despite the consuming heat, two crazy bodies contorted themselves around the court like porpoises, with the floor soon becoming a sea of perspiration. At the end of the match we lay outside in the sun to dry off and then to my amazement Godfrey leapt up and exclaimed that he still could not get his legs going quickly enough for the demands of a Test match. He demanded that we should continue and unfortunately I had not sufficient breath to decline. If only I had been firmer I might have saved him; but whereas a good night's sleep restored me to fitness, Godfrey developed a high temperature and required the doctor. What he thought was lethargy at the start had all along been a nasty infection.

Cricket Today, Cowdrey

TREVOR BAILEY

England's dour all-rounder made himself universally
unpopular with 68 in 458 minutes at the Gabba in
November 1958.

At five to three somebody in the magnificent Brisbane press box asked how long it was since Bailey had scored. 'At twenty past two,' answered George Duckworth. 'Today or yesterday?' yawned somebody.

Four Chukkas to Australia, Fingleton

FRED TRUEMAN

Fiery Fred was voluble even before he played Ashes
cricket, recalled Arthur Mailey.

'If I'm picked to play against your fellows,' he told me at the beginning of the last Australian tour, when I met him at an outlandish village match in north-east Yorkshire, 'I'll bowl like hell. If I hit them it will be too bad, but while I'm supposed to be a fast bowler I'm going to try and bowl fast. You can tell that to your papers out in Australia.' I found nothing wrong in that.

10 for 66 and All That, Mailey

Just before his Ashes debut at The Oval in 1953,
Trueman relished the encouragement of Keith Miller.

I was bowling in the nets and he had been watching me for some time. I remember him coming up to me when I had finished, patting me on the back, and saying, 'Keep bowling like that, my old sunshine, and you'll be all right.' Coming from a great bowler those words meant something.

Fast Fury, Trueman

Trueman also relished a rivalry with Miller's comrade Ray Lindwall.

I got four wickets for 86, so I made a fair contribution. I also got a very sore shoulder because Ray Lindwall violated the truce that exists between fast bowlers and let me have a bouncer. It hit my shoulder blade so hard that I thought someone had stuck a knife in it, but I didn't let him know he'd hurt me. I just made a mental note to pay him back and had to wait five years before the time came. He faced up to me in the Second Test at Melbourne in the 1958–59 series and I gave him one which reared up, struck his bat handle, clouted him between the eyes and flew up in the air to give a simple catch. Ray came to me after the match to complain and started going on about his age, so I told him I didn't squeal when he did me at The Oval. 'Christ!' he said. 'Do you remember that?' I said that I certainly did. 'Okay, come and have a drink on me,' he said.

Ball of Fire, Trueman

Neil Harvey recalled the fun in his rivalry with Trueman.

He was a fine bowler, probably the finest I faced.

Fred would do his melon a bit, but in a good-natured way. For example, if you played forward to Fred and missed he might say to you, 'Oh you're not bloody well good enough to nick 'em!' You'd come back with, 'Bowl the next one, Fred, and I'll hit you for four.' It was all in good fun. We're still good mates, old Fred and I.

Winning: Face to face with Australian sporting legends, Writer

Likewise Bill Lawry.

He always had plenty to say, most of it uncomplimentary. If he had deceived you with a fine delivery the rather colourful description that followed would flow something like this: 'It bloody well swung out, cut back off the track and you weren't good enough to hit it. You shouldn't be out here.'

Run Digger, Lawry

Even Robert Menzies appreciated his combativeness, presenting Trueman with a pewter mug for his thirty-second birthday.

England's team manager the Duke of Norfolk turned to his host and said, 'That was very generous of you, Menzies, but I would like you to know you have undone the hard disciplinary work of the last six weeks.'

Cricket Close-up, Beecher (Ed.)

PETER MAY

The captain who led England to the Ashes in 1956 was no showboater.

Peter Richardson, his England contemporary and a close friend, often wondered whether May really enjoyed cricket. The instinctive talents, sublimely expressed from boyhood onwards, kept his admirers enthralled, but he was never seduced by the acclaim. He would be quietly pleased if one or other of his glittering strokes was complimented. Richardson, batting with him on one occasion, offered words of praise. May, after some moments of thought, said, 'You're right, it did go rather well.' Richardson says, 'Peter did like to be noticed, but without fuss.'

Peter May: The authorised biography, Hill

SIR COLIN COWDREY

Five-year-old Colin Cowdrey was sailing home to England from India when the *SS Strathmore* hove into view.

What I can also recall most clearly is the change in my father's voice, for its tone, all at once, could not have been more reverent if he had been showing me the precise spot where Moses had delivered the tablets. He said, 'Don Bradman is on board that ship. He's bringing the Australian team to try and beat England.'

MCC, Cowdrey

Len Hutton became the surrogate for Cowdrey's
doting father when the 21-year-old embarked on
his first Ashes tour in 1954–55.

In the midst of it all, he found time for a quiet word
of reassurance with Colin Cowdrey's parents who
had come to see off their son, the youngest member
of the party. Cowdrey has never forgotten Hutton's
kindness and thoughtfulness at that time, not least
because his father died three weeks later. Not a lot
was said but it was Hutton who quietly took the
bereaved young man under his wing and made him his
golf partner on the Sunday after their arrival. Cowdrey was told to equip himself for a rough reception
when he went into bat. 'You're a young player with
quite a reputation. They're going to try and rough you
up a bit.'

Len Hutton, Howat

The serene Cowdrey was hard to rough up, even
for the fearsome 1958–59 Australian dragger
Gordon Rorke . . .

The big difficulty as the batsmen saw it was that Rorke,
the biggest dragger of all time, ended up bowling from
about sixteen yards. He was, I may say, a bit hostile
from there. Just after Colin Cowdrey was out in the
last Test, an elderly gentleman went up to him and said,
'Excuse me, Cowdrey. Do you mind if I offer you a bit
of advice?'

'Not a bit,' said Colin, tactful as ever.

'This man Rorke,' said the old fellow. 'All you people are playing him the wrong way. I've been watching you and him. The answer is to play forward all the time. To put your left foot right down the pitch to him.'

'Thanks for the advice,' said Colin, sounding as if he meant it. He thought for a moment. 'There's only one problem. If I put my front foot too far down the pitch I'm scared that Rorke might tread on it!'

Over to Me, Laker

. . . or when brought to Australia sixteen years later in 1974–75 as an emergency to face the killer duo Lillee and Thomson.

He bade a cheerful 'good morning' to Thomson, who looked at him as if he was mad, calmly avoided the inevitable first-ball bouncer, then took another short one on his backside without the hint of a flinch. Between overs he strolled down the pitch, greeted me as if we were neighbours out for a Sunday walk by the river and chuckled, 'This is good fun, isn't it?'

The Autobiography, Lloyd

TED DEXTER

Debonair Dexter sometimes gave the appearance of not caring about his cricket, although he became as keyed up before a game as anyone.

In 1961, the photographer Henry Cartier-Bresson asked to spend a few days with me to take photographs of my normal working day in the cricket season. He came to Sussex on the train, took photographs in the nets, and in the dressing-room. I found him an interesting and charming man and we managed to entertain each other adequately for the first day or two. On the third day I was due to drive to Birmingham for the First Test against the Australians. I do not believe my French friend knew what he was getting involved in when he said he would accompany me. Thoughts of the impending game came crowding into my mind as we drove up the M1. Conversation became strained, limited to yes-and-no answers. At one moment he asked whether I always drove so fast, and I was surprised to see the speedometer well up over the eighty mark. I drove him to the match on the following morning and my conversation had dried up completely. I do hope that Monsieur Bresson understood that it was those Aussies who restrained my talking, and that I was not suddenly bored by his company.

Ted Dexter's Cricket Book, Dexter

RICHIE BENAUD

For the first six years of his Test career Richie Benaud was an underachiever, only occasionally giving glimpses of his abilities – as at Scarborough against T.N. Pearce's XI in 1956.

Playing themselves in against Bedser's and Bailey's steady bowling, Benaud and his partner had raised 51 in the first hour when a Yorkshire fieldsman passing the wicket between overs remarked, 'What the matter, laad? Art playing for average?' The taunt was answered by a soaring six off Wardle, the first of 11 sixes.

Green Sprigs, Robinson

In the 1958–59 Ashes series he was made captain – without even his selectors having much confidence in the side they picked.

Just before we went to Brisbane for the First Test match, in December 1958, Sir Donald Bradman, the master of Australian cricket, said, 'I only hope we can at least give you a decent game.'

Over to Me, Laker

Benaud, however, came into his own, a shrewd and innovative leader from the very first over at the Gabba.

Pitching on a grassy strip the first ball rose to hit left-hander Peter Richardson on the shoulder. Before a second ball Benaud brought mid-on into close forward leg, a few yards from the batsman's hip. A field change before a ball touched the bat.

On Top Down Under, Robinson

He also developed a priceless reputation for luck.
He decided to bat at Brisbane but, when he lost the toss and saw England do so instead, discovered first-day conditions ideal for his pacemen. The same happened in Melbourne. He cringed on losing the toss in Adelaide on a bone-jarring flat pitch, and couldn't believe his ears when May elected to bowl. 'Pardon?' asked Benaud. 'You can take strike,' May repeated. Australia made 476.

The Summer Game, Haigh

In the Fifth Test at Melbourne in February 1959, he was surprised by the selectors' decision to make Les Favell twelfth man.
Richie looked incredulous and said, 'You've left me with four fast bowlers.' Sir Donald chuckled merrily and said, 'That's your worry.'

Fifteen Paces, Davidson

So, Benaud defied cricket precedent by inserting England.
Just before the captains left the dressing-room to toss, Bradman walked over to Benaud and said, 'It's never been done before, did you know?' Benaud answered with another question, 'What hasn't?'

'No captain has ever sent England in to bat in Australia and won the match,' replied The Don.

'Well,' said Richie, with a broad grin on his face to match Sir Donald's, 'there's always a first time, you know.'

A few minutes later we knew Benaud was not bluffing. 'We are in the field,' he snapped, 'so let's get into 'em.' We did. The gamble paid off and England scored only 205.

Ins and Outs, O'Neill

Benaud's victory ended a drought in Australian Ashes success.

I remember Richie Benaud saying to me at the end in something like bewilderment, 'I've played three series against England over nearly six years and I've never known what it's like to win one before.'

A Game Enjoyed, May

His relationship with his star bowler Alan Davidson was uncanny . . .

Richie Benaud always seemed to get the best out of 'Davo'. They liked each other and I'm sure there were times when he was bowling for Richie. There was one occasion when he had been bowling his heart out for a long spell on a very hot day. 'Just one more over, Al, pal,' said Richie. 'Bowl him another like that fourth one last over which moved in then left him. You're doing wonderfully.' Davo had his eyes shut. 'Just put the ball in my hand,' he said, 'and show me which way to go.'

Parson's Pitch, Sheppard

. . . while his relationship with his manager on the 1961 Ashes tour, Syd Webb QC, was tense at best.

He [Webb] bridled in particular at a hyperbolic report by Ern Christensen of the *Sydney Sun* of a telephone interview with Benaud, especially as the Fairfax tabloid was Benaud's employer. And, before the team headed to Canterbury, Webb summoned Benaud and waved an air-letter at him: it was, he said, from Bradman, empowering the manager to make all future press announcements. The captain would be limited to discussing on-field matters. In retrospect, Benaud feels that he erred: 'The sensible thing for me to have done would have been to ask to see the message and from whom it had come. Instead, I said something to the effect that, if that was what the board wanted, then there was nothing I could do about it.'

On 18 June, the Australians were scheduled to visit the estate of the new Governor-General, Lord De L'isle. Benaud arrived late, having visited London for further treatment, and walked into the usual press posse. But when Tom Goodman of the *Sydney Morning Herald* inquired after his shoulder, Benaud replied blankly, 'I'm afraid you'll have to ask the manager about that.' The journalists exchanged meaningful glances. When the team returned to the Abbot's Barton Hotel in the evening, Webb was closely interrogated. The manager insisted that the move had come at Benaud's request. 'Richie spoke to me about the great volume of work he was doing. He said that he preferred his press interviewing to be limited to on-the-field matters and asked that I do the rest. I agreed.' The journalists returned to Benaud, asking if he was happy with the situation. 'If I answered that question I'd be commenting, wouldn't I?' he replied, deadpan.

Nobody was fooled. Percy Beames wrote in *The Age*: 'The Board of Control has never been keen on captains appearing in print and I am certain that in some way Benaud has been given an unofficial reprimand.' English pressmen delighted in the whiff of scandal. Beneath the headline 'Gag Slapped on Benaud', the *Evening News* featured a picture of Australia's captain with sticking plaster over his mouth. Brian Chapman commented in the *Daily Mirror*: 'The Australian manager, Mr Syd Webb, said the decision was made to lessen the burden of work on Benaud. My answer is . . . PHOOEY!'. . . But it was not a fight Webb was likely to win. With his journalist's nous and his public relations skill, Benaud was simply too poised. Subtly, Benaud and assistant manager Ray Steele, an intelligent and personable lawyer, were taking over the running of the tour. 'We were bloody lucky to have Ray,' says Colin McDonald. 'He carried the tour for Richie. Like us, he realised pretty early that we didn't have a manager. Syd simply didn't have a clue. He was a joke. And Benaud pushed his authority to the limit because, in a stand-up confrontation, he knew he'd win and Syd'd go to water.' Percy Beames recalls, 'Richie really played it for all it was worth. I'd ask him, "How's your shoulder, Rich?" And he'd say, "Well, Perce, I'll just go and find out from Mr Webb." And he'd walk off for a bit, come back and say: "Mr Webb says that my shoulder is fine."'

The Summer Game, Haigh

BOB SIMPSON

With Australia needing a draw at Old Trafford in 1964 to retain the Ashes, captain Bob Simpson compiled 311, exactly as he had foretold.

At their pre-match dinner at the Stanneylands Hotel, Simpson explained his policy simply: 'We'll win the toss and bat for two days.' Simpson slapping his leg after the toss on Thursday morning indicated that the first part of the plan had been executed. And an exchange as Rex Sellers strapped on Simpson's pads suggested that the second part was taking shape in the captain's mind. 'Can I get you a drink?' asked Sellers. 'Yeah, I'll have a Coke,' Simpson replied. 'And I'll have one when I come in tonight, too.'

The Summer Game, Haigh

The innings included, belatedly, his maiden Test century.

Eventually I was within one stroke of that unattainable goal. The ball popped up and I turned it to fine-leg. I looked around. Someone had stopped it surely, or some fieldsman had swooped from no-where to pick up an impossible catch. But no, the ball was on its way and so were my legs, carrying me to the most wonderful of all scores. 'You beaut, I've got it at last,' I thought. 'Thank God that's over. I can now get on with making some runs.' And make some runs I did.

Captain's Story, Simpson

BILL LAWRY

Simpson's opening partner, Victorian Bill Lawry, drove crowds crazy.

One evening during the Fifth Test of the 1964 Ashes series, Jack Fingleton and Neville Cardus were returning from dinner in Soho when their cab became marooned in a theatre crowd. A young dandy rapped impatiently on their vehicle with the handle of his umbrella. As the writers watched in astonishment, their driver leapt out and flattened the fop with a quick one-two. When Fingleton summoned the courage to commend him, the driver replied, 'I've been watching that Lawry all day down at The Oval. I'm in no mood to put up with any more bloody nonsense.' Watching Bill Lawry bat could have that effect. In the six years between his Test debut and his nomination as Australian captain, he had steadily stripped his game to the essentials. He was an international synonym for stubbornness, a butt of barrackers' humour. 'What's the matter, Lawry?' a Sydney Hillite hollered one day during a particular strokeless stretch. 'Have you taken the Pill?'

The Summer Game, Haigh

Rod Marsh, likewise, found that Lawry was no laughing matter when he proposed chasing 469 for victory in the Adelaide Test of 1971.

In my naivety I thought we could get them if we really had a go and I made the mistake of saying that to Lawry. The dour Victorian said through gritted teeth, 'There is no possible way that will happen.' I blundered on, undaunted by this firm retort, 'Hey, hang on, what happens if we don't lose a wicket and we're 180 in the first session? There's no way we're going to be, but we might just be in a position at the start of the last session where we still need 200 runs but we've got nine wickets in hand. We could win it then with a big slog, couldn't we?' I think I took things as far as that to see if I could draw some positive thought from Lawry, and to put some meaning into the last day of a Test match. Bill told me I certainly had a lot to learn about Test cricket, which was right, and added, 'There's no way we would even be thinking about winning the game from here, because we'll lose it if we do.'

You'll Keep, Marsh

The next day he became the first Australian captain
to be sacked mid-way through an Ashes series.

Bill Lawry rose early in the Australian team's Adelaide
hotel on 4 February 1971. The Melbourne flight for the
Victorians who'd just played in the Sixth Test against
England didn't depart until 10.50 a.m., so the Australian captain had planned an early-morning visit to
the residence of Bert Minards, a local with whom he
shared his zeal of pigeon fancying. In Adelaide Tests
gone by, the non-drinking, non-smoking Lawry had
preferred Minards' company to the traditional rest-
day sojourn at Wyndham Hill-Smith's winery. 'A lovely
man with a lovely home,' Lawry recalls. 'We'd sit there
by his grapevines and talk pigeons for the day.' Before
heading out, Lawry went to see Sam Loxton, who'd
joined Australia's selection panel on Ryder's retirement
in September 1970, and in whose company he'd spent
most of the previous day watching the draw's last rites.
But Loxton, he was told, had taken the early flight out.
'That's strange,' he thought. 'Why would Sam take the
5.06 a.m. or whatever out? That's unlike him. Oh, well.
Better get moving.'

Just over an hour later, the telephone rang in the
room occupied by Lawry's fellow Victorians Stackpole

and Redpath. It was cricket writer Alan Shiell, a former state player known to all as 'Sheffield'. 'Is Bill round?' Shiell asked.

'No, Sheff, he's not,' said Stackpole. 'Why?'

'Well, there are quite a few changes to the Test side,' Shiell began, then dropped his bombshell: 'Bill's been dropped and Chappell's been made captain.'

When Stackpole put the phone down, he turned to Redpath. 'Bill's been dropped,' he said. 'Jeez, how are we gonna tell him?'

As if on cue, Lawry knocked at the door and walked in with a breezy, 'G'day boys!'

Stackpole tried to be as sensitive as possible, 'Bill, you'd better sit down.'

'Why?' Lawry replied. 'Have I been dropped?'

Stackpole was amazed. Lawry hadn't broken stride. When Stackpole confirmed that he had been omitted from the side for the Seventh Test, Lawry said merely, 'Well, I thought I might have been. The selectors usually come over for a word after the Test and last night they didn't.'

It wasn't a front, either. Lawry genuinely didn't feel it was the end of the world. He was an uncompromising cricketer, to be sure, but he had been brought up to believe that, if one suffered a check, one got on with it. He says, 'I've no anger at all about being dropped. I hadn't been playing well that series, and I had no compassion when I was dropping players as a selector. I was disappointed that I'd been with the selectors (Loxton, Neil Harvey and Sir Donald Bradman) in the dressing-room most of the previous day. But I should probably have woken up when Sam hadn't been in his room next morning. In our day, everyone was dignified. It was the way we'd been brought up by Jack Ryder, Neil Harvey, Len Maddocks, Colin McDonald, to take the good with the bad.'

The Summer Game, Haigh

GEOFF BOYCOTT

Yorkshire's equally stubborn opener scored 657 runs at 94 against Lawry's Australians in 1970–71, sometimes taking self-sufficiency to extremes, as the *Daily Mirror*'s Peter Laker recalled.

I was talking to Basil D'Oliveira in the Gazebo Hotel with Clive Taylor (the late cricket correspondent of *The Sun*) and Bob Taylor, who was number two wicket-keeper on the tour, and Boycott approached us with a big smile saying, 'If you ever want any advice, my door is always open.' Dolly was suddenly furious and grabbed Boycott by the shirt front, snarling, 'You, you bastard. I know all about your advice.'

Then Basil told us the astonishing story involving Gleeson, the Australian bowler of 'funny stuff' – right-arm spinners – which all the tourists had been having trouble sorting out. Dolly said he had been batting with Boycott and, between overs, had said to him that he thought he had finally worked Gleeson out, giving the details. Boycott (said D'Oliveira) replied, 'Oh I sorted that out a fortnight ago, but don't tell the other buggers up there,' indicating the players' dressing-room.

Boycott, Mosey

All was forgiven when he became the first batsman to register his hundredth first-class century in a Test match, against Australia in 1977 before his home crowd.

His innings contained all the elements which had brought so much criticism down the years, yet this time selfishness was described as dedication. The gates slammed shut early on a packed and expectant crowd, whose nervousness conveyed itself in a roar of applause which greeted little more than a defensive push. It was released in a burst of emotion surpassing anything the old ground had experienced whenever Boycott pierced the field. Caught up in it, the human being inside the brittle shell of the run machine walked on air with unsteady legs at the close of play. 'I did not think it possible, but they did,' he said, indicating through a window the milling throng on the field. 'They willed me to do it. I have hardly slept, knowing that so much was expected of me and worrying in case I let people down. I know this, the hall porter at the hotel is glad it's over, because I had him making tea all night.'

Boycott: A cricket legend, Callaghan

After 63 not out in a day at Perth in 1978, Boycott's mailbag was also bursting.

Jack Birney, a member of the House of Representatives, and one of Australia's most publicity-conscious politicians, dropped me a little note – 'You have done for Australian cricket what the Boston Strangler did for door-to-door salesmen' – which was a compliment if not a very original one.

Put to the Test, Boycott

DOUG WALTERS

Teenager Doug Walters took the cricket world by storm.

From the moment Walters entered Test cricket as a nineteen-year-old against England at the Gabba in December 1965, he batted with the same unflustered intent of a man mowing his lawn. The Don was regularly invoked as he proceeded coolly to 155. The headline in Rupert Murdoch's new daily, *The Australian*, screamed: 'Toast of the Test'. Which he was: when Wally Grout ran a book on how many telegrams the youngster would receive by lunch the following day, Queenslander Peter Allan won with a bet of close to a hundred. Slazenger signed him at once on a £1000 annual contract. Walters made 25 and 115 in the Second Test and, by the Third in front of his home crowd, was firmly installed as a national favourite. Coming out as nightwatchman at the SCG, David Sincock had an intimation of Walters' new popularity. 'I remember I got a standing ovation and I couldn't understand why. Then I looked up at the board and saw Doug's name in the slot. I thought, "I can relate to that. I wish it *was* Doug out here."'

The Summer Game, Haigh

Walters regarded dismissal sardonically . . .

Walters played a quick and handy innings which came to an end with what one writer described as a 'wild village ya-hoo'. When good humouredly challenged on this matter by manager Ray Steele, Walters answered without a smile, 'It was an attempted lofted drive forced on me by the ball dropping quickly in flight.'

Tigers Among the Lions, Chappell

. . . and success much the same, even when turning the Perth Test of 1974 on its head with a century in a session.

I'd been 3 when we resumed after tea and when Bob Willis came in to bowl the last over before stumps I was 93, so if I could hit 10 runs off that over I would have scored a century between tea and stumps. I got a top edge attempting to pull Bob's first ball – four runs. Six to go. Willis had been pounding in three or four bouncers an over so I got on the back foot hoping he'd dig one in and I could get hold of it. But no, he kept them all well up. Then, with the last ball of the day, he let me have a bouncer. Whacko! I connected and belted Bob over the fence for six.

Winning: Face to face with Australian sporting legends,
Writer

Ah yes, the dressing-room. Now wouldn't that be a scene, I thought. The guys would mob me, say 'Bewdy, Doug' and all that sort of stuff. They'd probably douse me with champagne. I'd be a hero among my peers. I rather fancied that.

Surprise! When I walked into the room I found it empty. Not a soul in sight. You bastards, I thought. Here's a man hitting a six off the day's last ball to complete a century in a session, and you haven't got the decency to be there to hero-worship me when I get back. You probably didn't even watch the last over. Where are you, you sods?

Surprise number two was when Ian Chappell appeared from a toilet shower and gave me a blast. 'You dopey bastard!' he said. 'What do you mean by playing a totally irresponsible shot and getting out on the last ball of the day? Haven't you learned anything about team first, individual second?'

Jesus, that's lovely, I thought. Not only had he not seen the last over, but he'd stuffed up what happened anyway. Chappelli glared at me for a couple of seconds. Then he broke into a huge grin and gave me a hug – the pre-arranged signal for the rest of the guys to emerge from hiding in the showers.

One for the Road, Walters

IAN CHAPPELL

The sacking of his predecessor Bill Lawry set the tone of Ian Chappell's captaincy career.

The night I was appointed captain of Australia I said to my wife Kay, 'They'll never get me like that.' The selectors didn't even afford him the courtesy of hearing the news direct, rather than on the radio or from another player. The episode moulded my attitude to the job of being captain of Australia. From the moment I was appointed I was determined I'd retire before the selectors deposed or dropped me.

Chappelli: Ian Chappell's life story, Chappell

He cut a swathe through England in 1972, impressing critics and cricketers alike.

From the moment of our arrival in Britain, Ian caught the eye as a progressive dresser and thinker. I fancy a few of the peers and dignitaries took a second look every now and then, but I think they ended up liking what they saw. He sailed through his first baptism, speech-making in the hectic round of receptions that always accompany the start of a tour in England. In the meantime, Ian had let us know his intentions to run a happy ship when he told us, 'My door will always be open to you till 3 a.m., to talk over any problems you might have. After that hour there's no way I'll talk to you.' Often when we had a game off and were having a late night, as 3 a.m. rolled around one of the blokes would say, 'Hey, we've only got five minutes to see Bertie!'

You'll Keep, Marsh

Chappell, however, knew how to keep his troops in line, as Rod Marsh recalled.

I was very pleased with my form with bat and gloves. But it wasn't until I had been pulled into line by Ian Chappell. I misgloved a couple of balls in a short space of time in the first innings and he hopped into me quick and lively, saying, 'Come on, you're not out here for your good looks, you know.' That came as quite a shock to me and I was furious. But later I realised I had deserved it and it certainly had the right effect because the standard of my work improved markedly.

You'll Keep, Marsh

Ian Chappell proclaimed his resolution with a hook shot that also got him out a few times, but once bitten he was never shy – as he showed at Lord's in 1972.

I had a stack of letters telling me to stop hooking, including one from my grandmother, and she wasn't the greatest expert on the game. The day before the start of the Second Test I had a net and got Jeff Hammond to bowl short to help me decide what to do. I remember a guy behind the net saying to me, 'Even your mates are trying to bounce you out.'

I still hadn't made up my mind when I was padded up and waiting to go in after we'd bowled out England for 272. In came Kenny Barrington and, bugger me, even he told me to stop hooking. He told me to wait until I'd got fifty before I even thought about it. I thought, 'I know he's trying to help, but the day I accept advice from an Englishman will be a first – so I'll hook. But will I?'

I knew I was going to get a few and, sure enough, the first one hit me as I was caught in two minds. Then John Snow hit me and that decided me. I went for everything and I reckon about 40 of the 56 came from hooks. Looking back it was important for the other batsmen, especially Greg and Graeme Watson who had also got out hooking at Old Trafford. The more short stuff I got the more I hooked because I was now sure it was the best way to establish a domination we badly needed after the way Snowy got after us in 1971.

The Innings of My Life, Bannister (Ed.)

His determination to go his own way puzzled Alan McGilvray.

I once asked him why he was so determined to be different, why he would not conform. He simply said that he didn't think he had to. 'If you received a parking fine would you feel compelled to pay it?' I asked, trying to get things in perspective. 'I wouldn't own a car,' he responded. This was about the only level of conversation you could ever get from him on the matter.

The Captains of the Game, McGilvray

Mind you, McGilvray had no reservations about his leadership.

He was utterly selfless and every bit the team man. When it came to playing winning cricket Ian Chappell was the master manipulator. In the fifty-odd years that I have watched Test cricket played around the world I have seen no better captain.

The Game is Not the Same . . . McGilvray

GREG CHAPPELL

Greg Chappell was smart enough to heed some very good advice early in his career.

In those days I was strong on the leg side – not the off. Sir Donald Bradman was a South Australian selector but he didn't speak to anyone except Ashley Mallett, the best spinner I've seen. Anyway, he walked through as usual and I said, 'Good morning, Sir Donald.'

He stopped, turned and said, 'You'll never be a good player with a grip like that.' I asked if he had any suggestions. He did and showed me and said it'd feel a bit uncomfortable at first, but it would be easier with practice. He walked off but stopped at the door and said, 'I've only given this advice to one other player. He didn't take it and he's no longer in the team.' I rushed to the nets. It was uncomfortable but it got easier. It's the grip I've used ever since.'

The Bedside Book of Cricket Centuries,
Smith

His 108 on debut in Perth established him as an individual in his own right.

At an after-play press conference high in the grand-stand at the WACA Ground, Greg Chappell gave a telling pointer to the battle he had waged within to make it as a Test cricketer. 'Maybe now I can stop being Vic Richardson's grandson or Ian Chappell's brother,' he said. 'Maybe now I can just be Greg Chappell.'

The Captains of the Game, McGilvray

Towards the end of his career Greg Chappell seemed to make runs at will.

Australia drew in Perth and won in Brisbane, so Greg led the team to Adelaide [1982–83] in great spirits. He rang his father Martin and apologised for forgetting his birthday the previous week. 'I'll make it up to you,' said Greg. 'I'll make a hundred against the Poms here.' Greg had never made a Test hundred in Adelaide. Martin duly received his gift of runs, 115 of them.

Greg Chappell: Cricket's incomparable artist,
McGregor

DENNIS LILLEE

Perth's Dennis Lillee, who took 5–84 on his Test debut at Adelaide in January 1971, knew he had lots to learn. Lillee has pace, courage, tenacity and that late outswinger. With proper coaching and nursing he could become great. His whole attitude is admirable, especially when catches go astray. And he is fine in the field – determined and confident. After the Seventh Test at Sydney he came across to the M.A. Noble Stand to ask Keith Miller for Ray Lindwall's address. 'He might be able to teach me how to bowl,' he said.

> *Captains Outrageous? Cricket in the seventies,*
> Whitington

Four years later, Lillee formed a terrifying duo with Jeff Thomson, recovering the Ashes in Sydney.

During that Test there was a big shout from Keith Fletcher in the front dressing-room (there are two in Sydney). 'Hey lads,' he said, 'the spinner's on.' We all rushed to see what was happening, and there was the fast–medium Max Walker just bowling an over so Thomson and Lillee could change ends. Fletcher it was who walked out to bat in the match to be greeted by Lillee. The two had been involved in an incident when Lillee, who was batting, had been hit on the arm. As Fletcher went out to bat now, Lillee said, 'Good luck, Fletch. You're going to need it.'

> *It's Knott Cricket,* Knott

Then it happened . . . Lillee bowled another bouncer which did not get up as much as Fletch anticipated and it hit him straight on the head as he took his eye off the ball. We had all been watching proceedings on the edge of our seats in the dressing-room and I will never forget Geoff Arnold jumping up and shouting, 'Blimey he's just knocked St George off his 'orse.'

G'day Ya Pommie B. . . . . .! and Other Cricketing Memories, Lloyd

In the second innings Dennis Amiss felt powerless.
The first ball was an enormous bouncer which flew over Marsh's head and hit the sightscreen one bounce. I thought, 'Shit, we've got a contest here.' It was a lethal wicket. I kept telling myself, 'Come on, Dennis, fight it out!' I was fending and ducking but managed to get 30 playing my best innings of the series. Suddenly I was out caught Marsh bowled Lillee again! It pitched off stump. I had to play it. It bounced and left me. Why did I keep getting unplayable deliveries from Lillee? He used to say, 'Amiss? I could bowl him out with an orange!' He had such an edge over me I was ready to give up the game.

The Zen of Cricket, Francis

Lillee became a ruthless perfectionist, as tough on himself as on batsmen.
I remember facing him in the Centenary Test at

Melbourne where, bowling with six slips, a square cover, short-leg and deep fine leg, he never strayed to the leg-side of middle stump and never bowled wide enough of off stump to be left without risk. At Headingley he bowled several balls quite wide on the other side. Having bowled them he would chide himself, 'Come on, Dennis. What is that, Dennis?'

Phoenix from the Ashes, Brearley

Lillee did not like the sense that his powers were fading, as Allan Lamb recalled in 1982–83.

He even apologised to me for not causing me more trouble than he actually did. It happened on a boat trip he organised. He tossed me a can of lager, sat down and said, 'I used to bowl better than that.' 'You don't have to tell me that, DK,' I replied. 'I saw you bowl on television when you were at your peak and I know your record. That's good enough for me. You're the best.'

Lamb's Tales, Lamb and Smith

JEFF THOMSON

Jeff Thomson's speed in the 1974–75 series had a devastating impact on Mike Denness's English batsmen.

When David Lloyd came back into the dressing-room after his dismissal as I was padding up, I said, 'Well played, David.' He replied, 'Bloody hell, captain, you never get any balls in your own half.'

Any cricketer getting out in a Test match, or any other game, is obviously annoyed with himself. He may come in and throw his bat down or just sit in silence, inwardly cursing himself for getting out. But on this occasion, within seconds of his dismissal, Lloyd's body was quivering. His neck and the top half of his body in particular were shaking. He was shell shocked, suffering from the effects of never having to move around so quickly in all his life. It was the reaction from his continual ducking and weaving to get out of the firing line.

I Declare, Denness

Thomson intimidated journalists . . .

One of the most distinguished and lordly English cricket correspondents effected an introduction to him at a reception later in the series and received for his trouble an acid, 'Are you one of those Pommie —s who've been writing all that — about me?' Exit one startled journalist.

Thommo, Frith

. . . and even past players – as recalled by John Edrich.

I remember Jim Laker sitting in the Noble Stand at Sydney watching Thommo's first three overs. He told us he'd never seen anyone bowl so quickly. He was white-faced with shock – and he didn't have to bat!

The Zen of Cricket, Francis

Thomson's Bankstown mate Len Pascoe knew him well, especially when Thomson was asked to pitch the ball up to Geoff Boycott a couple of years later in England.

Thommo, though, has always been a creature of habit and promptly let Boycott have a couple of short ones. Greg was furious and made his feelings quite plain. 'Oh well,' said Lennie, with wisdom beyond his years. 'Ya can't expect a leopard to change its stripes!'

The Gloves of Irony, Marsh

ALAN KNOTT

In the Ashes of 1970–71 England's keeper Alan Knott was almost infallible, not missing a chance until the final Test when he failed to stump his opposite number Rod Marsh off captain Ray Illingworth.

Keeping so much to Illy, I have come to know instinctively what he was going to bowl and this miss (at this stage of the game) must have been a big disappointment to him. At the end of the over with a wry smile he said, 'Well, at least you've proved you're human.' Under the circumstances this was a remarkable thing to say, for though you have trained yourself to sweep such mistakes out of your mind it always helps if someone makes an understanding remark like that.

Stumper's View, Knott

David Steele recalled his power and his politeness at Headingley in 1975.

He came in and slogged Thommo for 6. He said, 'What have I done?' I said, 'You've hit him for bloody miles.' He looked worried. 'I shouldn't have done that.' I said I wished I'd done it.

The Zen of Cricket, Francis

ROD MARSH

Rod Marsh's Test debut at Brisbane in 1970 turned into a disaster, redeemed somewhat by the humour of his team-mates.

Late that day I tasted my first blood in Test cricket, catching Boycott off Gleeson. As I took my pads off in the dressing-room at the close of the day's play I was pretty satisfied with myself. I had kept well and had the scalp of the great Boycott on my belt. How things changed the next day. I dropped three catches – Edrich, Fletcher and D'Oliveira – all sharp chances but all well and truly catchable. I was devastated as one after the other went down. I felt embarrassed because I knew Ian and Doug Walters were insepara-ble mates of Brian Taber. After the match I was having a beer with Doug Walters who quipped, 'Well, Bac-chus, if you'd caught them all you'd have got a world record.' Tremendous!

You'll Keep, Marsh

Marsh's career was all about those mates.

I remember that when Rod Marsh retired in 1984, A.B. asked him why he had decided to call it a day and Marsh said, 'Because my mates have retired.'

Deano: My call, Jones

Marsh was also loyal to his craft, as Jack Russell learned when England left him out for a batsman/ backstop in 1991.

As I mulled over the significance of my omission, I met up with the great Australian keeper Rod Marsh. He couldn't believe that I'd been dropped and rubbished our management in the press and on television. It was reassuring to have such enthusiastic support from such a distinguished quarter, but I had no answer when he said, 'What are they doing to our craft, Jack? Don't they understand wicketkeepers?'

Unleashed, Russell

DAVID STEELE

Summoned from obscurity, bespectacled, grey-haired Northants batsman David Steele personified English grit in the Ashes of 1975.

I floated out through the Long Room. People were looking at me. I could hear them muttering, 'Who's this old grey bugger?' Thommo stood with his hands on his hips. I said, 'Good morning, Thommo.' He said, 'Bloody hell, who have we got here, Groucho Marx?'

I didn't hear the crowd. I always had tunnel vision. Whenever a colleague held up play because someone walked in front of the sightscreen or moved in the crowd I used to ask them why they were looking in that direction. They should have been watching the bowler with the ball in his hand. A herd of elephants could go past and it wouldn't bother me. I hit a four early on that morning and the crowd erupted. It sounded a long way off. Beautiful feeling. I loved it, knowing I was in command.

The Zen of Cricket, Francis

MIKE BREARLEY

No less grey, but known mainly for his grey matter,
Mike Brearley could nonetheless be ruthless.

In 1979 in Sydney we had a disastrous first day. We had batted very badly then fielded and bowled even worse. As we were hobbling off at the close, Mike Hendrick, one of the senior players, was distraught and said, seemingly to nobody in particular, 'We all need a right bollocking.' 'He's dead right there,' said Brearley, and he let us file into the dressing-room, quietly closed the door and tore into us, collectively and one-by-one. Such livid anger from this civilised man trebled its impact, and we went out and played tremendously tight next day.

The Autobiography, Gooch and Keating

DAVID GOWER

On that 1978–79 tour, his first, was David Gower, who made batting on a bouncy, seaming pitch at Perth look uncannily easy.

As Gower said, seventy per cent of Hogg's deliveries were coming chest-high. One ball hit Gower in the neck, just under the helmet. I feared the blow might unsettle him, yet the very next ball he played with easy timing for four on the off-side. With the second new ball, Hogg bowled three consecutive deliveries that cut away and went through at chest- or shoulder-height. Gower started to play at them, then took the bat inside. He said later, 'I had no chance of hitting them, because they did so much.' But in the next over he hit Hogg for two fours square on the off side – one off the back, the other off the front foot – a mark of his class.

The Ashes Retained, Brearley

Gower always gave the appearance of a light heart, even ten years later as the unfortunate captain during an Ashes defeat, especially at lunch on the second day of the Old Trafford Test when Australia was 1–329.

There sat the England captain calmly sipping a glass of champagne. 'I'm having a toast,' he announced, 'to the first English wicket for a day and a half.'

Under the Southern Cross, Boon

By the last Test the ease had given way to indifference. There were no team meetings, he failed to turn up for practice before The Oval, and during that match was severely distracted by media pressure. At one point he called on the twelfth man to go to the press box and find out who they thought ought to bowl next. When the message came back, Gower laughed uproariously and continued to let Nick Cook get merrily milked.

Opening Up, Atherton

GRAHAM GOOCH

On 99 in the over before tea on the first day of the Melbourne Test of February 1980, Graham Gooch fell six inches short of a maiden Ashes hundred.

I pushed it towards mid-on. I obviously thought it was travelling faster than it was. I called and set off. Kim Hughes came round and fielded it and I know I'm struggling. I was out by about six inches. I glumly led them all in to tea. Ian Chappell looked at me as though I had a screw loose. 'What, don't you like scoring centuries or something?'

The Autobiography, Gooch and Keating

Gooch became the best English batsman of his generation, even in the opinion of Shane Warne . . .

Gooch was a player I really enjoyed competing against. I am still not sure whether he read me as well as some of the others, but he had his own method, knew the strokes he could get away with and stayed in through sheer application, determination and pride in his country and performance. I used to call him 'Mr Gooch' when he was batting, out of respect more than anything else.

My Autobiography, Warne

. . . although, as Gooch learned when meeting Harold Larwood, not everyone treated him with such deference.

I know I'm getting old, but I didn't laugh as much as Darren [Gough] did when Harold said to me, 'You must have seen Hedley Verity bowl.'

The Autobiography, Gooch and Keating

ALLAN BORDER

Dismissed cheaply during the Perth Test of 1979, young batsman Allan Border couldn't contain his disappointment.

The old WACA pavilion had steps leading up to the players' balcony, with the home dressing-room to the right, the visitors to the left. I had not been to the ground as anything else but a visitor, and I wasn't thinking too clearly anyway as I climbed those steps with a wretched failure weighing heavily on my mind. I opened the door with a bad-tempered, hip-and-shoulders shirtfront, threw my bat onto the floor, ripped off my gloves, kicked them as far as I could and unleashed a scathing verbal attack on Poms in general and their cricketers in particular. I had just exhausted my vocabulary of expletives when the horrible truth dawned: I was in the England dressing-room.

Allan Border: An autobiography, Border

Border became the ultimate batting survivor, at one stage during the 1981 Ashes series batting thirteen hours without dismissal.

While I was fielding at silly mid-off, Border gave me an indication of the high standards he set himself: he drove Willis past cover for two, but when he came back was muttering to himself, 'Bad shot, bad shot. Too wide. Concentrate.'

Phoenix from the Ashes, Brearley

Border was not a successful captain, however, until on the 1989 Ashes tour he turned over a new, more abrasive, leaf – as he later explained to his rival David Gower.

He said to me, 'David, the last time we came here I was a nice guy who came last. I've been through all sorts of downs with my team, but this time I thought we had a bloody good chance to win and I was prepared to be as ruthless as it takes to stuff you.'

The Autobiography, Gower and Norrie

IAN BOTHAM

The great all-rounder was also a chivalrous opponent, recalled Dirk Wellham, who made a hundred on debut at The Oval in 1981.

After I had been on 99 for 15 minutes, the drinks break came and brought some relief from the seemingly endless tension. I drank, chatted about nothing and returned to pick up my bat and began to pull on my gloves. As I composed myself to continue, a voice from nearby said, 'You've done all the hard work, don't throw it all away now.' Disbelieving I looked up as Ian Botham walked past. Botham, the nemesis of Australia's batsmen and the man who had been trying harder than anyone to dismiss me in my first Test for 99! Ten minutes after the resumption, my instincts took over and I punched a shortish delivery through to the cover boundary. It was hard to believe that I had scored a century in my first Test. It was *Boys' Own* stuff and I didn't know what to do or where to look. The first man to shake my hand was Botham, saying simply, 'Well played.'

Solid Knocks and Second Thoughts,
Wellham

All the same, no-one forgot the experience of being dominated by him, not least Merv Hughes, who went for 22 in an over as Botham charged to 138 at the Gabba in November 1986.

Cricketers have a black humour in the darkest times but Hughes was not cheered to hear his team-mate Jones's call when he tossed the ball back to him from mid-off after Botham had pulled him for six. 'Jeez, Merv, that one went so far it should probably have qualified for frequent flyer points.'

Merv Hughes: The full story, Keane

By 1989, however, Botham was a shadow of the cricketer he had been, falling spectacularly at Old Trafford to Trevor Hohns' leg breaks.

If he hadn't been bowled he would have been stumped by the acreage of his farm in Northumberland. Apparently he came in and said he'd got his bat stuck in his pad. Graham Gooch looked up and asked him, 'Where was your pad, Beefy? On your fackin' head?'

Opening Up, Atherton

MERV HUGHES

Hughes was fast and fierce even in low-key games, like one in 1989 against Nottinghamshire.

Merv was bowling a fiery spell and followed each delivery with a few comments, 'What sort of fucking shot was that?' and, 'The next one will take your fucking head off.' Just the normal sort of verbal intercourse between intelligent, sensitive cricketers. This went on for a few overs until, at the end of one over, the umpire went to hand Merv his jumper and with a smile said, 'And that, gentlemen, is the end of another fucking over.'

Diary of the Ashes 1989, Lawson

Hughes didn't get the last word in with umpire Dickie Bird during the Sixth Test at The Oval either after being no-balled for bowling three bouncers at Robin Smith.

A.B. came flying in from mid-wicket and as I walked past I heard:

A.B: 'What's going on, Harold?'

Dickie: 'That's three in a row!'

A.B: 'Why didn't you say something to Merv last ball instead of just no-balling him?'

Dickie: 'I did.'

Then I copped the blast from A.B.

South African Tour Diary, Waugh

IAN HEALY

Keeper Ian Healy not only played a good game but talked one too.

Healy's sledges were always humorous and worth listening to. Once, when captaining Queensland, he told the bowler he wanted a fielder 'right under Nasser's nose' and he proceeded to place him about six yards away. In Melbourne in 1998–99, Mark Butcher had moved down to number three from his usual opening berth, but each innings he was in by the second over. As he took guard in the second innings, Healy gleefully piped up, 'Not much different at number three is it, Butch?'

Opening Up, Atherton

MARK TAYLOR

Mark Taylor was not the most recognisable Australian cricketer when he was appointed Australian captain.

A day later when he called into a pub in Glen Innes to meet some of his wife's family, the publican studied him as he ordered two beers. 'Jeez, you look like Mark Taylor,' the publican mused. Taylor smiled, 'People say that, but I'm better looking, aren't I?'

Inside Edge, August 1994

Mark Taylor arrived in England in 1997 on the end of a long lean streak, and in the second innings of the Edgbaston Test was assuredly on his last chance. He was inspired to a century by a timely message from Kieren Perkins.

I mentioned that before the Test we had watched the video of Kieren's 1500 metres freestyle victory in Atlanta. On the second day here a fax arrived from Kieren in Brisbane. In it, he talked of our similarities, how he felt before the final in Atlanta, how he doubted himself. 'Just get out there and do it . . . believe in yourself,' Australia's greatest swimmer advised me. 'And beware of the "Fud" factor (fear, uncertainty and doubt),' Kieren advised. 'You are there because you are the best and they [the critics and detractors] are not,' he wrote. 'You can do it and I know you will.'

A Captain's Year, Taylor

SHANE WARNE

Shane Warne's first ball in an Ashes Test at Trent Bridge in 1993 to Mike Gatting is perhaps the most famous in Test history.

With the ball to Gatting all I tried to do was pitch on about leg stump and spin it a fair way. As it left my hand it felt just about perfect. When a leg-break works really well it curves away to the leg side in the air before pitching and spinning back the other way. I knew I'd bowled Gatt and I could tell from the look on Ian Healy's face behind the stumps that the ball had done something special, but it was not until I saw a replay that I fully realised just how much it had done. After stumps the England players came into our dressing-room for a drink, and Gatt looked at me and said, 'Bloody hell, Warnie. What happened?' I'm afraid I didn't have much of an answer for him. 'Sorry, mate. Bad luck.' Then we both laughed.

My Own Story, Warne

Warne's hat-trick in the Boxing Day Test of 1994 caused consternation.

The silence in the dressing-room was broken by Phil Tufnell, who was the next man in after the hat-trick ball, and who had got a duck in the first innings. Tuffers stood up, turned to the manager and said, '— me, Fletch, I'm on a pair and a quadruple here!' He survived the quadruple ball but not his pair.

Fraser's Tour Diaries, Fraser

He never relaxes on the field, as the England coach David Lloyd recalled in this vignette of the Ashes of 1997.
I recall observing Warne standing at second slip, clapping his hands and going round the team, calling out their surnames and goading them into greater effort. As they closed in on victory to level the series at Old Trafford, he sensed the mood was too subdued, so he shouted so all of Stretford could hear, 'Come on, Australia. This is what it's all about.'

The Autobiography, Lloyd

Warne's successes bothered one Englishman in particular . . .
Phil Tufnell was constantly in a flap. For a start, Warne spun the ball twice as far as Tufnell, who often looked innocuous in comparison. 'That bloke's making me look ordinary! He's ruining my career!' Tufnell constantly complained.

Opening Up, Atherton

. . . but he is a generous opponent.
How well you are going to do depends on how much

you want to listen to him and worry about him, but he is great to face because he gives you respect. If you do well against him he is not one to give you abuse. He will just say, 'Shot,' and after the game or your innings he will come in and say, 'Well played.'

A Year in the Sun, Vaughan

STEVE WAUGH

Steve Waugh was once thought vulnerable to fast bowling – publicly, by England's Mike Atherton, before the Brisbane Test of 1994. He [Waugh] would not let that stand.

I saw him in a bar there – I was going out of my way not to speak to him and he was probably doing the same. I was pretty hurt by what was said so I went up and said, 'I think it's about time this stuff stopped. Let's just forget it and get on with the cricket.' And he said, 'Good idea. I'm sorry I said those things in the paper and let's start from now.' It was good that things got sorted out. We went back to square one. He's tough out in the middle; he's got lots of pride. England need more like him.

Inside Sport, February 1995

Waugh's 108 and 116 at Old Trafford in 1997 were made in spite of a horrid pitch and an English plan to surround him with silence.

We felt he revelled in a hostile atmosphere and sledging merely fuelled his adrenalin. He arrived at the crease and soon realised this. 'Okay, you're not talking to me, are you? Well, I'll talk to myself then.' And he did, for 240 minutes in the first innings, and 382 minutes in the second.

Opening Up, Atherton

Steadily, Waugh drove Darren Gough crazy.
Steve Waugh is so hard to bowl at. You can bowl him maiden after maiden and think you've got him tied down then he smashes two fours. Some bowlers wear batsmen down. He's a batsman who wears bowlers down. I remember thinking, 'How the hell do I get this man out?' I do every time I play against him.

Dazzler, Gough

Although Waugh made 152 undefeated runs in the Boxing Day Test of 1998, Alec Stewart found him inconsolable in defeat.
I went across to the umpires to shake hands, and also to Steve Waugh. 'Well played, mate,' I said. 'Doesn't matter, does it?' he replied, completely dejected.

A Captain's Diary, Stewart

When Waugh was on 98 with one ball remaining of the second day of the Sydney Test in 2003, his rival captain Nasser Hussain wanted him to reflect on it.
The crowd was going absolutely ballistic and it was getting pretty dark. So I thought, well, drag it out as long

as possible. I'm not sure if Steve Waugh does sweat, but if he does sweat, let him sweat a little bit longer on it. I ran up to Dawson and said, 'I've got nothing to say to you actually, we're just trying to stall here.' I finally said to him as I walked off, 'Bowl it full and straight and quick.' I thought Steve would go for his favourite shot which is the slog sweep over mid-wicket. I wandered past Steve and he was steely-eyed. And then Dawson bowled and it just had a fraction of width on it. It was a ball that most of us in world cricket would have patted back. His hands just nailed it through the covers and then pandemonium set in.

Never Say Die, Waugh

GLENN McGRATH

Glenn McGrath added his name to the famous Lord's honour board with 8–38 in 1997, thanks to some hasty improvisation.

The board is in the visitors' dressing-room and it commemorates every batsman who has scored a century or any bowler who has bagged five wickets in an innings there, and I must admit I still get goose bumps when I remember how the Australian coach Geoff Marsh beat the ground's sign-writer to his job straight after we dismissed the Poms for a measly 77 by scribbling my name on a piece of scrap paper and plastering it to the board!

Pacemaker, McGrath

ADAM GILCHRIST

Adam Gilchrist came in on a pair but under pressure
to get quick runs at Brisbane in 2002. He quickly put
both to rights.

We were 359 in front and Stephen had lifted me two
places up the order to have a crack at getting us up to
a declaration. But I was facing a dreaded pair and all I
wanted to do was get off the mark. My last pair of ducks
was in Calcutta in that famous Test where we made India
follow-on then not only lost the Test but also the series.
The sports psychologists would say that I shouldn't have
been thinking about this as I approached the crease in
Brisbane some eighteen months later, but I was.

The fieldsmen, who had been scattered around the
edges for Haydos, were brought in close to try and stop
me getting off strike. I blocked the first ball, then the
next one was 'the right delivery'. I was off the mark
with a six.

Walking to Victory, Gilchrist

MICHAEL VAUGHAN

When Justin Langer unsuccessfully claimed to have
caught Michael Vaughan at cover on 19 at Adelaide
in 2002, the stage was set for a bitter day.

To say Langer was angry is a huge understatement. He
was so red-faced I thought he had turned into something out of a giant packet of matches – this short
strand of white with a big red blob on the end of it. For

the rest of that morning session Langer called me every name under the sun. That fired me up and made me determined to make him pay for it. I also told him during the height of the verbal abuse that a year earlier he had got away with something similar against the West Indies at the Sydney Cricket Ground. Most of the Australians, I think, agreed that I was perfectly entitled to do what I had, but Langer would not let it drop and all day kept on giving me plenty.

A Year in the Sun, Vaughan

RICKY PONTING

After a day scoring 156 at Old Trafford in August 2005 to take Australia to the brink of safety, Ricky Ponting had to wait to see if he'd blown it.

I was calm, seeing the ball clearly, my feet moving well, and there was no way I was going to get out. It was my desire to take that responsibility that cost me my wicket. Facing the last ball of a Stephen Harmison over I knew he was going to bowl me a bouncer – that was his best chance of stopping me getting bat to ball and making it to the other end to retain the strike. When the bouncer came I tried to paddle it away for a single to fine leg, but it brushed my glove on the way to Geraint Jones. It seemed an eternity before umpire Billy Bowden gave me out, and I lingered for just a second or so before dragging myself off the ground unable to believe what I had done. The draw was in sight and I had contrived to get myself out. I could not face going out onto the balcony to watch the last four overs. I just stayed in my seat. It was agony, but gradually the last pair, Lee and McGrath, got down to the last ball of the match, and when Lee survived there was a collective shout, 'Yes, Binga!' Michael Kasprowicz rushed up and hugged me, and Justin Langer said, 'That's the best innings you have ever played.' But nothing sank in for a long while after the match.

Ashes Diary 2005, Ponting

2 | AN ASHES TWENTY20

In discussions of the heritage of the Ashes certain matches recur endlessly. Selection of the best invites challenge. The Tests represented in this chapter may not actually be the greatest, but they are the most storied, from Australia's act of lese-majesté in the very first, at The Oval in 1882. The Oval 1948 was a fearful whitewash, but it did contain the oft-retold tale of Bradman's swansong. Headingley 1989 may not have been an epic of grandeur, but the players in it remember the game as a turning point, a final exorcism of the Botham demon of eight years earlier.

There are no Tests included from the 1990s, not because there were not good ones, but because those that were tended to be short-lived English rallies against the Australian tide of events, and thus of little practical meaning. But Edgbaston 2005, the final selection, was definitively great, almost too recent for history, but surely the stuff of it.

153

THE OVAL 1882

England's A.P. Lucas describes the turning point
of The Oval Test of 1882 involving W.G. Grace,
Australians Billy Murdoch and Sammy Jones,
and umpire Bob Thoms.

Murdoch played a ball to leg for which Alfred Lyttelton ran and W.G. from point went up to the wicket.
S.P. Jones completed the first run and, thinking the ball
was dead, went out of his ground to pat the wicket.
Grace whipped the bail off and Thoms gave Jones out.
He was furious and so were several of his side, but one
of the Australians later on admitted he would have
done the same thing if he had been where Grace was.

> *The Memorial Biography of Dr. W.G. Grace,*
> Gordon, Hawke and Harris

And when A.N. Hornby's Englishmen needed 85 in
their second innings to win, the incident became the
casus belli: Fred Spofforth and Harry Boyle ignited
the Ashes with Australia's first win on English soil,
as David Frith describes.

'This thing can be done!' growled Spofforth. As W.G.
and Ulyett built England's score (to 2 for 51), Spofforth
switched to the pavilion end in place of Garrett, the
fast–medium bowler. The breakthrough came when
Ulyett touched a fast one to Blackham, who held the
catch low down. W.G. went next, caught at mid-off
from Harry Boyle's bowling for 32, and a tremor

of alarm swept through the English camp. With six wickets remaining, England needed 32 more as the Hon. Alfred Lyttelton went out to join A.P. Lucas, the hour-hand of the clock dropping slowly to five, the ground becoming firmer for the bowlers.

Spofforth and Boyle tightened their grip on the situation. There was an eerie silence about the ground; England's waiting batsmen sat huddled, shivering in the cold air. As maiden over followed maiden over the tinkle of hansom cabs could be heard outside.

Stalemate was broken by a tactical ploy. Though England required only 20 to win, the Australians gave a single with a misfield so that the bowlers could have fresh targets. Soon the dividend was delivered. Spofforth charged in on his angled run, eight menacing strides. Over went the arm and the ball crashed through Lyttelton's guard and took the top of the middle stump.

A.G. Steel entered and had to pass Spofforth's baleful glare as he walked to the crease. Within minutes he was on his way back, caught-and-bowled halfway down the pitch by Spofforth, whose slower ball had claimed another victim. His next ball bowled local hero Maurice Read. England 70 for 7: 15 needed.

A yorker first ball to Bill Barnes almost did its work, but the batsman chopped down on it. Then three byes drew everyone's attention to the boldness and magnificent teamwork of Spofforth and his wicketkeeper Blackham throughout the innings in having no long-stop despite the delicate position. The bearded Boyle, medium pace round the wicket, turning from leg, continued to bowl tightly and Murdoch stuck to this attack, praying that the burly Barnes would not unleash one or two tension-breaking hoicks through mid-wicket. Then Spofforth broke through again, forcing Lucas to play on to one which turned a lot from outside the off. When Barnes was caught at point off his glove off Boyle, England were 75 for 9.

Edmund Peate, Yorkshire's slow left-arm bowler, came in, his captain A.N. Hornby having told him to leave everything to C.T. Studd, one of England's finest batsmen held back to number ten and now stranded at the non-striker's end. Peate was expected to exercise caution. He had an almighty swing and got two runs. One ball left, then Spofforth could do his worst on Studd. But it never got to that. Peate irresistibly thrashed again . . . missed . . . and it was all over. England all out 77. Boyle 3–19 off 20 four-ball overs. Spofforth 7–44 off 28, 14–90 in the match. Australia winners by seven runs. For the first time Australia had humbled the full might of England and small boys were forgiven for believing that F.R. Spofforth had horns in his head.

The Fast Men, Frith

The sensations of victory were savoured by George Giffen . . .

While the tension had lasted the spectators rarely gave

vent to their feelings and when Peate, the last man, was out they seemed unable for a moment or two to realise that England had actually been beaten. The great crowd was like a man stunned. But they soon forgot their sorrow to applaud us, and we had cheer after cheer from those healthy British lungs. A small coterie of Australians who sat in the pavilion were wild with joy; and I remember Mrs Beal, the mother of our manager, running down the steps and I, being the first who came along, although I had contributed as little as any to the victory, found her arms around my neck and a motherly kiss implanted upon my brow.

With Bat and Ball, Giffen

. . . and Tom Horan.

He [Grace] played an excellent 32 himself when England were set 85 to win, and it was after that Horan records he saw him looking a bit downcast for the only time. W.G. said to him, 'Well, well. I left six men to get thirty odd runs and they could not get them.'

The Memorial Biography of Dr. W.G. Grace,
Gordon, Hawke and Harris

The vast concourse rushed the ground and Boyle was fairly carried into the pavilion by several enthusiastic Australians. I am only speaking the truth when I say that we were as heartily cheered as if we had won the match on an Australian ground before an

Australian public. Cries of 'Massie', 'Murdoch', 'Spofforth', 'Boyle' and 'Blackham' were heard again and
again from the tremendous throng in front of the pavilion, and each of these players had to go out and bow
his acknowledgements amidst multitudinous shouts of
'Bravo, Australia', 'Well done, boys', and so on. Never
shall I forget the wild excitement of the moment; how,
for instance, our manager Charlie Beal in rushing out
to congratulate us sent the man at the gate head-over-
heels; how one man dropped dead in the pavilion from
over-excitement; how not only the Australians but
Englishmen rushed into our dressing- room and shook
hands with us all around; how they mingled champagne, seltzer, and lemons and passed the drink round
like a loving cup; and how, true sportsman that he is,
A.N. Hornby came up to Murdoch and said, 'Well, old
fellow, it would have been the proudest moment of my
life to have won, but I cannot help congratulating you
sincerely on the splendid uphill game you played and
your well-merited success.'

Then when we were leaving the ground how the
crowd around our conveyances cheered us to the echo;
how they almost took Spofforth off his legs in their
desire to pat him on the back and shake hands with
him for his really superb efforts with the ball; how the
ladies from the windows in Kennington Road waved
their handkerchiefs to us, and how all the way back to
the Tavistock [Hotel] the passers-by looked at us as if

we really had done something to make us famous for all time.

The Australasian, 21 October 1882

The famous obituary, the handiwork of Reginald Brooks, ensued.

In affectionate Remembrance
OF
ENGLISH CRICKET
WHICH DIED AT THE OVAL
on
29th AUGUST 1882
Deeply lamented by a large circle of sorrowing
friends and acquaintances
R̄ĪP̄
NB – *The body will be cremated and
the ashes taken to Australia*

The Sporting Times, September 1882

SYDNEY 1894

When Australia's John Blackham and England's Drewy Stoddart tossed at Sydney in December 1894 they had no hint of what was to follow.

'Someone will be swearing directly, Jack,' Stoddart said as he watched Blackham flip the coin, 'I hope it's you!'

My Dear Victorious Stod: A biography of A.E. Stoddart, Frith

Syd Gregory's 201 in four and a half hours seemed to have set Australia up beautifully.

By the day's end at 6 p.m. admirers had collected 103 pounds to recognise the size and quality of Gregory's innings. Handing over the money George Reid said, 'If we had left the list open for a week I believe we would have got enough to set him up for life, but it was thought better to crown his performance with a spontaneous expression of admiration. When I say no grander innings was ever played on the ground I feel glad for the sake of the Old Country that our friend is no taller, for if he had been a Bonnor he would have got into millions.'

On Top Down Under, Robinson

After a titanic struggle in which England had followed-on, Australia needed 64 to win on the final day with eight wickets in hand.

But as Sydney slept the elements took a hand. The Australian cricketers went down to breakfast at the Baden Baden Hotel, Coogee, with great anticipation. 'It's all right, boys. The weather is beautiful!' roared Ernie Jones, who was first out of bed that morning.

Giffen was confident too as he looked through the window at the bright blue sky – until he bumped into his skipper. Blackham, who had worried about the weather throughout the previous day, had a face 'long as a coffee-pot', and forecast bad things as they took off for the SCG, the carriage leaving deep furrows in the soft ground. It had rained heavily during the night. The uncovered pitch was saturated, transformed into a batsman's nightmare.

Some of Stoddart's men, feeling the match was lost, had got drunk on the Wednesday night, and it now fell to the captain to get the booziest of them all, Bobby Peel, sobered up for action. He was put under a cold shower, then told of the duty which lay before him now that a blazing sun on the wet pitch had given England an unexpected opportunity to fight back for a victory. Peel, as oblivious as any to the night's rainfall, at first thought someone had watered the pitch. As it gradually dawned on his befuddled brain that England was back in with a chance, he is supposed to have said to his skipper, 'Give me the ball, Mr Stoddart, and I'll get t'boogers out before loonch!'

Stoddy's Mission: The first great Test series 1894–1895, Frith

Which he did, taking 6–67 as Australia's last eight wickets fell for 36 runs.

The crowd were all on their feet, yet the silence, except for the roar when a wicket fell, was the tragic stillness of death, and for an hour people suffered, in silence, that unpleasant sinking about the waistband which is a manifestation of anxiety, and almost painful while it lasts. Blackham walked up and down the balcony like a caged lion, muttering 'Cruel luck – cruel luck,' and George Giffen, half-dressed, stood with a singlet in one hand and a shirt in the other, blankly watching the procession. In short, the team were thoroughly cut up seeing the victory thus snatched away. 'The rain beat us,' said some of them. 'No, the sun beat us,' said Blackham. Those who bet were heavy losers, a well-known Sydney jockey dropping £100, while another was fool enough to lay £40 to £5 on the Australians on Thursday morning. He was an admirable judge of horses but a poor judge of cricket.

The Australasian, 21 December 1894

OLD TRAFFORD 1902

In a low-scoring match on a wet wicket, the opening partnership of 135 in 78 minutes between Victor Trumper and Reg Duff, confounding England's scheming skipper Archie MacLaren, was vital.

MacLaren often reconstructed Victor's innings for me in our many talks together, a match-winning achievement if ever there was one. When MacLaren won the toss (in a three-day match remember) the wicket was soft after rain – no 'covering' in those olden times. My plan, narrated MacLaren, was to keep Victor quiet for two hours. Lockwood was unable to bowl more than a few overs before lunch, because the ground was so damp that he could scarcely find a foothold. So, MacLaren commanded his other bowlers, F.S. Jackson, Tate, Braund and Rhodes, to keep Victor quiet until lunch, whatever else you do. Thus one of cricket's subtlest skippers with his tactics put into force by experienced and skilful masters of spin and length, sought to reduce Trumper to inactivity. The field was set to stop the fours, on a turf which robbed strokes of much power. 'In the second over,' said MacLaren, 'Victor drove Jackson over the sightboard into the practice ground, and I couldn't ruddy well set one of my long fields in the practice ground, could I?'

Cricket: The great ones, Arlott (Ed.)

England, 0–36 at lunch on the final day, needed only 87 to win, but Australia's Joe Darling remained confident.

We were sitting at lunch when Archie came into the room. 'Ah, Joe,' he said to Darling, our skipper, 'I think we've got you this time.'

'Oh, have you?' said Joe. 'Why, we've only got to get two or three of you out and the rest will shiver with fright.'

The Game's the Thing, Noble

England got as far as 3–92, but six wickets for 24 to Hugh Trumble and Jack Saunders included a miraculous catch of Dick Lilley by Clem Hill.

I raced after the ball with not the slightest idea of bringing off a catch, but with the full determination of saving a fourer. Almost on the boundary, after having run the best part of twenty-five yards, I threw everything to chance and made a dive at the leather. No-one was more surprised than myself to find the ball stuck in my hand. As a matter of fact for the fraction of a second I could hardly believe I had brought off the catch. Poor Dick Lilley passing me on the way to the pavilion said, 'Oh, Clem, what a bally fluke!' For appearance sake I had to reply, 'Never on your life!' But the England wicketkeeper knew the truth and spoke it.

Maurice Tate, Brodribb

Last man Fred Tate needed to score 4 to win, but entered the annals as the loser of his only Test.

Now Saunders ran in with his left arm extended parallel to his body, signifying to his comrades 'a fast one coming'. It pitched straight and came on through as poor Fred Tate played forward, too late. The ball, keeping low, sent the leg stump somersaulting. The massed crowd sat horrified and silent at the spectacle and even the Australians were momentarily bemused, not fully aware they had won by just three runs. Suddenly they leapt in the air excitedly, shaking hands as they sprinted for their dressing-room.

Victor Trumper and the 1902 Australians,
Brown

The wife of Major Wardill, who had been doing some crochet work prior to the last stages of the match, involuntarily ran one of the needles through the palm of her hand. My mother [Hugh Trumble's wife], who was sitting with Mrs Wardill, often told me that the strain and suspense were impossible to express adequately in words.

The Golden Age of Cricket: A memorial book of Hugh Trumble, Trumble

THE OVAL 1902

The fastest Ashes century, a match-winning 104 in 75 minutes by Gilbert Jessop with England 5–118, was inspired by an unusual wager.

Personally I was most uncomfortable for I had foolishly embarked the night before at dinner at the Great Central Hotel, which one or two of us had made our quarters for the match, on a wager which bordered on the ridiculous.

In pleading guilty to so grave a misdemeanour as betting I throw myself on the mercy of the court, for though betting at cricket is an anathema to me, on this occasion it was not so much the desire quickly to become proprietor of lordly demesne as it was to assist in the laudable object of raising drooping spirits.

We had sat down to dinner that night before an open window from which could be perceived a cloudless sky giving hope of a welcome change in the weather. The first glass of 'Pommery' had scarce time to produce that feeling which for want of a better word may be described as more-ish, when pitter-patter, pitter-patter, the change came. It rained harder. When the flow had subsided save for an intermittent trickle, I rashly offered to take 10 to one that I for one would make 50, and 20 to one as regards double that figure. As this seemed such a clear case of money for nothing the offer was snatched up immediately. Let me say at once that the sum at stake would have sufficed to have paid for no more than the paint on the lodge gate of the aforementioned demesne.

A Cricketer's Log, Jessop

Richard Binns narrates the breathless last-wicket stand of the Yorkshiremen George Hirst and Wilf Rhodes.

As Rhodes walked out of the pavilion gate, Hirst walked away from the crease to meet him, and they exchanged a few words as they approached the wicket again together. 'We'll get 'em in singles,' said Hirst, and thus briefly, as hard-headed businessmen might settle the upshot of a deal, they decided their plan of campaign. Rhodes began with a lucky four through the slips, and he put the spectators' hearts into their mouths a second time when he cocked up a ball in the same direction just short of Armstrong, who made a great but fruitless effort to reach it. Risk, however, was reduced to a minimum. Run by run victory was brought nearer. A single by Hirst was converted into a two through an overthrow due to the fieldsman's excitement. Three wanted. Another single to Hirst brought him opposite Trumble. One to tie. Hirst played the first ball of the over without scoring; the second he placed cleverly between the bowler and mid-off and the two batsmen had dashed across before the fieldsmen could get to the ball. Two balls later Rhodes drove forcibly and cleanly to the same spot on the off-side – England had made her 263 and the match was won by a wicket!

Great Cricket Matches, Buchanan (Ed.)

SYDNEY 1903

England doubled Australia's first innings before a brilliant fightback led by Victor Trumper, with an unbeaten 185, which included one of the most controversial dismissals in Test history when Clem Hill was run out, described by England's captain Pelham Warner.

Braund was bought on to bowl, but his first over was a sensational one. The first and second balls Trumper cut magnificently for four, the third went for four byes, the fourth was hit past extra cover to the ring, the fifth was played back to the bowler, and the concluding ball of the over was again forced away past mid-off. Three had been run when Hirst returned to Braund, who threw at the wicket while the fourth run was being made. He missed the stumps and the batsmen were off again for the fifth – a dangerous one seeing that Hill had overrun his wicket by yards. The ball was splendidly returned by Relf to Lilley, and on the unanimous appeal of those in the vicinity of the wicket, Hill was given out by Crockett. Hill had rushed past his crease, and when Crockett told him he was out he showed by his manner that he was greatly surprised by the decision. Hill did not say a word in protest to Crockett, but the way in which he walked back to the pavilion could not possibly have left anyone in doubt as to what he himself thought of Crockett's ruling. Immediately after Hill had reached the pavilion a perfect storm of groans and hisses came from the members in the pavilion, and this chorus of disapproval was immediately taken up by the 'rinkers'. A minute or two later I walked to the pavilion with the intention of asking the members to desist, but instead of them listening to me the 'booing' became louder than ever. At this moment Noble, who was next in, came from the pavilion and we walked together to the pitch. We both sat down for a few minutes waiting for the disturbance to subside. During these moments Noble and I were talking the matter over, and I told him that we should be compelled to leave the field if the demonstration against Crockett did not cease. After a while the noise abated somewhat and Noble advised me to go on with the game. The moment we started play the noise became, if possible, greater than ever, and shouts of, 'How much did you pay Crockett, Warner?'; 'Have you got your coffin ready, Crockett?'; 'Which gate are you leaving by, Crockett?' rent the air.

It was a difficult situation, but I think that, on the whole, I acted wisely in not withdrawing the team from the field. People in England, however, can have no conception of the yelling and hissing that went on that afternoon right up to the drawing of stumps; even such hardened Test match players as Hirst and Rhodes were upset.

How We Recovered the Ashes, Warner

Trumper's innings almost revived Australia.

When he played his great innings of 185 not out against Warner's team in 1903–04, Braund was bowling leg theory with most of the fieldsmen on the on-side. Victor stepped to leg and continually back cut him to the fence. Braund afterwards said, 'It didn't matter where I pitched the ball, Trumper could hit it to three different places in the field.'

The Game's the Thing, Noble

MELBOURNE 1907

Test cricket might have had its first tie half a century earlier but for an errant throw by young Gerry Hazlitt, after a last wicket stand of 39 between Sydney Barnes and Arthur Fielder, recalled by the former.

It was like this. When we wanted two runs to win, Fielder was facing Armstrong and played one to Saunders at rather deep mid-off. Although it was quite a sharp run we made it easily through. The next ball I drew away to leg and played Armstrong with a gentle push on the off-side. He was bowling leg stuff with only two men on the off, Hazlitt at deep mid-off and cover nearly square with the wicket and I judged it to be a safe move. On playing the stroke I dashed off for the run, which was really a run and a half, but imagine my consternation to find when halfway down the pitch that Fielder was still leaning on his bat, dreaming no doubt of the run he had just made. I shouted, 'For God's sake, get off, Pip' and off he went like a hare, but in the meantime Hazlitt had dashed in and grabbed the ball and, had he kept his head and just lobbed it to the wicketkeeper, Fielder would have been out by yards. Instead, however, he had a wild shy at the sticks, missed, and the match was over. I have often thought that if he had been run out the verdict would have been I had lost my head (and the match) at the critical moment. Pip kept on running flat out and my last view was of him disappearing into the crowd around the pavilion. Had not the pavilion been in the way I think he would have finished up in England and been the first to bear the good news.

Cricketer International, February 1978

TRENT BRIDGE 1921

Jack Gregory established his reputation in England
during a single over in the first Test, which sped the
hosts to a two-day defeat.

The match was only four or five overs old, the score
was up to 18 when Gregory whipped one away off the
seam, Knight moved his bat but not his feet and Carter
took the thick snick in triumph. Not a happy moment
for Ernest Tyldesley, also in his first Test, rushed into
the breach before a proper breath could be drawn. This
was unkind luck enough, but his first ball was worse,
it was one of Gregory's fastest and it spat savagely back
from the line of the off-stump. Tyldesley's defence was
as good as any number three's in England, but though
he came down hard on it he was too late for anything
but a thick inside edge, and it had his leg-stump in the
spasmodic smother.

The next ball beat Hendren, and the last of the over,
testified to by all responsible spectators as the best and
fastest of the whole cumulative sequence, shot his off-
stump yards out of the ground, a completely unplayable
back-break delivered at the peak of speed. *The Cricketer* solemnly declared that this ball would have
bowled the best batsman in the world at any time of an
innings; no doubt Hendren would have gladly endorsed
this sentiment with his initials and the date if, in the
heat and horror of the moment, he could have recalled
either to his memory. England 18 for three; with that

single over Gregory destroyed the morale of English cricket for the best part of a season.

Warwick Armstrong's Australians, Mason

England reeled from the shock of Gregory and his partner in pace Ted McDonald.

England's selectors were Reggie Spooner, a Golden Age batsman of famous charm; Harry Foster, oldest of the famous Worcestershire cricket family; and John Daniell, Somerset's captain. The last was a famously unconventional character, a former rugby international prone to sweeping damnations like, 'If you look at the hind leg of a syphilitic chicken you will see a better cricketer.' The cowardice they perceived at Trent Bridge appalled them. When, having resisted honourably for ninety minutes, Yorkshireman Percy Holmes was bowled by McDonald while shrinking towards square- leg, Foster fumed to Home Gordon, 'So long as I have influence in choosing England, Home, that man never bats in another Test.' He did not.

The Big Ship, Haigh

TRENT BRIDGE 1938

Australia was 6–194 in reply to 8–658 when Stan McCabe turned the match on its head with 232 out of 300 added while he was at the wicket.

That was the signal for McCabe to take the match in his own hands. For the next couple of hours his batting was enchanting. It held everyone under its spell, bowlers as well as spectators. From the players' balcony, Bradman called to a few of his team who were inside the pavilion, 'Come and look at this! You've never seen anything like it.' In the press box, Woodfull was moved to write, 'It is a pity that the whole cricket world could not see this double-century.'

The 30 000 who were lucky enough watched wonderingly as the vice-captain added 170 while his last four partners scored 38. The arrival of Fleetwood-Smith was accepted as an infallible sign that the innings was drawing its last breath. Instead his advent inspired McCabe to unfold the most dazzling half-hour's batting of the match. Hammond spread five fieldsmen round the boundary yet could not prevent fours – McCabe had so many strokes and guided them so surely. The Englishmen fared little better when, near the end of the overs, they drew in to encircle him with a net of infielders trying to block the singles he needed to get the strike at the other end. Fleetwood-Smith rose to the occasion by surviving 18 balls and collecting 5 runs. Stan scored 72 in the last thrilling 28 minutes – something unheard-of in Test cricket even in the days when Bonnor and Jessop were denting pavilion roofs. McCabe's 232 in 235 minutes (34 fours, one six) is the fastest double century in Test history. Despite the urgency of the chase for runs there was not one slogging hit, in fact no show of force because of the precision of his timing. It was power without violence, dash without slap. When McCabe returned to the pavilion, Bradman greeted him with, 'If I could play an innings like that I would be a proud man, Stan.' Surely the highest tribute ever paid a batsman.

Between Wickets, Robinson

BRISBANE 1946

Don Bradman had made a sketchy start in the first post-war Test when umpire George Borwick gave him a reprieve that changed the course of cricket history. Bill Voce was bowling. Bradman had got 28, and suddenly attempting one of his favourite strokes, a drive just wide of cover-point, the ball flew from the top edge of his bat and straight towards second slip where Jack Ikin caught it beautifully.

Now I want to be precise about this. I was in the best position on the field, even better than the umpire himself, to see exactly what happened. I watched the ball bounce from the turf onto the top edge of the bat and go from there straight into Ikin's hands. According to the Laws of Cricket it was 'Out!' Ikin held the ball waiting for Bradman to leave the crease. He stared at the ground and did not move. Astounded, Ikin called 'Owzat?' The umpire looked straight at him and said, 'Not out.'

Everyone on our side looked in blank amazement, and Hammond in particular seemed to be wondering what to do next. Bradman still looked down. The point was this. The umpire, according to subsequent statements, supposed that the ball had been chopped down from the bat onto the ground, and had bounced. But you do not have to play cricket for years to know that a ball chopped down at that speed bounces steeply up. It does not travel parallel with the ground at chest height.

I am not intending any slight to Don, nor suggesting anything except that umpire Borwick made a mistake. All human beings make mistakes sometimes. All the same, it was an unfortunate moment at which to make one.

Cricket Campaigns, Yardley

After Bradman's 187 in Australia's 645, Brisbane's notoriously fickle weather turned foul and Sidney Barnes enjoyed a famous practical joke.

Those who went through the Brisbane storm of 1946 will never forget it. It was a terrifying experience and, in no time, the cricket ground was a sheet of ice. The dressing-room there is next to the members' pavilion, the scene of so many rows in the cricket world and as hard to enter as paradise. This is fenced with barbed wire and once led an English pressman to term it Belsen.

Drinks in the dressing-room are contained in a large tub with a block of ice in its middle. Barnes struggled out with this block of ice in the middle of the storm and tipped it over the fence into the sacred pavilion. Down it slithered on the grass among all the hailstones. The eyes of the members bulged. They think to this day that it came down from above, and had you known that storm you might have believed it, too.

Brightly Fades the Don, Fingleton

Bradman, Ian Johnson recalled, relished the weather as an opportunity to avenge past indignities.

He was in the highest spirits, chuckling and laughing as the rain cascaded down. I remarked that surely he was not concerned about the rain when we had more than 600 runs on the board.

He replied, 'Ian, the first time I played against England in 1928 they scored 521, caught us on a wet wicket and got us out for 120. With a lead of over 400 they batted a second time and left us over 700 to make in the last innings. Then they invented Bodyline for my special benefit and, the last time I played against them in England, England made over 900 before Hammond declared and I broke my ankle while bowling and couldn't bat. Just this once we have them in trouble. Do you really blame me for being so happy?'

Cricket at the Crossroads, Johnson

Keith Miller was less impressed.

When I started cricket with Australia after the war everyone was happy to be alive. We went to Brisbane for the First Test in 1946. It was a mud heap for England. I was bowling on the worst sticky ever and I was frightened of hurting someone. I got seven wickets or something in the first innings. Blind Freddie could have got wickets on that track. I remember hitting Bill Edrich and Wally Hammond. Edrich, a chunky, gutsy little chap with a DFC was getting battered from pillar to bloody post. Hammond and Edrich held us up for a little while. Bradman came over to me and said, 'Bowl faster, bowl faster. Get them out.' He told me later, when you play Test cricket you don't give these Englishmen an inch, play it tough, flat out the whole way. 'Grind them into the dust' were his words. I thought to myself that a war had just gone and a lot of Test cricketers and future Test cricketers had been killed and here we are just after the war, everyone is happy and now we have to grind them into the dust. So I thought, 'Bugger me. If that's Test cricket then they can stick it up their —' Don kept up this incessant will-to-win, which just wasn't my way of playing cricket.

Howzat! Sixteen Australian cricketers talk,
Butler

HEADINGLEY 1948

Australia was 3 for 68 replying to England's 496
when Neil Harvey, in his first Ashes Test, began
the counterattack.

As he came to the wickets and passed Miller, Harvey

made a typical remark, 'What's going on out here, eh? Let's get into them.'

Brightly Fades the Don, Fingleton

Don Bradman, watching from the pavilion, was seen many times to hold his head in disbelief. He did not expect the onslaught to last so long. His concern was that Neil was trying his luck on-driving against Laker's off-spin. Afterwards Harvey had the temerity to tell his captain, 'They were half volleys, weren't they?'

The Bedsers: Twinning triumphs, Hill

To Alan McGilvray fell the job of describing Harvey's century.

I imagined the scene in the Harvey home back in Melbourne's Fitzroy. Neil had six brothers and devoted cricketing parents, and I knew they would be beside themselves listening to the torment of those overs through the nineties. I remember the overwhelming need to reassure the folks at home. I described the twenty minutes Neil was stuck on 99 as if I were in the Harvey lounge-room, like the local clergyman in a time of real crisis. 'Don't worry, Mrs Harvey,' I was saying. 'Neil can do it. He'll be OK.'

The Game Goes On, McGilvray

When Harvey's roommate Sam Loxton himself fell seven runs short of a maiden Test century he also spared a thought for the folks back at home.

Returning disconsolately to the dressing-room, Loxton flung his bat into the corner and cried, 'There goes the old man's axe through the radio.'

Cricket Capers, Goldman

Australia was set 404 to win and looked insecure against the chinamen of Denis Compton.

Then came a most incredible over from Compton. This is worthy of close description because I think it ranks as Bradman's most uncomfortable over in his whole Test career. Bradman failed first of all to detect a bosie. He snicked it very luckily past Crapp at first slip for four, an accident of a stroke. Up came another slip and Bradman glanced Compton for four. Next ball he failed to pick Compton's bosie again, played for the off-break, snicked it as it went the other way and was missed by Crapp, yes, Crapp in the slips. The last ball of the over beat Bradman again completely and rapped him on the pads. Phew! What an over of excitement this was!

Brightly Fades the Don, Fingleton

But England's captain Norman Yardley had his distractions that day.

There was a personal thrill for me on the last day of that Leeds Test, for my second child – and first son – was born that day. My wife had travelled up from London

to Bridlington so that what we hoped would be a Yorkshire cricketer of the future should have the proper
qualification. When the news came through Don Bradman gave me a handshake and his good wishes. I must
admit to a lot of relief and happiness. Perhaps a Test
match is not the best time for such affairs.

Cricket Campaigns, Yardley

Arthur Morris was anything but distracted.
All the press'd said, 'Thank God, this is the day we've
been waiting for where we finally beat these Australians.' Suddenly you get that perverse feeling that you
want to stop them and, before you know it, you can
take on the world. They weren't bowling all that badly
but, when you're batting well, you make your own
rubbish, and we just kept going. Yardley, he had to go
for a win so the field was always in, and I hit twenty
fours in my first 100.

One Summer, Every Summer: An Ashes journal, Haigh

When Morris was out for 182, Bradman took
command, heading to an unbeaten 173, but leaving
the tyro Harvey to hit the winning boundary.
I was at the crease with Bradman at the end and hit
the winning run. I wasn't used to hitting winning runs
in Test matches and was totally unprepared when the
crowd invaded the pitch at the end. As Bradman hared
past me to avoid their clutches I cried out, 'What do

I do now?' He replied, 'Son, we get out of here.'

Winning: Face to face with Australian sporting legends, Writer

THE OVAL 1948

Donald Bradman went to the wicket in his last Test
needing four runs to become the only batsman in
Test history to average a hundred every time he was
dismissed. Warwickshire's Eric Hollies was the bowler,
Rex Alston and John Arlott the BBC commentators.

Alston: The crowd settles down again – they've got
forty minutes – forty minutes more left to play and
Bradman is now taking guard, Hollies is going to bowl
to him and John Arlott shall describe the first ball, so
come in, John.

Arlott: Well, I don't think I'm as deadly as you are,
Rex, I don't expect to get a wicket. But it's rather good
to be here when Don Bradman comes in to bat in his
last Test. And now, here's Hollies to bowl to him from
the Vauxhall End. He bowls, Bradman goes back across
his wicket and pushes the ball gently in the direction of
the Houses of Parliament which are out beyond
mid-off.

It doesn't go that far, it merely goes to Watkins
at silly mid-off. No run, still 117 for one. Two slips, a
silly mid-off, and a forward short-leg close to him
as Hollies pitches the ball up slowly (voice rises) and
(sudden applause) he's bowled. (Applause continues.
Several comments off-mike. Applause dies.)

(Slowly and distinctly) Bradman, bowled Hollies, nought. Bowled Hollies, nought. And – what do you say under those circumstances? I wonder if you see the ball very clearly in your last Test in England on a ground where you've played some of the biggest cricket of your life, and where the opposing team have just stood round you and given you three cheers and the crowd has clapped you all the way to the wicket. I wonder if you really see the ball at all.

Arlott: The authorised biography, Allen

On the Australian balcony, during all this, was Barnes. He had gone into the dressing-room, whipped up his camera before taking his pads off, and from the balcony filmed the last Test innings of his captain. There is no more enthusiastic photographer than Barnes. Adjusting his camera he entered the dressing-room, unbuckled his pads with his skipper and told him he had got all his innings!

Brightly Fades the Don, Fingleton

Fingleton and O'Reilly, the main thorns in Bradman's side over the years, were in the press box. When Bradman was out, said a fellow commentator who was with them at the time, 'I thought they were going to have a stroke they were laughing so much.'

Bradman: An Australian hero, Williams

Arthur Morris had a closer view, as he is apt to remind interlocutors.

When the subject of Bradman's duck is inevitably raised, Morris says, 'I often say to people, "Yes, I was there." "Were you playing?" "Yes, I got 196."'

The Invincibles, Allen

SYDNEY 1954

England came to Sydney in December 1954 after defeat by an innings and 154 runs at the Gabba, where Len Hutton had sent Australia in.

Someone remarked to Hutton after England had been beaten by an innings at Brisbane that he looked very glum. 'Come on, Len, snap out of it,' this chap said. Hutton replied, 'It's all very well for you to tell me to snap out of it. I know it's only a game but there are millions of cricket-lovers back in England in the middle of floods and gales and blizzards and this is a nice thing to happen to them, isn't it?'

Way of Cricket, Benaud

'Hutton is a muttonhead!' Plum [Warner] exploded back in St John's Wood, and E.W. Swanton wrote an article of such severity that he was excluded from the captain's counsels for the rest of the tour.

Sins of Omission, Synge

With 101, Peter May turned the match England's way
by sheer willpower.

I did make a profound statement to Colin Cowdrey
as we walked out after lunch. 'If I had the chance to
play the innings of my life, I would like to do it this
afternoon.'

A Game Enjoyed, May

Australia wrested a first innings lead of 74, but the
experience of being hit on the head by Ray Lindwall
turned Hutton's young fast bowler Frank Tyson into
a match-winner.

The previous day he had turned his back on a bumper
from Lindwall and took a fearful crack. We watched
horrified as he went down like felled timber and lay inert
and still. There was a hush around the ground and it
took quite a time to get him to his feet and back into
our dressing-room, where he was stretched out on the
massage table surrounded by medics and anxious team-
mates. When he came out of his concussed state I swear
there was a new light in his eyes as if a spark had been
kindled deep down inside him. I am not given to fanci-
ful imagination, and the fact is that when he resumed
bowling the next day he was a yard, maybe a yard and
a half quicker than before. His pace on that decisive and
extraordinary day in Sydney was nothing short of fright-
ening. After one ball Evans and the slips exchanged
significant glances and moved back several paces. Soon

after the English fielders were saying, 'If we can get Ray to nut Frank again, there'll be no holding him.'

Fifty Years in Cricket, Hutton and Bannister

When Australia set off after 151 with eight wickets preserved on the final morning, Tyson promptly made inroads.

He bowled Jim Burke in his second over, Hole four deliveries later, caught Benaud at square leg, then bowled Archer off an edge after lunch. A piquant contest was promised when Lindwall faced the man he'd decked not twenty-four hours earlier. But Tyson was too shrewd: cringing from a retaliatory bouncer, Lindwall was yorked.

Neil Harvey held fearlessly firm, cutting cleverly, reproving anything on his pads, but barely able to acquaint himself with partners before they vanished. When last man Bill Johnston entered at 2.30 p.m. with 78 needed, Harvey finally seized the match, commandeering the strike where possible and backing his judgement. At one stage Tyson motioned his fine leg finer and dropped short, but Harvey hooked anyway, over Bailey's head and the fence on the first bounce.

As Johnston trusted in his homespun technique, the target was halved in 40 minutes. Harvey was in sight of his century and, after a dozen devastating overs, Tyson nearly spent. 'I hadn't thought at the start that we could get 70,' says Harvey. 'But, after Bill stuck round for a while, I started having a few ideas. Tyson was just about rooted by that time and I didn't consider Bailey a problem. They'd have brought Statham back but Bill could have handled him, because he played pretty straight.' As Tyson took the ball for his 19th over, Johnston said, 'I'll try to hang round at least for your hundred because I think Frank's had it.'

But there was no fairytale Australian victory, nor the century Harvey merited. After three deliveries, Statham advised Tyson, 'Try one a little closer to his body and a little shorter.' Johnston's self-protective, one-handed glide ended in Evans' gloves. Tyson's 10th wicket of the match for 130 runs at 3.11 p.m. brought victory by 38 runs. Without conscious irony, *Wisden* reported that Tyson had 'won the match for England because he kept his head.'

The Summer Game, Haigh

MELBOURNE 1955

Everyone wanted to know what happened to the pitch during the Third Test in January 1955, but only one man, journalist Percy Beames, knew the culprit: Albert Ground curator Jack House.

Happy as they were at rolling England for 191, the Australians were staring daggers at the pitch. The little moisture binding it had disappeared and, without a covering of couch, it was threatening to disintegrate. Harvey muttered to Benaud as they walked off, 'I don't reckon we'll be able to play on this on Monday.' The chances faded further when record temperatures and an infernal northern wind on New Year's Day baked the pitch to a crumbling crust. Though Victorians Johnson and keeper Len Maddocks saw Australia to within 4 runs of the lead, the captain grew more anxious. 'We went in on Saturday and the wicket was doing all sorts of things,' says Johnson. 'When I was in with Len toward the end of the day the ball was starting to fly off the cracks.'

Melbourne's hottest night-time temperature of ninety-six degrees Fahrenheit was recorded that evening and players sought shelter on the rest day: Harvey had Benaud, Davidson and MCC player Jim McConnon to his home in Heidelberg; Tyson headed for the beach at Point Leo; Johnson spent a fretful day in Middle Park: 'I was thinking, "God! What's this wicket going to look like on Monday?"' At the Collins Street offices of *The Age*, Percy Beames was filing for Monday's edition when his telephone rang. It was Bill Vanthoff, an old friend with whom he'd played VFL football for Melbourne twenty years earlier. He sounded distraught. 'Percy, something terrible's happened,' the MCG curator said. 'Jack House's flooded the square. He's put too much water on.' Beames was stunned. Such a watering was completely at odds with Law 10 of MCC's 1947 Code: 'Under no circumstances shall the pitch be watered during a match.' He went at once to his editor, Harold Austin.

The story was sensational. But Austin did not want to be the cause of controversy jeopardising Anglo–Australian cricketing relations. 'Do you think it will affect the game?' he asked.

'It might,' Beames replied.

'Do you think there was any evil intent involved?' Austin asked.

Beames said honestly, 'No, I don't.'

Austin thought a moment, then proposed, 'Then we won't run the story. What we'll do is black [print in bold] a paragraph saying that watering a pitch during a match is illegal.' Beames was full of admiration, 'I thought to myself that it showed what a great editor Harold Austin was. He was more interested in the game than in a scoop for his newspaper.'

Johnson arrived early on Monday to inspect the wicket. It looked surprisingly firm and the cracks seemed to have closed. He ran his spikes along it. It was moist. He fetched his deputy, Morris. 'This has been watered,' Johnson said.

'Crikey,' Morris said. 'So it has.'

As Johnson and Morris went to notify VCA secretary Jack Ledward, umpires Col Hoy and Mel McInnes arrived from their digs at the Commercial Travellers' Club in Flinders Street. Hoy blanched and McInnes advised from the corner of his mouth, 'Say nothing to anybody.' The secret was out and the press box was in pandemonium. Englishwoman Margaret Hughes, writing for Sydney's *Daily Telegraph*, recalled, 'Pressmen could be seen rushing here and there, chatting together in groups, snatching phones – the inexplicable feather-bed state of the wicket had been explained – "It had been watered."' Beames knew that there was no holding his story.

With the pitch momentarily tamed, Hutton and Edrich mopped up England's arrears themselves. The tourists led by 119 at the close with seven wickets remaining, and all talk centred on what had changed the wicket's spots. And next morning Melburnians awoke to the bold *Age* headline: '**Test Pitch Watered During Game.**'

The Summer Game, Haigh

Tyson then swept through the Australians again, as Evans remembered.

It was a pleasure to stand there when Keith Miller came into bat. The conversation went like this: 'Morning, Godfrey.' 'Morning, Keith.' 'I hope that bastard comes off soon!' We hadn't been able to frighten Keith before.

The Zen of Cricket, Francis

Tyson's 7–27 was deplored by at least one local entrepreneur.

In the last innings Australia needed 239 to escape defeat, but England's speedmen Frank Tyson and Brian Statham dismayed the batsmen by making some balls shoot and others kick. They ripped through the last seven wickets in two hours, dismissing Australia for 111 when wicketkeeper Evans caught last man Johnston off Tyson the last ball before lunch. A crowd of 50 000 drifted away and nothing looks so empty as the vast MCG without onlookers. In the umpires' room Mel McInnes and Colin Hoy were changing when a sad-looking character came in and asked, 'Who was the chap who gave Bill Johnston out?'

'I was,' said Mel.

'Well, I'm the caterer and that decision of yours cost me 10 000 bloody pies.'

Cricket's Fun, Robinson

OLD TRAFFORD 1956

Some Australians were looking forward to the
Old Trafford Test of 1956, as Jim Laker recalled.

Even Sir Donald Bradman was misled by the Old Trafford pitch in 1956. I was drinking a cup of tea in the pavilion when he returned from inspecting it. 'What do you think of the track?' I queried.

'It's nice and flat, isn't it?' joked Bradman in return and then, more seriously, 'It's just what our fellows have been looking for. They will get a packet of runs out there.'

Spinning Around the World, Laker

Other Australians, including Keith Miller, approached their task fatalistically.

The umpires were Frank Lee and Emrys Davies, who maintained a very high standard during the series. I walked over to Frank and said, 'I think three days will see this through. You'll be paid for two days you won't have to work!' Whereupon Frank answered, 'That's funny, I had just said to Emrys, "This game will go for about three days," and Emrys replied, "I was going to say the same thing to you."' But for the rain the game would have been over in two and a half days. The first ball I bowled on the opening morning sent up a puff of dust when it pitched – the writing on the wall could not have been larger. I felt sorry for the groundsman. He had so much publicity that he became a world figure overnight. He confided to me one morning, 'I'm fed up with it. They won't even give me five minutes to cut my throat.'

Cricket Crossfire, Miller

When Laker took 9–37 in the first innings, Australia was 375 behind and the cause was lost. Ian Johnson, however, endeavoured to rally the team.

He said with some feeling, 'We can fight our way back. We need guts and determination. We can still save the match.' Miller, sitting in the corner of the room, lifted his head from a racing guide and commented indifferently, 'Bet you 6/4 we can't.'

Fifteen Paces, Davidson

As Laker ploughed through the Australians a second time, Godfrey Evans noted, his spin partner Tony Lock was driven to distraction.

It wasn't just the spin that did the Aussies. It was the aura of the man. He was the only person who looked like getting wickets. I remember Tony Lock catching one at short-leg and cursing under his breath, 'Well bowled, you bastard!'

The Zen of Cricket, Francis

When rain that had looked like saving Australia relented, Johnson knew who to blame . . .

It was when commenting on this burst of sunshine and other allegedly divine intervention by the weather on our behalf that Ian Johnson, nodding towards the Rev. David Sheppard, made his famous remark, 'It's not fair! You've got a professional on your side!'

A Game Enjoyed, May

. . . and when batting Ray Lindwall knew not to bother complaining.

I went in to bat in the second innings and said to Godfrey Evans, 'What's going on, Godfrey?' And he said, 'Nothing. It's not spinning.' And I got three balls that spun so far he couldn't stop them and they went for byes. I said to Godfrey, 'Thanks, Godfrey. Not turning much, is it?'

Ray Lindwall: Cricket legend, Ringwood

After Laker had taken 10–53 in the second innings to complete an unequalled 19–90, he became a celebrity – briefly.

For the next two or three hours I did not have a second to ruminate on what had happened. There were celebration drinks with the players and officials, congratulations all round and photographs. There was a press conference, appearances on the radio and television. I did not get to my car until 8 p.m. And there, scores of people were waiting for autographs of souvenir scorecards. Finally I headed south at about 8.30 p.m. – alone. I was left to myself and my own thoughts. I had to drive through the night, for I was playing the next day – against the Australians! I phoned my wife twice en route. I knew she would be worried in case I celebrated too generously. She need not have concerned herself. My celebration dinner consisted of a bottle of beer and a sandwich in a pub near Lichfield. I sat in the corner of a crowded bar for fifteen minutes while everyone talked of the Test match. No-one spotted me. Beyond asking me how far I had to go, the landlord said nothing.

Spinning Around the World, Laker

The Oval Test followed close on Laker's Old Trafford triumph.

The fourth ball of the match was whipped off his legs by Colin McDonald and Tony Lock brought off a blinding catch at leg slip. Laker turned to Sheppard with that wry smile and said, 'I haven't really got anything to play for now in this match.'

Laker, Mosey

OLD TRAFFORD 1961

Richie Benaud and Neil Harvey led Australia to England for the last time in 1961 with high hopes that began onboard ship.

'Have a good look at it,' I said to him, 'because neither of us might ever see it again.' 'You're right,' he replied, 'so we'd better make it a good one.'

Willow Patterns, Benaud

Australia and England arrived at Old Trafford 1–1, after a big England win at Headingley, which Benaud tried to exploit.

Memory of the Third Test was still raw. But, rather than consign it to memory, Benaud sought to exploit it. On the team notice board at Manchester he pinned one of the more damning Australian newspaper reports of Trueman's triumph, one alleging that Benaud's team was in disarray. It was a favourite Benaud ploy and never failed to elicit a response. 'The reaction was good,' he remembered, 'though some of the language wasn't.'

The Summer Game, Haigh

Australia trailed heavily on the first innings and desperately needed a good start.

He [Benaud] walked up to Bobby Simpson and myself with a cheerful grin and said, 'We are 177 runs behind England. We must have a big stand to start our second innings and stay in the game. I know you two can do it.' I cannot speak for Simpson but I know that instantly I felt we could do it, and we did.

Run Digger, Lawry

Australia led by only 150 runs with one wicket in hand on the final morning, but against the odds was given runs to bowl at by Alan Davidson and twenty-year-old Graham McKenzie.

The game was firmly in England's grasp. At the wicket, Davidson was looking like 'an old, old man'. McKenzie, who had been receiving treatment from masseur Arthur James for his sore leg, was taken by surprise when the three wickets fell. He had to rush to get his pads on, but he knew the prospects of Australian victory had almost disappeared.

What followed was like a story from a *Boys' Own Annual*. Carefully keeping McKenzie away from the danger man David Allen, Davidson for one of the few occasions on tour revealed his undoubted batting ability. First he saw Statham out of the attack. Close, his replacement, tended to overpitch his off-breaks allowing Davidson and McKenzie to score fairly freely.

Meanwhile Allen, after nine overs, had conceded only two runs, and Davidson decided to hit him out of the attack. Twenty runs came in a single over – 6, 4, 4, 6. By now McKenzie was batting confidently and England's grasp was weakening by the minute. Finally it was Flavell who managed to bowl McKenzie for 32, leaving Davidson 77 not out. Together they had added 98 runs in 102 minutes, stretching Australia's lead from 157 to 255.

> *Garth: The story of Graham McKenzie,*
> Jaggard

Davidson, breathless but triumphant as he tossed his bat into a corner proclaimed, 'We'll do these jokers, Rich.'

> *A Tale of Two Tests,* Benaud

When Ted Dexter led England majestically to 1–150, wicketkeeper Wally Grout had doubts about his captain's optimism.

I sent a look of disgust down the wicket to Richie and reminded him at the end of the over that I had money on this match, and if he kept bowling that stuff I was going to do my dough. Benaud, serene as ever, said, 'Stick with me, Wal, we're going to win this game.' He sent Ted a similar ball in the next over and even Dexter must have had some compassion for Benaud as he slammed it to the fence. The next ball looked a 'dead ringer' for the other two and Ted again played the cut. But the ball carried top spin and skidded from the bat into my gloves.

I will never forget that moment. The way I clung to that ball it could have been gold bullion, and Benaud's broad grin from halfway down the wicket said as plainly as if he had yelled out, 'I told you!' I have never doubted the man since.

My Country's Keeper, Grout

Bowling round the wicket into the rough, Benaud then dismissed his rival captain Peter May to speed an unlikely Australian victory.

It was no good trying to keep him quiet, we had to get him out and quickly. I reasoned that there was just a chance if I could land on those rough spots to him that I could trap him. The first ball didn't land in the rough at all but on the leg-stump and May played it back down the wicket. 'Get it out further, you idiot,' I said to myself. The next ball did land in the rough and as May tried to sweep it the ball dug into the turf and whipped back towards leg-stump. I saw all this from where I had run to the on-side of the wicket . . . there was that terrible fraction of a second as I waited for the ball to hit the leg-stump and then an unrestrained yell of joy.

A Tale of Two Tests, Benaud

Australia won by 54 runs with twenty minutes spare when Davidson bowled Statham with a change of pace. 'I think it was the best Test I played in,' he says. 'We were never in it. It was Bill [Lawry] who gave us the chance. For his innings at Lord's I'd have given him the VC, but his 102 at Manchester was worth at least the Military Cross.' But it was Benaud who was the toast of a dressing-room that hugged itself in disbelief. O'Neill filled the bath and laughed, 'Go on, Rich, dive in. With your luck, you won't even get wet.' The location made victory sweeter still. On the ground where Laker had prostrated them in 1956 the captain and Harvey sipped champagne on the players' balcony. The obligatory telegram from the Prime Minister arrived: 'Congratulations on the most brilliant fight-back I can ever remember. My warmest greetings to you and the team.' But dignity was maintained. As celebrations continued over dinner at the Midland Hotel, E.W. Swanton of the *Daily Telegraph* breezed past and asked, 'Would it be all right with you chaps if I had a photographer come and take your picture?'

'By all means,' Benaud replied. Then, as the snapper arrived, the skipper said solemnly, 'One moment. Bottles off the table, gentlemen.' Coffee cups were positioned, the picture taken, and retention of the Ashes savoured.

The Summer Game, Haigh

HEADINGLEY 1964

Australia was 7–178 chasing England's 268, with
Peter Burge feeling his way painfully against spinners
Fred Titmus and Norman Gifford. But then, as Hawke
joined him, the brawny Queenslander saw a way out.

Burge saw Dexter signal that he was about to take the
new ball. For Burge it looked like a reprieve, a release
from the straitjacket imposed by the spinners. He
walked down the wicket to Hawke. 'Ted's taking the
new ball. Let's make the most of it. The spinners will be
back soon enough. We've just got to take it out on this
new ball.'

Innings of a Lifetime, Barker

Hooking and pulling with abandon, Burge added 105
with Hawke and a further 89 with Grout, remembered
by the latter.

Peter and I were leaving the dressing-room to resume
the innings when I heard Simmo say to somebody, 'The
old feller will do it.' The faith of Bobby's inspired me
to square cut Freddie Trueman's first ball to the fence
and hook his next to the opposite boundary, which
prompted Ted Dexter to bark at Freddie from back-
ward square leg, 'Why are you dropping them short to
this fellow?' Later in the innings, Trueman the number
one gamesman walked in from leg-slip between overs,
took a long look at the pitch and said to me, 'I wouldn't
like to be you fellows batting on this in the second

innings.' I said, 'The way you are bowling, Freddie, we won't have to,' one rare occasion when I had the last word with him.

My Country's Keeper, Grout

Burge's 160 in five and a quarter hours, with 98 in boundaries, had secured Australia a lead of 121, and himself a lasting renown. 'I think, after that innings, I finally felt accepted by the cricket aristocracy,' Burge remembers. 'Because when we got home for the next summer in Australia I got an invitation to The Don's place. I knew I'd been accepted because he thanked me for what I'd done. Don had this theory that, while you should always beat England in Australia, to really succeed you had to beat England in England.'

The beating was still to be done as England began its second innings, and Barrington and his Surrey comrade John Edrich built a patient stand in the afternoon that stymied the tourists. The home side was only 33 in arrears with nine wickets remaining at tea, and news that Margaret Smith had lost her Wimbledon crown seemed an ill omen for Australia. But McKenzie had Edrich taken down the leg-side with the first ball on resumption, and Veivers picked up a doleful Dexter and a defiant Barrington before the close. Wrote English journalist Denzil Batchelor, 'The more I analysed the day's play the more convinced I became that it was not in bowling superiority or batting supremacy that the Australians eclipsed us. It was in sheer intestinal fortitude, or to put it more briefly still: guts.' After Australia's six-wicket win on 6 July, Batchelor commented even more concisely: 'As for Burge, he *was* Australia.'

The Summer Game, Haigh

THE OVAL 1972

Trailing 1–2 and without hope of reclaiming the Ashes against Ray Illingworth's seasoned XI, Ian Chappell's youthful Australians dedicated themselves to winning the last Test at The Oval.

At the team meeting before the last Test Ray Steele [manager] gave another stirring speech. He seemed to find the right words and pick the mood of the players. 'We will be remembered as a good – maybe great – side if we win this one and draw the series. But if we lose we will become three-to-one losers and that will reflect badly on us, both individually as we play on and hope to retain selection, and as a team which failed. Win here and we will be known as winners.' Then Doug Walters, who had sadly been dropped after a run of failures, piped up from the back. He had borrowed a pair of glasses and, looking over the rims in true Ray Steele style, he mimicked the team manager's words after the loss of the First Test: 'Take this lying down . . . Pig's bloody arse we will!' It brought the house down. Ian Chappell also lifted the spirits of the players at that team meeting.

"I think we are the better team, and if we go home two-all we will have been seen as the better team," I told the boys.'

Chappelli Speaks Out, Chappell and Mallett

Ten wickets from Lillee and centuries from the Chappells, and later a poised partnership between Rodney Marsh and Paul Sheahan completed the task, as Marsh recalled.

I was facing Tony Greig and poked one just behind square-leg off my toes for the winning single. 'You little beauty,' I thought, and then went into an uncontrollable dance of victory. I kept on jumping and waving my bat, whooping it up like a child. The rest of the day and the night was the same. I ran into Paul the following morning and he made some comment about how well we were knocking over the champagne the night before. As I don't drink champagne, I asked, 'What champagne?' He laughed and replied, 'At dinner time, don't you remember we sat together?' It was news to me.

You'll Keep, Marsh

Rod Marsh jumped up on the dressing-room table and gave his famous, joyous, ringing rendition, guaranteed to flush the face, stand hair on end and make dry eyes brimful:

Under the Southern Cross I stand
A sprig of wattle in my hand
A native of my native land
Australia, you fucking beauty!

Greg Chappell: *Cricket's incomparable artist,*
McGregor

Despite retaining the Ashes, the English team next
door had a sense that their time had gone.

The England dressing-room was a very sober place
at the end of The Oval Test match as we packed to
go our separate ways while listening to the sounds
of the Australian champagne celebrations in their
dressing-room almost directly overhead. Not only
because we had failed to win the series. Throughout that summer we all felt we were taking part in a
long drawn-out farewell party. The time was drawing
nearer when the old firm under Ray Illingworth was
having to break up.

Cricket Rebel, Snow

BRISBANE 1974

England's Tony Greig recalled how he first learned
of Jeff Thomson, and sensed that the 1974–75 Ashes
series might be tougher than anticipated.

I shall never forget as long as I live wandering up
to [Sydney's] King's Cross at midnight with Bruce
Francis and Keith Fletcher to buy the Sunday papers.

We took them back to the hotel and opened them in the coffee lounge, and then sputtered over our cups. In one of the papers was a huge article by Thomson referring to blood on the pitch. Pommie blood, and the fact that it wouldn't bother him if he hurt a few batsmen. The seeds had been sown.

Wisden Cricket Monthly, December 1982

Greig took on Lillee and Thomson as only he knew how.

Edrich, however, played a brave innings, taking blows on elbow, hand and body while Greig launched himself into a characteristically impudent one which started when he greeted Lillee with a polite, 'Good morning, Dennis' when he arrived in the middle. The fast bowler replied, 'Get up there – now it's your turn!' Greig motivates himself by provoking people and now he rode his luck in superb style, standing up to hit the ball rather than prod uncertainly at it, and he played a series of marvellous strokes through the covers, hitting the ball on the rise every time. All the time Greig did his best to upset Lillee with his theatrical antics. Once he pretended to head a bouncer away and when he drove him through the covers for four with a really high-class stroke he shouted, 'Take that, Lillee!' and signalled the runs for good measure.

In Search of Runs, Amiss and Carey

On the way to 110, Greig rallied the tail with plain speaking.

I was bubbling over with adrenalin when Underwood came in to bat, walked up to me and said, 'Well, what do you reckon, mate?' I told him, 'It's a straightforward question of fighting for your life.' I will never forget the way he looked at me, going slightly pale and said, 'Thanks a lot.'

One thing Underwood does correctly is to get his front elbow up. Well, the first ball was an absolute flier from Thomson. It rose up off the pitch and passed through the crook of Underwood's arm between his elbow and his ear. How it didn't kill him I still don't know. There was a look of absolute death on Underwood's face as he came down the pitch and said to me, 'Mate, you're spot on right.'

Wisden Cricket Monthly, December 1982

Thomson, however, had the last word in the second innings.

The hero of the first innings, Tony Greig, now entered, but this was not to be an occasion for a repetition of his earlier heroics. With the north-easterly breeze, Thomson produced the most devastating delivery of the game: a yorker which pitched on the ideal blind spot in line with the leg stump and ricocheted off the batsman's pads to shatter the stumps.

Test of Nerves, Tyson

MELBOURNE 1977

The Centenary Test had miraculous qualities off the field as well as on, with every former Ashes player a guest – a daunting notion, as Rod Marsh observed.

Every time you walk into the Hilton Hotel you see 400 blokes who have probably been better cricketers than you, and you probably feel a little insignificant among all the greats.

The Game is Not the Same . . . McGilvray

The oldest, 84-year-old Percy Fender, had a particularly memorable visit.

In spite of his failing eyesight, limiting his vision to a few metres, Percy succeeded in seeing passages of play in the Test first hand; asked into the Melbourne Cricket Club committee room, he was invited to look through the gargantuan binoculars which stand immutably rooted to their pedestal in the viewing room. Glancing through these almost astronomical lenses, he discerned fleeting glimpses of the white-clad players on the field. 'I can see, I can see,' exclaimed Percy. 'Just wait till I see that doctor in England who told me I was almost blind.'

The Centenary Test, Tyson

Australia also made a miraculous recovery, bowling England out for 95 in reply to its 138. But perhaps the most miraculous recovery was by Rick McCosker

who, his jaw broken by a mis-hook in the first innings,
made an unforgettable appearance at the crease
in the second innings swathed in bandages – after
counselling from Greg Chappell.

I had spoken to Rick McCosker in his room at the hotel
that morning and was pleased to hear that he was not
only prepared but wanted to bat. The doctor said he
wouldn't be risking further damage if he went out to
the crease, provided he used a runner and didn't receive
a direct hit on his fractured jaw. The hero's welcome
that Rick received was to be expected, though we were
less gratified by the series of bumpers with which he
was greeted by the England attack. Not only did Rick
defy the England pace men, he batted with confidence
and flair, hooking two bumpers to the fence and ducking safely under the others.

The 100th Summer, Chappell

Man-of-the-match in the Centenary Test with 174,
Derek Randall showed monastic self-discipline.

Every night there was a party, giving rise I am sure to
many a hangover among the ex-players. I kept away
from it all, partly through professional desire to do
well, but partly through the fact that my basic shyness
filled me with a dread of having to meet and chat to
so many famous personalities. So the introvert side of
Randall, a great surprise to those who had only seen
me in the field, came to the fore. I spent each evening

in my comfortably furnished Hilton room, watching uncomfortably similar Australian soap operas and eating food which might have seemed nothing special to those who had come from England, but to a home-loving man hot-foot from three months among the curries of the East seemed the height of luxury.

The Sun Has Got His Hat On, Randall

Rod Marsh took a hand too.

Randall, edging Greg Chappell, was given out caught behind on 161, but Marsh immediately called him back as he walked, intimating that the ball hadn't carried, a fact that we had not appreciated from the pavilion. Apparently Greg Chappell had remarked to Marsh, 'Have you gone all religious?'

It's Knott Cricket, Knott

Dennis Lillee claimed 11–165, but he received at least as much attention for seeking the Queen's autograph.

When I introduced them, he produced a paper and pen from his blazer with the comment that he hoped she didn't mind, but he wondered if she'd consent to giving him her signature. The Queen was naturally taken aback, but gracefully told him that she had better not in front of all the people watching as she had a tight schedule to keep. They had a bit of a laugh and I am sure the Queen wasn't affronted in any way – and I'm sure Dennis wasn't put out because she wouldn't sign: although Buckingham Palace did subsequently send an autographed photo to Dennis after the game.

The 100th Summer, Chappell

The players were also preoccupied with who had, and who had not, signed with Kerry Packer's World Series Cricket.

In Melbourne, I learned later, the best illustration of the secrecy was provided with a dialogue between Greg Chappell and Rod Marsh, respectively captain and vice-captain of the Australian team. Chappell had accepted a Packer contract during Australia's short tour of New Zealand, but Marsh signed only days before the Centenary Test. As they walked out together at the MCG, Marsh said, 'Enjoy it, mate. It'll be the last one we play at this ground.' Chappell feigned innocence, but Marsh retorted, 'You must know what I'm talking about. I've signed – haven't you?'

My Story, Greig

HEADINGLEY 1981

Australia led by Kim Hughes made 9–401 on a pitch sure to deteriorate.

I thought Hughes was right when he said after play, 'Four hundred was worth about a thousand on this pitch.'

Phoenix from the Ashes, Brearley

Australia then bowled England out for 174, leaving
Hughes with the option of enforcing the follow-on –
a decision watched by his coach Peter Philpott from
the BBC's Test Match Special box.

Eventually Trevor Bailey put the question to me, 'Peter,
will you enforce the follow-on?' I paused and felt sorry
for Kim Hughes, whose final decision this would be
and who would live with the responsibility. My reply
was something like this. 'Trevor, the English batting
is shattered with confidence so low that I don't think
Australia can ignore the psychological advantage of
enforcing the follow-on. But I wouldn't like to be batting last on that wicket with more than 100 to 120 to
get.'

    A Spinner's Yarn, Philpott

Not that it seemed to matter when England slid to
7–135 in their second innings and odds of 500–1
were quoted by Ladbroke's against an English victory.
At that point, however, Ian Botham was joined by
tailender Graham Dilley.

'You don't fancy hanging around on this wicket for a
day and a half, do you?' I said to Graham Dilley when
he walked out to join me. 'No way,' he replied. 'Right,'
I said. 'Come on, let's give it some humpty.'

    The Incredible Tests, Botham

After Ian Botham with 149 not out and Bob Willis
with 8–43 had led England to a 17-run victory, even
England captain Mike Brearley felt sympathy for his
rival.

Kim kept saying, 'I suppose me mum'll speak to me.'
Pause. 'Reckon me dad will, too. And my wife.' Pause.
'But who else?'

Phoenix from the Ashes, Brearley

MELBOURNE 1982

Australian hopes in the Fourth Test of the 1982–83
Ashes series at the MCG hinged on a last-wicket
alliance of tailender Jeff Thomson and Allan Border,
whose form to that stage had been wretched. But
the former stuck round and Border's touch steadily
returned when England's skipper Bob Willis decided
to concede him singles.

Counselling his colleague through the day's last 45 minutes, Border began relishing England's misdirection.
'When the partnership had started the Poms had been
full of the joy of living. By stumps they were showing a
little strain.' The sight of 10 000 queuing for a day that
could end in a ball cheered Border and Thomson next
morning as they performed ritual nets.

Willis' plan remained to defend against Border but,
as the scoreboard flashed the run requirement at thirty-
second intervals and a second new ball was survived,
confused fielders began colliding. With the crowd

20 000 just after noon and the target reduced to a single stroke, Willis bowled his fiercest and most frugal over with Border on 60. The left-hander glanced a couple to deep fine leg but could not appropriate the strike for Botham's 26th over. Mid-pitch conferences at 12.20 p.m. confirmed the air of imminent decision and Thomson took fresh guard pondering the possibility of a boundary.

Border recalled the next few seconds and the uncanny collaboration of Botham and slipsmen Tavaré and Miller with clarity. 'When he [Thomson] hit it, my initial reaction was that it was going over the top and for four. Then I thought, "It's in Tavaré's hands and we're gone." And when it bounced out of his hands I thought, "Beauty, we're back in it." Then all of a sudden, Miller was there.' England had won by three runs.

Border also recalled Marsh's dressing-room prowl – peering beneath kits, behind doors and in lockers – and its explanation, 'I'm looking for four runs.' The atmosphere next door was no better. Wrote Allan Lamb, 'I know callers expected to witness scenes of absolute mayhem, with England cricketers dancing with delight knocking back champagne as if Australia was going to run out of the stuff at any moment. Instead, even half an hour after the match had finished they found the room like a morgue. Most of us just sat around staring into space hardly saying a word.'

The Border Years, Haigh

HEADINGLEY 1989

Before the First Test at Headingley in 1989, where
Australia had been defeated in 1972, 1977, 1981 and
1985, nerves preyed upon even senior players such as
Geoff Marsh, as his roommate David Boon recalled.

'It was the weirdest thing,' Boonie said. 'It was still
early, only about six in the morning I think, and I had
this sort of sixth sense about something. I opened an
eye and there was Swampy, in his helmet and gloves,
with his bat, in the bollocky, and he's practising his forward defence in front of the mirror.'

Ashes Glory: Allan Border's own story,
Border

Marsh's young partner Mark Taylor was unfancied
in his first Ashes innings.

In the days before the game I went along to the tent of
Ladbroke's, the bookies, and checked out the odds for
different players: who'd get most wickets, score most
runs, make the first 100, etc. I ran a finger down the
'most runs' list down to 33/1 – Moody and Hughes.
I didn't even make the list!

Time to Declare, Taylor

Captain Allan Border set the tone for his team with
a sparkling 66.

In 118 balls Border blew away any residual smog
hanging from Headingley 1981. Australia had lost

Marsh and Boon in an overcast half-hour since lunch on the series' first day when Border approached the pitch with that walk that would make him recognisable in a balaclava. At once his driving was unbridled, almost reprimanding. As DeFreitas gaped at a six over point, Border was unblinking. 'The six was an accident,' he wrote, 'but the thinking behind it wasn't an accident. Who knows, maybe the shot and its psychological impact rubbed off on the rest of the team?' Partner Taylor was certainly inspired to fluency. Border pumped his hand as the opener posted a maiden Test half century in 165 minutes. The captain even fell with a brisk normality: after fetching DeFreitas from outside off stump to mid-wicket, he reacted like someone who'd simply dialled a wrong number.

The Border Years, Haigh

Taylor it was who scored the first hundred, and Steve Waugh the second: his maiden century in twenty-seven Tests.

Underneath that unflappable demeanour was a turbulent whirlpool of emotions as Waugh crept closer to shaking the monkey off his back. 'I had no saliva. I thought if I don't get it now I'm going to collapse.'

When the moment of truth arrived the climax was more Python than Hollywood. Waugh said he tried to smack his chewing gum away with his bat in celebration, but when it came to the big moment the man who had just flayed the best bowlers in England was not up to the task. 'I spat the chewie out and went to hit it and missed,' he recalled sheepishly. 'It was about the only thing I'd missed after the first couple of balls.'

Waugh Declared, Gately

The Australians were ruthless. England's keeper Jack Russell recalled Border setting the example of brooding hostility.

Border made a conscious decision not to fraternise with us during the 1989 series. The method used at Leeds was silence. The Aussie players just stared at us out in the middle. There was simply no recognition; it was unnerving and unpleasant. Terry Alderman, who had played at Gloucestershire the season before, barely exchanged a word with me all series. 'Good morning' was all I'd get – and that was on one occasion.

Unleashed, Russell

A cocky England, holder of the Ashes, careened to a 210-run defeat, and Allan Border's team celebrated the lifting of the Headingley hoodoo.

As the dressing-room was being flooded with champagne, Clem, A.B. and myself couldn't help feeling we had taken revenge for what had happened to us here in 1981. However, we didn't have much time for private reflection as Merv began spraying everybody with champagne and beer. A.B. was in the middle of a television interview on the balcony when he was drenched with a can of XXXX. Tub said he had now played three Tests for two wins and a draw and he couldn't understand why everyone says Test cricket is so hard.

Diary of the Ashes 1989, Lawson

EDGBASTON 2005

Leading 1–0 in the series, Australia went into the Second Test confident. But during the warm-ups, recalled captain Ricky Ponting, a stray cricket ball on the outfield had dire consequences for his star fast bowler Glenn McGrath while Ponting and vice-captain Adam Gilchrist were inspecting the pitch.

As we were standing there, Gilchrist turned around to the group away to our right and said, 'McGrath's down.' McGrath is a practical joker and at first neither of us thought anything of it, but when the curator moved away from the pitch to get transport to take McGrath off the field we began to realise something was seriously wrong.

Ashes Diary 2005, Ponting

Nonetheless, Ponting elected to send England in on winning the toss, a decision that England's coach Duncan Fletcher couldn't believe.

I do not usually watch the toss taking place, so while I was pottering around the dressing-room I heard the shout go up that we were batting. I thought to myself, 'Great toss to win, Vaughany.' It was then I was informed that Ricky Ponting had won the toss and inserted us. It was a complete shock. What was he thinking? There had been no doubt in our minds that we were going to bat.

The Ashes Regained, Fletcher

At the end of a Test played at breakneck speed
Australia was three runs from victory, with its brave last man Michael Kasprowicz facing Steve Harmison.
Everybody playing, watching, televiewing, or, worse still, listening to radio, with the imagination running riot, is in a cold sweat. Harmison bounds in again and sends down a pig of a delivery. The batsman is help-less. He falls towards the off, trying to parry the rising ball, and a split second later Geraint Jones plunges for-ward to take the catch. England has won by two runs, the narrowest margin ever in an Ashes Test match. Pandemonium.

The Battle for the Ashes 2005, Frith

3 | GAMESMEN ALL

Cricket is a game that prides itself on obedience to the forms of correct behaviour, even if condoning their violation is just as much a habit. From its inception, the Ashes has been an arena pushing its protagonists to the limits of what is felt acceptable: the stakes are high, the spoils worth enjoying, and the incentives acute.

In recent time the media has obsessed over batsmen not walking for low catches, and sledging. As J.A.H. Catton's story of the Lord's Test of 1896 and Jack Hobbs's story about Warwick Armstrong in 1909 suggest, however, these have long histories. W.G. Grace, too, knew all the lurks and used them unblushingly. If Australians are sometimes regarded as the quintessential gamesmen, they have had some handy English teachers.

W.G. Grace was the original gamesman.

Playing for Gloucestershire against the Australians at Bristol, in 1890, he [Grace] went in first and, after the usual preliminaries, took strike to J.J. Ferris, who opened the bowling. To the first delivery he played forward and just touched the ball, giving Trumble at slip a chance, which he accepted.

Dr Grace, knowing he was out, immediately commenced to pat the pitch where the ball lodged, evidently to convey the idea that he was waiting for the ball to be returned to the bowler and for the over to be continued; but as this was not done he stood and enquired what was the matter, whereupon he was told he was out. With an apparent air of surprise he exclaimed, 'What! How's that, Umpire?'

'You're out,' the umpire replied. Grace laughingly retorted, 'I did not carry the bluff far enough.' Besides enjoying the reputation of being the finest cricketer that ever played the game, Dr Grace was one of the keenest and knew every move on the board.

The Quest for Bowlers, Turner

But Australians, as this incident recounted from the Lord's Test six years later shows, caught up quickly.

Gregory and Trott did great deeds, but I shall always believe that Trott was caught in the slips by Hayward when 61. At that time the Press Box at Lord's was beneath the old grandstand scoring board, and the view was broadside, so that one could see the slip fielders at each end. It appeared as if Tom Hayward had made a clean catch – although the ball was near the ground.

He tossed the ball into the air, but Trott stood still, and on appeal one of the umpires gave him not out, as he was entitled to do. During luncheon I ventured to ask Hayward if the catch was above suspicion and for my pains I got this reply, 'Do you think I should have tossed the ball up if I had any doubt about it?'

William Gunn, who happened to be fielding close to the wicket, was equally sure that Trott must be out, and another cricketer, whose name I shall suppress went so far as to say that 'No-one but a — Australian would have stood still.'

Wickets and Goals: Stories of play, Catton

All the same, as the next Test showed when Australia ended the penultimate day in a strong position, cricket is a funny game.

As soon as stumps were drawn the late Dr Grace came into our dressing-room and said, 'Well, Trott, you are going to beat us, as now the weather is settled there will be a good wicket tomorrow.' During the night it remained lovely and fine and we went down to The Oval very sanguine of winning. One can well imagine our surprise when we found that there had been a 'local rain' of about 22 yards long and 6 feet wide, just where the wicket was. At first we did not realise what had happened, until we started to bowl on the wicket. England set us 113 runs to win and we made only 44. The wicket was absolutely at its worst in our second innings, and this in spite of the fact that it had not seen any rain since 3 p.m. on the Monday.

Test Tussles On and Off the Field, Darling

It could get even funnier if, like Charlie McLeod, you were deaf as a stump and run out when bowled by a no-ball. England's Prince Ranjitsinhji recalled the incident fifteen months later in Sydney.

The incident began by Richardson bowling him off a no-ball; the fullpitch, after hitting the wicket, travelled to short slip; the batsman, meanwhile, not hearing the call of the umpire, left his wicket and was walking away to the pavilion. The ball, being smartly fielded by slip, was thrown to the wicketkeeper, who, seeing the batsman out of his ground, pulled up the stumps and appealed for a run-out, the umpire answering the appeal against the batsman.

This incident gave rise to a lot of excitement, argument, and talk all round the ground, but, as usual, the majority of critics harped on a point that had no bearing on the question. The great point was: was the ball dead or not at the time the man was out of his ground and the stump pulled up? If dead, the man was not out; if otherwise, the decision of the umpire was the right one. In this case the ball was in play the whole time, therefore the decision given was the only possible one.

The England team came in for much abuse, owing to what the public considered its unfair play and unsportsmanlike conduct in taking advantage of a batsman's mistake. It is needless to say that such criticisms came from persons who might do well to study the game more closely. Our opponents, the players, upheld our action.

With Stoddart's Team in Australia,
Ranjitsinhji

Jack Hobbs didn't find it very funny when he slipped setting off for a run at Headingley in 1909, and the Australians appealed unsuccessfully for hit wicket.

The Australians made a rare fuss. They gathered together in the field and confabulated. The chief offender was Warwick Armstrong, who got very nasty and unsportsmanlike, refusing to accept the umpire's decision. This upset me. I did not know whether I was standing on my head or my heels, with the consequence that two balls later I let one go, never even attempting to play it; and it bowled me. I still bear this incident in mind against Armstrong.

My Cricket Memories, Hobbs

It's probably best to make a bit of a joke of things, like Arthur Mailey.

Mailey hit the pads in a Test match at Adelaide Oval. 'How's that!' he demanded.

'Not out,' replied umpire George Hele.

'Bloody cheat,' muttered Mailey.

Hele almost leapt at him. 'Who's a cheat?' he barked.

'I am,' said Arthur, and all was well.

The Vic Richardson Story,
Richardson and Whitington

Although it was against the law, I must break down and confess that I always carried powdered resin in my pocket and, when the umpire wasn't looking, lifted the seam for Jack Gregory and Ted McDonald. And I am still as unashamed as a Yorkshireman who appeals for lbw off a ball that pitches two feet outside the leg-stump.

Anyhow I was in pretty good company. One day in Sydney, Johnny Douglas the England captain asked me to show him my hand. He held it for a while and then said, 'Arthur, you've been using resin. I'll report you to the umpire.'

I asked him to show me his right hand and, looking at the thumbnail, I noticed it was worn to the flesh on the outside.

'You've been lifting the seam, Johnny,' I said. My co-rebel grinned and the matter was dropped.

10 for 66 and All That, Mailey

But perhaps not too much of a joke, like Australia's slow bowler Chuck Fleetwood-Smith.

First the magpie call . . . arck . . . arck . . . arck . . . screeched out in a gravelly voice. The bewildered batsmen looked all ways wondering if they were about to get pecked on the back of the head from an overprotective maggie. Then the loud chants, 'Up Port Melbourne, Go Port Melbourne' in tribute to his favourite football team. Usually by this time the batsmen had realised they were in the vicinity of a madman. Chuck would wander off to first slip, drawing closer to the batsman and confusing him even more by raising his head to the sky and imitating the whipbird. If he saw someone he knew in the crowd his enthusiastic waving would be accompanied by the cry, 'Woop woop woop, gee up there, Bess, woop woop woop, Lord Hawke, Lord Hawke.'

And we were only in the second over. By the fourth over Chuck was giving a comic performance of his golf swing, strutting around with his bottom sticking out and playing to the crowd, miming his delight at getting a hole-in-one. By this time his team-mates and even his opponents were nearly sick with laughter.

A Wayward Genius, Growden

Some think it should all be left to the umpires.

I remember once when Don Bradman, fielding at cover point, saw the ball hit Denis [Compton] on the pad and up he went with his 'Howzat' and he was told 'not out'.

Denis, never loath to express a view, said, 'Don, how could you possibly see from out there?' Don answered, 'I couldn't, but it might have been out, mightn't it? That's for umpircs to decide, not me!'

The Gloves Are Off, Evans

As Ray Lindwall and Bill Edrich showed, however, some players are also capable of ethical debate.

Our conversation centred on the question of bumpers and the ethics of field setting on the leg-side for them. Then Bill asked, 'Tell me, Ray, what would you do if I bowled some bumpers at you?' 'Wouldn't worry me, Bill,' I assured him. 'I'd treat them with impunity.' The word seemed to amuse Bill but he said no more than 'We'll see tomorrow.' He did not forget. He happened to be bowling when I went in and, without so much as a nod, he bounced the first five balls at me. I swung at the first four and missed. The fifth rose a little higher and struck me on the hand. Still forgetting the leg-pulling of the previous evening, I called down the wicket, 'Hey, what's the idea, Bill? I can bowl these a bit, you know.' The bowler's face was a picture. 'No need to worry, Ray,' he sang out. 'Just giving you a few of your impunity balls.'

Flying Stumps, Lindwall

Colin Cowdrey recalled that the best sledges, like the one from his captain Len Hutton, often come from team-mates.

I looked around at the end of an over to see Vic Wilson, the twelfth man, calmly walking out to the middle. As I had not signalled to the dressing-room for anything, nor was it the drinks interval, I could only assume that Compton had indicated that he wanted some fresh batting gloves. Wilson, however, kept walking straight to my end. I was mystified. He reached into his blazer pocket, produced two bananas and gave them to me. I said, 'What the hell are these for?' Wilson replied, 'Well, the skipper thought you might be hungry. He watched you play a couple of wild shots just now. It rather suggests he is keen for you to stay out here batting a little longer.'

   MCC, Cowdrey

Never let anyone tell you that sledging is new. Fifty years ago Wally Grout was an expert.

Grout was keeping wicket when Ted Dexter made his debut in Sydney in 1958 and asked for what to Wal sounded like 'Two laigs, please'. Gloved hand to mouth Wally murmured to the slips, 'Blue-blooded ones, of course.'

   Willow Patterns, Benaud

His repartee flashed again when I beat Dexter with one that got up quickly. Dexter said, 'That was a good ball, Wal.'

'Naw,' said The Griz as he flipped the ball to slips. 'You just made it look good.'

Slasher Opens Up, Mackay

Dexter himself could vouch for the vehemence of Grout's appeals.

Wally and I had an amusing chat on another occasion when he was keeping to Richie's bowling at Leeds. Richie bowled a beauty, pitching leg, beating the bat, and missing the off-stump. A terrific appeal from Wally and Richie together practically convinced me I had hit it, though I knew I had not. The umpire was not convinced either and gave me not out. Wally came in for a drink that evening. 'You didn't really think I hit that one did you, Wally?' I asked. 'No, no, Ted,' he replied. 'Just clearing my throat.'

Ted Dexter's Cricket Book, Dexter

Grout also sledged umpires, such as Col Egar . . .

We were riding back into town from the cricket ground in the same car. We stopped at some traffic lights and I said to Col, 'You get out here, don't you?' Col looked out the window and said, 'No, this isn't my hotel.' I then read him a traffic sign attached to a post, 'Blind pedestrians cross here.'

Col took it as I knew he would – a good bloke Egar!

My Country's Keeper, Grout

. . . and even crowds, like that at Old Trafford in 1964.
A Lancashire member complete with cloth cap and pipe
looked up at the players' balcony and yelled, 'Declare,
Simpson, you bastard.' Wally Grout leaning over the
rail took a deep draw on his cigarette and enquired
drily, 'What about The Oval 1938?'

Bowled Over, Hawke

Yet, as Neil Hawke recalled, Grout was also the
consummate sportsman, as witnessed in the Trent
Bridge Test of 1964 . . .
Simpson had reminded me that I had right of way to
field a ball and it was the batsman's duty to avoid me.
I remembered this when Boycott played me on the
on-side and called for one. I darted after the ball and
poor old Fred Titmus crossed my line on a collision
course. He finished sprawled on the ground and Gra-
hame Corling picked up the ball and lobbed it back to
Wally Grout. Wally made a sweep with the ball over
the stumps without removing the bails and then lobbed
the ball back to me. From the covers came the startled
cry, 'I thought this was a bloody Test match!' which
suggested not everyone was in accord with Wally's
gesture.

Bowled Over, Hawke

... and also in the 1966 Melbourne Test.

Titmus, who had resumed batting at 23, would have been out at 35 but for the honesty of Australian wicket-keeper Wally Grout. He square drove a ball from Graham McKenzie towards third man where Doug Walters fielded and fired his return as the batsmen began a third run. Parks sent Titmus back as Walters' return screamed into Lawry who, seeing Parks was safe, hurled the ball to Grout's end and struck the wicket with Titmus out of his ground. But Grout in his excitement had already broken the wicket with his pad. No-one knew this but Grout, and as the crowd hailed the defeat of the fighting Londoner, Wal indicated to umpire Egar, who was in the act of raising his finger, just what had happened. Titmus won a reprieve and to this day I believe the crowd does not know it was because of Grout's sportsmanship.

The Quest for the Ashes, Mackay

Times got tougher and tempers flared more often in the 1970s as players, crowds and umpires became more outspoken and fast bowling frayed nerves. Ian Redpath managed to keep his feelings to himself while under bombardment from John Snow during his 171 at Perth in December 1970 – but only just.

Redders just ducked and weaved and occasionally got hit and every time he stood upright he swayed back, the old Adam's apple poking out, and he mouthed down the wicket to Snow, 'Get —.' He didn't say it loud but Snow saw it and smiled to himself. They didn't exchange a word, but Redpath must have got 100 bouncers that day.

Greg Chappell: Cricket's incomparable artist,
McGregor

Nobody restrained themselves when Geoff Boycott was run out at the Adelaide Oval the following month, as Alan Knott recalled.

Geoff ran for a sharp single to wide mid-on and Ian Chappell hit the stumps at the bowler's end. I was looking out square with the wicket at the time and so I had an excellent view, even if it was a distant one. I doubted whether Geoff had made his ground, but he was quite sure that he had done and when he was given out he threw his bat to the ground. Many umpiring decisions had gone against us in this series, decisions which could have made all the difference between winning and losing the Ashes. The pressures were now becoming intense and it only needed something like this for control to snap. I have no doubt that if Geoff had been left to pick up this bat and walk out quietly the whole incident would not have received the amount of unfortunate publicity it did. The Aussies crowded round, pushing and shoving at him and thumbing him off the field and the fielders' action made it obvious to the crowd there was real dispute in the middle. All the gesticulating I am sure helped to increase the volume of booing that dinned in Geoff's ears as he walked off the field.

Stumper's View, Knott

The hostility of John Snow when bowling to tailender Terry Jenner during the next Test, which was played in Sydney, caused one of Australian cricket's ugliest incidents.

As the first rose toward his ribs, Jenner gingerly fended it away with his bat. It ran around the corner for a single, giving Chappell the strike for four balls. Facing Snow again for the sixth ball, Jenner unhappily squirmed out of its way as it reared. Had he stood still, it would have struck him near the left armpit. The over count so far to Jenner: two short-pitched balls, at least one of which an umpire could have classed as intimidatory. To follow up Jenner's apprehensive wriggle from the sixth ball, Snow's field-setting was changed by bringing Willis from mid-off to the on-side. This made four leg-trap fieldsmen: deep leg (Underwood), leg-gully (Hampshire), close short-leg (Illingworth) and mid-on (Willis). Stepping back, Jenner stared at the reshuffle like a bird transfixed by a snake's mesmerism. Like every cricketer watching, he recognised the field adjustment as preparation for catching a mis-hit off a bouncer to come. It came. Banged down short, it cut in as it reared toward Jenner's collarbone. As he tried to duck beneath it, the ball struck the left side of his head near the back and rebounded toward cover. Jenner's collapse on the pitch brought a thunderous hoot from the keyed-up crowd.

The Wildest Tests, Robinson

After Snow had an altercation with spectators on the boundary edge and suffered a beer-can bombardment, Ray Illingworth led his team from the field, and umpire Lou Rowan had to coax him back.

Sitting side-by-side broadcasting, ex-captains Benaud and Lawry had made a small diversionary bet on the match. Illingworth's disappearance through the gate reminded Lawry of this. Turning to Richie he said, 'It's a forfeit. Pay up, Benordy!' The batsmen stayed at the wicket. Lillee, playing in his second Test, walked along to Chappell and asked, 'What do we do now?' Greg: 'We stay here until we are told to do something differently.'

The Wildest Tests, Robinson

At Perth eight years later Greg Chappell saw Dennis Lillee using an aluminium bat in practice the day before a Test.

'It was a real tinny thing, hollow, just didn't go,' Greg said. Greg had a mild shot at Lillee. He wasn't going to use that, was he? Lillee whipped around, 'What do you mean?' Greg's evil mind chimed: here was a way to get the boy stirred up. In retrospect Greg believed that had he told Lillee that in the interests of the team he should use his normal bat Lillee may, or may not, have used his favourite Duncan Fearnley. Greg did not know that the bat was cracked. Greg did know that Lillee at number nine would be bowling soon. He intended to let him bat for an over, take the bat off him and fire Lillee to fury when bowling. Events went awry. Rodney Hogg took a cracked bat out to Lillee who rejected it. Lillee came in for a new one and Greg sat like a sphinx knowing that one blink from him would set Lillee off. Rodney Marsh saved him the trouble. 'It's not like you to let people tell you what bat you can use,' he said deadpan.

Lillee stopped. Marsh was bloody right. Out he went with the metal bat again. 'Thanks for your help, Bacchus,' said Greg, exasperated. He looked round for Rodney Hogg to take another bat out, but Hogg would not have a bar of it. Greg then had the tiger by the tail himself. Fortunately Brearley had involved himself at the crease. When Greg arrived with the new bat Lillee heave-hoed the aluminium so, to Greg's relief, the Poms became the cause of it all.

Greg Chappell: Cricket's incomparable artist,
McGregor

Let's try and keep it all in perspective, like David Hookes and Tony Greig in the 1977 Centenary Test . . .
As I was walking off Greig said, 'Piss off.' I half stopped and turned round, spat the dummy and said, 'At least I'm an Australian playing this game and not a fucking

Pommy import.' No-one was more surprised than me when I later saw Tony Greig walking into our room carrying a bottle of beer and two glasses. 'Mind if I sit with you, son?' he said. 'Please do,' I replied. And he said, 'Well played.'

Hookesy, Hookes and Shiell

. . . and Merv Hughes and Robin Smith in 1989 . . .
Hughes, having Smith in trouble, snorted at him, 'Smith, you can't —ing bat.' Next ball, Robin smashed him for four, and as he was turning at the non-striker's end looked at Merv and said, 'Make a good pair don't we? I can't —ing bat and you can't —ing bowl.'

The Autobiography, Gower and Norrie

. . . and, finally, Merv Hughes again and Jack Russell.
The day before the Lord's Test I had a long chat with Alan Knott about my batting and he said I had to bat as though my life was at stake. Real mental grit, geeing myself up all the time. After that I kept talking to myself while at the crease – the Aussies must have thought I was a real nutter. I knew they would give me a lot of lip at Lord's because they sensed I would be vulnerable as a new boy. Merv Hughes gave me an almighty earful and I gave it back. That really helped me, it geed me up. When I slapped the loose ball to the boundary I would shout, 'Now go and fetch that!'

Declarations, Murphy (Ed.)

4 | BODY LINES

Devised as the irresistible force to Donald Bradman's immoveable object, the 'Bodyline' bowling of Harold Larwood, Bill Voce and Bill Bowes against Australia in 1932–33 not only recaptured the Ashes but made the Empire reverberate. As England under the implacable leadership of Douglas Jardine prevailed by the margin of four Tests to one, telegrams of the highest dudgeon ricocheted back and forth between the Australian Board of Control and Lord's, and events were discussed at the highest levels of government.

No batsman was comfortable against Bodyline. If Bradman contrived to average 56, his batting often seemed skittish and anxious; after a period in which batsmen had feasted on undemanding medium-pace on doped wickets, Larwood's hostility was simply irrepressible. He never played beyond the series, but he had done enough never to be forgotten. Likewise there remain pubs in Australia where public expression of admiration for Jardine would earn the speaker an invitation to step outside.

Everyone has a view of Bodyline, whether as
a stunning sporting drama . . .

To have seen Larwood in Australia is to have witnessed one of the greatest of all sporting occasions.

Express Deliveries, Bill Bowes

. . . a bowlers' rebellion . . .

Bodyline was not a cricket revolution that grew overnight. Unrest among bowlers because of the difficulties and injustices of their job had been simmering for years. It was purely a coincidence that Bradman, bringing to the game a particular outlook, should have synchronised with a period when the art of doped wickets was at its height. All it required to touch off the fire of bowling revolution was somebody like Bradman who could throw off into bold relief just how one-sided the game of cricket had become in its lauding of and consideration for the batsmen always at the expense of the bowler.

Cricket Crisis, Fingleton

. . . English perfidy . . .

Now we Australians are at a loss to understand why we alone of all the Empire are singled out for these continual attacks. We claim to be loyal to the throne, and to uphold the traditions of the British race. Also we pay our debts and are England's very best customer within the Empire. When danger threatened we were one of the first to respond to the call to the arms by the Motherland. Well then?

'The Sporting English?' Anonymous, 1933

. . . Aussie whingeing . . .

Bodyline itself was no more lethal or sustained an attack on the batsman's body than the more modern version practised by Lillee, Thomson and others, but it embittered relations to a remarkable degree and Jardine was the focus of hostilities.

Runs and Catches, Pawson

. . . a breach of cricket niceties . . .

One of the strongest arguments against this bowling is that it breeds anger, hatred and malice, with consequent reprisals. The courtesy of combat goes out of the game.

Cricket Between Two Wars, Warner

. . . or a correlative to the rise of fascism.

Bodyline was not an incident, it was not an accident, it was not a temporary aberration. It was the violence and ferocity of our age expressing itself in cricket.

Beyond a Boundary, James

Bodyline's origins lay at The Oval in 1930, when England's fastest bowler, Harold Larwood, noted Bradman's discomfiture when attacked on the leg-side from short of a length during a partnership with Archie Jackson.

There is nothing more heartening for the fast bowler than to get a little lift from the wicket. It is like icy champagne to the palate. Don didn't like the balls rising on his body. He was hit once or twice, but the real significance in his play was the fact that he kept drawing away. It wasn't all that obvious to me at first because I was mainly concerned with getting the ball up off a length, but I began to notice that he flinched. Others saw it too and we talked about it after the match. I thought Bradman was a bit frightened of the ball that got up sharply. I may have been wrong but that was my impression. I wasn't dropping them short – the ball was popping from a good length.

The Larwood Story, Larwood and Perkins

Larwood found a like spirit in Douglas Jardine, captain of the England team of 1932–33, educated at Winchester by Rockley Wilson.

In the classroom Rockley penetrated Jardine's harsh exterior and Jardine later paid many extravagant tributes to him. However, on the field Rockley found him extremely headstrong. Thirteen years later, on being told that his former pupil had been chosen as captain for what would prove to be the Bodyline tour, Rockley made one of his best-known quips, 'We shall win the Ashes – but we may lose a dominion.'

> *Great Characters from Cricket's Golden Age,*
> Mailes

Jardine, too, felt that Bradman flinched from harm.
As for the true genesis of Bodyline, the key moment had come some time earlier when D.R. Jardine, having watched film of the 1930 Oval Test match in the company of a gathering of MCC committeemen at Lord's, spotted Don Bradman's discomfort on the damp pitch and ejaculated, 'I've got it! He's yellow!'

> *Bodyline Autopsy,* Frith

Jardine began his tour by alienating the press, rebuffing their first request.
'Could we please have the team selections in good time, Mr Jardine? The evening papers in Sydney and Melbourne go to press at midday.' The effrontery of these Australians was staggering! Was he to supply names for the convenience of some reporter, for the sake of Sydney and Melbourne? He lost his temper with the man. 'Do you think we've come all this way to provide scoops for your bloody newspaper?'

> *Bradman and the Bodyline Series,* Docker

When journalist Claude Corbett criticised his team for taking the field late in their opening match at Adelaide, and was sent for by the English captain and his manager Plum Warner, the feeling emerged as mutual.

Jardine said, 'Mr Corbett, I have received a number of letters from Australians, abusive letters. These I disregard. I have also received a letter from an English friend of mine living in Australia. Of course, I shall reply to him. In view of what I have told you, is there anything you would like me to add to the letter as a comment from yourself?' Corbett said, 'Yes, Mr Jardine. There is something you can add. You can tell him from me that my comment is "Go and get f—!"'

The Larwood Story, Larwood and Perkins

Stan McCabe watched the early stages of Australia's innings in Sydney with a growing presentiment.

Stan McCabe was sitting in the front seats of the members' enclosure with his mother and father as the early batsmen began to be hit about the upper bodies by balls from Larwood. Wickets began to fall, and as the 22-year-old McCabe left his parents to don his pads, he called to his father, 'If I get hit, Dad, stop Mum from jumping the fence.'

The Vic Richardson Story,
Richardson and Whitington

His fearless 187 not out heartened the tailenders who stayed with him.

Bill O'Reilly was next and was greeted by Stan with the following advice, which should be enshrined in our cricket folklore for all time, 'Don't worry about him [Larwood], he's not as fast as he looks – I'll handle him.' Bill took guard and the first delivery received from Larwood cannoned onto the shoulder of his bat before he had time to lift it. O'Reilly, stupefied, called down the pitch to McCabe. 'Not so bloody fast, eh? I'll say you can handle him.'

Stan McCabe: The man and his cricket,
McHarg

Lunching on the rest day with 'Chappie' Dwyer, McCabe was unmoved by press praise for his defiance.

At that lunch, Chappie remarked jokingly, 'I suppose you have a swollen head after reading all that praise in the press.' 'But I haven't read the papers,' replied Stan. 'I thought there might be a lot of exaggerated praise in them it would be better for me not to read.'

Fours Galore, Whitington

Three English players scored centuries in the First Test at the SCG: Herbert Sutcliffe, Wally Hammond and the Nawab of Pataudi, whose five-and-a-quarter hour 102 tested a few of the locals' patience.

After watching him potter round for an hour and a half for about 25 runs and then, for a similar period, without any improvement, Vic Richardson said to him, 'Pat, what's wrong? Aren't you seeing them too well?' 'I'm waiting for the pace of the wicket to change a bit.' 'Good God!' said Richardson. 'It's changed three times while you've been in.'

The Larwood Story, Larwood and Perkins

Bill O'Reilly, a teacher at Kogarah, received an insight into the implications of the series immediately after the SCG Test.

Early defeat in the Sydney Test meant that O'Reilly, 'being a very, very good and I should say unsophisticated public servant,' went back to work for the half-day to take his boys to the St George Sports Ground for their afternoon games. 'They all got their gear out and they went down onto the four grounds,' O'Reilly remembered, 'and each one of the bowlers or each one of the captains set a Bodyline field straight away. And I thought to myself, "Well, I'm not going to interfere. I'll let them have a go and find out how they like it."'

Wisden Cricket Monthly, January 1995

Bradman at the time was locked in a struggle with the Australian Board of Control.

He had agreed to write for R.C. Packer's Associated Newspapers, but the Board had then refused to grant him its permission. It seemed for a time that the Don might not be available to play against Jardine's men. There was one very tempting offer from overseas. An English newspaper group cabled him an offer of £3000, a huge sum for those days, if he would abandon any hopes of playing in the Tests and cover the series for them.

By that time Associated Newspapers were under fire for 'holding Bradman to his contract', and some members of the Board had begun to flinch under the steady bombardment of abuse and criticism. They asked A.G. Moyes, then the sport editor of the *Sun*, to introduce them to R.C. Packer, of the editorial board of the newspaper group, so that they might ask him to release Bradman from his contract. Packer agreed to do so, but Bradman steadily insisted that he was under a moral obligation to fulfil the contract. His only offer of concession was to accept the English bid, drop out of the Tests and write for the overseas newspapers and pay the huge fee over to Associated Newspapers.

Packer rejected this and said, 'You must play, Don.'

He answered, 'You can't force me to write, but there's nothing in the contract which allows you to force me to play.'

Packer replied that Associated Newspapers only wanted him to forget about writing and play for Australia. He spoke so persuasively that Bradman at last agreed to break his own inflexible rule.

Bradman: A biography, Page

Bradman's return for the Second Test at the MCG
was followed the breadth of the continent; Yorkshire's
towering right-arm paceman Bill Bowes had the job
of bowling the first ball to him.

Every step he took toward the wicket was cheered, and
Bradman, a cunning campaigner, came from the dark-
ness of the pavilion and walked towards the wicket
in a huge semi-circle. He was giving the crowd time
to quieten and also accustom his eyes to the glare.
He was cheered as he took up his guard, cheered as
he looked round the field to see the disposition of
the fieldsmen. The cheering continued at the same volume as I ran up to bowl. It was deafening. I had to
stop in the middle of the run-up and wait for the noise
to subside. To fill in time I asked my mid-on to move
up to silly mid-on.

Once again I began my run. Once again came a terrific roar. Once again I had to stop. This time I moved
my fine-leg fieldsman to the boundary edge. I saw Don
eyeing those changed positions with a look of determination. Then the thought flashed into my mind, 'He
expects a bouncer – can I fool him?'

I ran up to bowl with the most threatening expression on my face that I could muster. Don stepped across
the wicket intending to hit the ball out of sight. But, as
the ball flew towards him, he realised it was not a
bouncer at all. In a manner that only a really great
batsman could achieve, he changed the elevation of

his intended shot and got a very faint edge on the ball, but his defensive move was ineffective. He was bowled out.

The crowd was stupified. Bradman walked off the field amid a silence that would have been a theatrical producer's triumph. The spell was broken by a solitary woman's clapping. The feeble sound rippled above the hushed throng and then an excited chatter broke out all over the ground. And it was then I noticed Jardine. Jardine, the sphinx, had momentarily forgotten himself for the one and only time in his cricketing life. In his sheer delight at this unexpected stroke of luck he had clasped both his hands above his head and was jigging around like an Indian doing a war dance.

Express Deliveries, Bowes

A coda from the historian Manning Clark.

The batsman at the bowler's end when it happened was Jack Fingleton, whom I liked very much – I got to know him later when he was a political journalist in Canberra. He told me that in the great hush that descended on the ground when Bradman was bowled, Bowes just put his hands on his hips and turned around to Jack and the umpire and said to them in broad Yorkshire, 'Well I'll be foocked!'

Extra Cover, Egan

The second innings was a different story as
Bradman powered Australia to victory, recalled
Walter Hammond.

As he walked in you could see 'Not this time!' written in letters of fire across the sky! And when he had leisurely played himself in, he made 103 not out from a total of 191. How well I remember him staring down the pitch as I bowled over after over, trying to keep the runs down and rest the fast bowlers. I took 3 for 21 that innings, but with Don I could do nothing, even if he could do little with me.

Cricket My Destiny, Hammond

With the series at 1–1, the Adelaide Test was one
of the most furious ever played. The crowd, noted
Jardine, was involved right from the beginning of
Tim Wall's opening spell.

One of the fast bowler's deliveries, which kicked awkwardly, struck Sutcliffe on the shoulder, to the huge delight of the crowd, which applauded vociferously. Indeed, it was frequently noticeable throughout the tour that a blow from the ball, so long as the victim was an Englishman, was the signal for a demonstration of public approval, while if an Australian happened to be the victim, the English bowler was often as not booed and 'counted out'.

In Quest of the Ashes, Jardine

When Larwood bowled during Australia's reply, he at once hit Woodfull a fearful blow over the heart, watched by non-striker Bradman.

The batsman staggered back and the crowd howled with rage. Not just the ordinary punters but grey-haired members were up on their feet, shouting imprecations. Jardine walked across to sympathise with Woodfull and then made his way to Larwood at the other end. Hammond was already there, telling Larwood not to be put off by the crowd's behaviour. 'Well bowled, Harold,' said Jardine, loud and clear, as much for the non-striker's ears as for Larwood's.

Douglas Jardine: Spartan cricketer, Douglas

The content of the visit paid by Pelham Warner to Woodfull, leaked to a journalist, has become part of the game's folklore.

Warner went up to Woodfull and said, 'We have come to say how sorry we are and to offer our sympathies.' Woodfull answered curtly in some such words as, 'I don't want to see you, Mr Warner. There are two teams out there. One is trying to play cricket. The other is not. This game is too good to be spoiled. It is time some people got out of it. Good afternoon.'

Bradman: A biography, Page

Another story current in Adelaide that weekend related how Jardine too had paid a visit to the Australian dressing-room. Not on any errand of sympathy, however. The door was answered by Vic Richardson with just a towel round his waist. 'I would like to speak to Woodfull,' Jardine demanded. 'One of your men called Larwood a bastard. I want an immediate apology.' But Richardson only looked at him derisively, turned and called out, 'Hey, which of you bastards called Larwood a bastard instead of Jardine?'

Bradman and the Bodyline Series, Docker

Larwood brought the crowd's rage to a climax when he felled Bert Oldfield with a bouncer, although, as he remembered, the blame for the injury was not all his.

I had stopped bowling Bodyline and the field was set mostly on the off. I wouldn't have pitched one short at Bertie, only he could bat and he had settled in. The last thing I would have wanted to do was hit him. I pitched it short on off-stump. Bert swung at it, going for a hook, but it came off the wicket slower than he expected. He had spun almost right round, having just about completed the stroke, when it hit him on the right side of the temple. I think the result would have been worse had the peak of his cap not broken the force of the ball. I was the first one up to Bert. I might have broken even with Gubby Allen. I was very upset. It was Bert's fault and he was gentleman and sportsman enough to admit it at once. I am certain the ball came off the edge of the bat and that he walked into it. I was frightened how serious Bert's injury might be; I was also frightened at the abuse and barracking of the crowd. It was so bad that Maurice Tate, who was sitting in the enclosure, got up and went into the dressing-room saying, 'I'm getting out of here – someone will get killed.'

The Larwood Story, Larwood and Perkins

Next man in was Bill O'Reilly.

After taking minutes to force his way through the recalcitrant members, O'Reilly's whiff of Larwood's pace was short, sharp and pungent. 'I stayed for about five or six balls before he rolled me over and, when he hit the off-stump . . . I saw the off-bail just disintegrate as it went. So I bent down and picked up all the pieces and brought them back in my pocket as a souvenir.'

Wisden Cricket Monthly, January 1995

The temper of the Test recalled by Larwood . . .

Feeling continued to run so high that I was not surprised when I went into an Adelaide theatre one night and overheard a small child saying to her mother, 'Mummy, he doesn't look like a murderer.'

The Larwood Story, Larwood and Perkins

. . . by Jardine . . .

On the occasion of drinks being brought out into the

field an Australian barracker made one of the few humorous remarks which we were privileged to hear on this tour. Seeing the Australian captain about to offer me a drink, he shouted, 'Don't give him a drink! Let the — die of thirst!'

In Quest of the Ashes, Jardine

. . . by Sutcliffe . . .

The crowd would hush as Larwood walked back to the point where he began his run, and then there would, for a fraction of a second, be absolute peace as Larwood swung around to begin his attack. The sound of his boots hitting the ground in his run could be heard – in the slips you were conscious of the breathing of the men alongside you, conscious, I say, of the rustle of Ames' gloves when he rubbed his hands before completing his stance – and then, the ball delivered, the crowd had its say.

For England and Yorkshire, Sutcliffe

. . . and by future Prime Minister Robert Menzies.

I was chatting to the man next to me whom I didn't know. He was quietly spoken, cultured and most interesting. We spoke of many things before the game started. That was the day Woodfull was struck by Larwood. I looked at the man again and he was a changed person. He was on his feet and his face was choleric. He shouted, he raved, he flung imprecations at Larwood and Jardine because of what his eyes had just seen.

Cricket Crisis, Fingleton

England regained the Ashes in the next Test in Brisbane in unremitting heat by bringing out the champagne early, recalled the winning captain.

I make no secret of claiming that this, the second day of the Fourth Test, is the greatest day which English cricket has known for twenty years. We were indebted to our manager, Mr R.C.N. Palairet, for a very good suggestion. He did not often say much, but what he did was always as helpful as it was sound. On this occasion, in view of the terrific heat, he suggested that our bowlers should be given half a dozen sips of champagne. All of us, I think, are agreed that the less use made of stimulants in all sport the better, but on this exceptional occasion the champagne proved an unqualified success.

In Quest of the Ashes, Jardine

Their first innings had been underwritten by an immortal innings from Eddie Paynter, who rose from a hospital bed to which he had been confined by tonsillitis.

No sooner had the invalid buckled on his pads soon after tea than Allen was out. To thunderous applause the little man under the wide-brimmed panama transported himself slowly to the wicket, pale and trembling. Ames, equally astonished, greeted him. Woodfull patted Paynter on the back and sportingly offered him a runner but he declined. He held on for the remaining seventy-five minutes, making 24 precious runs, Larwood's passive partner in a partnership of 55 after Ames was out. He then tugged his pyjamas back on, donned his dressing-gown and returned to hospital in a bit of a daze. He felt appreciably better the next day and, pockets bulging with tablets and gargle mixture, he returned to the Gabba. With the steady – and often fortunate – Verity he continued the England resistance, playing strokes to all parts, taking England into the lead, stopping twice to gargle and take his medicine, and receiving great cheers when he reached 50. On a pitch rendered tranquil after Jardine ordered the heavy roller at the start, the pair were still together at lunch, Paynter having picked up most of his runs on the leg side. When Paynter finally fell at 83 there was the rare sight of Australian cricketers clapping an England batsman as the small figure withdrew to the dressing-shed.

Bodyline Autopsy, Frith

England began its fourth innings chase with an obdurate innings by their captain in which he spent 82 balls without scoring, recalled by Bill O'Reilly. Facetiously I congratulated him with, 'Well batted, Douglas.' Looking straight into my eyes he said, 'Really, Bill, really. Don't you think I was like an old maid defending her virginity?' With my sails windless my reply was, 'Sorry, Douglas, I am too short in experience to answer that question.'

'Tiger', O'Reilly

For the final Test at Sydney Larwood the batsman was on show, falling just short of the feat of a century as nightwatchman in unlucky fashion.

The pitch had improved and by excellent batsmanship he went on to compile 98 runs. Then unexpectedly, in a flash, came one of those dramatic moments that help to make cricket so fascinating. Eager to pass his century, Larwood stepped out to smite P.K. Lee, a right-handed spinner, to the boundary. Alas, owing to a slight mistiming, the ball whizzed off the edge to Bert Ironmonger of all fieldsman at mid-on. Now it was alleged jokingly that Bert had never held a catch in his life. Certainly in this match he had consistently put the ball 'on the carpet' when chances had come his way. As the ball whirred from Larwood's bat, we groaned inwardly feeling sure Bert's frantic grab at it would be abortive as usual. To our astonishment – and the utter astonishment of Bert himself – his brief nerve-racking juggling ended with the ball still between his fingers! And Larwood was out, most unluckily, with two runs short of the century after an innings deserving of that coveted honour. To cap everything, Bert's reaction to his success was as extraordinary as the catch. At that period in Test history a prominent firm was presenting money prizes for feats on the field, including a pound for every catch taken. And Bert, finding the ball still between his finger, let out a yell that one imagined might have been heard at Toowoomba. 'Whoopee! I've won a quid! I've won a quid!'

The Rattle of the Stumps, Oldfield

The ghost of Bodyline was exorcised by the exits of Jardine and Larwood, and the possibility of retaliation on Australia's 1934 Ashes tour – as hinted at in a meeting involving Lord Hawke and Australian Board of Control representative Dr Robert Macdonald.

MacDonald pointed out that the board was entitled to know beforehand whether the English team would use the tactics, because it might be necessary for Australia to include four fast bowlers to maintain the shock attack from both ends in the Test matches.

Lord Hawke, 'Reprisals, by gad!'

Macdonald, 'Not reprisals – reciprocity. Action and reaction on a mutual basis.'

Between Wickets, Robinson

In the 1934 Lord's Test when Bowes had bowled Woodfull a few softening bouncers and Bradman was coming to the wicket, the following dialogue occurred.

R.E.S. Wyatt: 'Bill, I've just had a message from the pavilion. "Ask Bowes not to bowl short."'

Bowes: 'And what do you say as captain?'

Wyatt: 'Well, if they want it friendly, perhaps they'd better have it that way.'

Sins of Omission, Synge

Bradman's magisterial progress resumed, though not to everyone's satisfaction.

Jardine was present as a journalist at the Leeds Test against Australia in 1934. One spectator looked up at the press box as Bradman moved inexorably on to his triple century and called out, 'We want you out there, Jardine.'

Hedley Verity: Portrait of a cricketer, Hill

In later years Jardine mellowed and was a guest at a dinner held for the 1953 Australians by Robert Menzies.

At one stage Menzies began a story, 'As you all know, I am the man in Australia who has most often had the legitimacy of his birth queried . . .'

'Surely, sir,' came the voice of Jardine, 'I still hold that honour.'

The Summer Game, Haigh

He even grew to like Australians . . .

'Though they may not hail me as Uncle Doug, I am no longer the bogeyman – just an old so-and-so who got away with it.'

The Wildest Tests, Robinson

. . . and insisted that the 4–1 winning scoreline flattered England.

'You know, we nearly didn't do it. The little man was bloody good.'

Bodyline, Derriman

5 | TRAVELLERS' TALES

Australia and England are at opposite ends of the earth yet culturally far closer. Cricket tours to and fro have thus been quite lengthy and solemn undertakings, where the differences have stood out for the general similarity of the language, history and values. In days of yore, too, when intercontinental travel was the preserve of the wealthy, cricketers were among a privileged few, and set out to enjoy their good fortune.

This chapter recalls the days when cricketers toured rather than simply took trips to play cricket. It also recalls the advice of Sir Robert Menzies: 'Great Britain and Australia are of the same blood and allegiance and history and instinctive mental processes. We know each other so well that, thank Heaven, we don't have to be too tactful with each other.'

Getting to England by ship was always an adventure, and players sometimes made it more. Murdoch's 1882 Australians shared the *SS Assam* with dramatist Haddon Chambers and involved him in some of their more dangerous pranks.

One day in the Suez Canal when the vessel was moored to the bank for hours, Mr Chambers and Mr Spofforth went ashore by means of 'swarming' along the steel hawser employed for the purpose of mooring. On the return journey of the adventurous pair, their companions who were lining the side of the vessel wickedly began shaking the heavy hawser and produced so violent a vibration that Spofforth, who was lightly clad, let go his hold and swam to the ship. But Haddon Chambers scorned so base a surrender to the enemy! Hanging onto the steel cable with all his strength and at the risk of severe injury to his hands, he successfully resisted all efforts to dislodge him and finally arrived on board again by this means amid the loud cheering and louder laughter of his fellow passengers.

Cricket of Today, vol. 1, 1902

Getting to Australia tested land-lubber Englishmen, too, like Arthur Shrewsbury's men of 1886–87.

As was to be expected, several of our team were unwell for two or three days at first. Amongst the worst by a long way being Gunn, although Barlow, Lillywhite, Briggs, Bates, Read and myself have been far from well and consequently have been absent from the dinner table on more than one occasion. Gunn talked of leaving the ship at Naples as he said he could not stand the journey, but of course now that he is all right he doesn't think anything of the kind. It was like a transformation scene, seeing him being led about one day and the following day dancing, romping and singing round the deck having forgotten all about being ill.

'Give Me Arthur': A biography of Arthur Shrewsbury,
Wynne-Thomas

Coming home was an adventure, too. Jack Blackham and Hugh Trumble of the 1893 Australians attracted interest even while they were returning through North America.

They stopped at Winnipeg for two or three days and in their hotel had quite a long interview with a deaf-and-dumb cricketer. The latter was an enthusiast and when he found that Blackham was Blackham and Trumble Trumble his joy was great. The pencil and paper questions and answers were kept up for a long time, much to the entertainment of several gentlemen present, and finally Messrs Blackham and Trumble said Good-bye after the strangest and most silent cricket interview ever experienced by them.

The Australasian, 13 January 1894

Likewise Sid Emery in 1912 as the players neared
Minneapolis, recalled by team-mate Charles
Macartney.

On our way back, the train stopped near a small town
named Theodore and from the windows we saw a bear
chained to a post nearby. Sid Emery thought he would
like to get a picture of this bear, so taking his camera he
left the train and set off.

To secure a good picture he advanced within the circle made by the captive in his wanderings about the
post at the full length of his chain. While trying to focus
his camera Sid took his eyes off the animal which at
that moment was standing at full height against the
post. Looking up a minute later Emery discovered
the bear almost upon him, and in a wild effort to get
out its reach, tripped and fell. The bear made a savage
lunge at him with its paw, but fortunately Emery was
able to roll out of its reach and escaped in the nick of
time. He returned to the train fully determined never
more to photograph a bear!

My Cricketing Days, Macartney

Shipboard life was shared by the Australian and
English teams of 1921.

Fresh from their five successive victories against Douglas' team, the Australians went to England in 1921; in
fact, the two teams travelled on the same ship to the
Mother Country. Warren Bardsley was the champion

at deck quoits. Makepeace as 'A Pirate', Hendren as 'Tarzan of the Apes' and Fender as 'Rasputin' excelled themselves at the fancy dress ball. We were well represented, too, with, to mention only a few, Bardsley as a mixture of W.G. Grace and 'The Ancient Mariner', Johnny Taylor as a 'Chinese Mandarin', and myself as a young lady. We had our own jazz band, conducted by Percy Fender. Bardsley played the saxophone, or an imitation one, and I think that is where he first took a fancy to the instrument, which he has since cultivated to some purpose. Parkin kept the ship alive with his fun. He operated the 'tote' every day on the ship's run, and was the most successful auctioneer in the Calcutta sweep that I have met on any voyage. How he kept up his fire of jokes for over two hours at that job without tiring his listeners I don't know, but he did.

My Cricketing Days, Macartney

The Australians almost lost a team member when their overland journey through Europe hit Paris, as Bert Oldfield recalled.

We had decided to get out at Invalides station but, to our surprise, Ryder was taking his time and was left in the train. The door had slammed quickly, as it does on all overseas undergrounds. I was detailed to follow him on the next train and restore him to the team. When I arrived at the next station, Ryder was surrounded by a host of railway officials and I found him gesticulating and saying, 'Me losee my friends' in quaint pidgin English and continuing to try and explain his dilemma. One of the officials said to him, 'If you would please speak zee good English I would probably understand you, yes!'

Behind the Wicket, Oldfield

Some players, like George Bonnor, were quicker getting over the effects of travel than others – here recalled by manager Charles Beal.

Soon after leaving Malta an army officer was talking about throwing a cricket ball 100 yards. Bonnor in his usual grandiloquent way said, 'A hundred yards! A hundred yards! Why, I could jerk it!' And so he could. After a little talk it culminated in a wager of 100 pounds that Bonnor could not throw 115 yards or more with the first throw on the first day he landed on English shores. Old Caleb Peacock of Adelaide was stakeholder.

We got to Plymouth and it was a fine day, so Bonnor, Murdoch, Garrett and myself got off the boat, the others going on. We tried to get a 5¼ oz cricket ball but could not get any lighter than 5½ oz. Before finally agreeing to the ground we went to several places including the Hoe, but that was down hill – all right for Bonnor, but it did not suit the other party. Then we went to the racecourse but that was slippery and of course did not suit us, so at last we arrived at the Barracks at Plymouth. As it was gravel and there was no wind we agreed the conditions were fair.

We got hold of the quartermaster – he happened to have a record in the army, he had thrown 107 yards I think. When we told him what the event was he became deeply interested. Bonnor got the quartermaster to put a pile of newspapers down as a target about two feet high at a distance of 120 yards to aim at. He was going to throw without taking his waistcoat off. It showed the cool belief he had in his powers. I insisted on his stripping to his singlet, though he didn't like the idea. He was toying with the ball. 'A man of my inches not being able to throw this little thing 115 yards!' Well, he threw 119 yards 7 inches and won the wager. I remember the quartermaster begged for the ball and we gave it to him. He never dreamt that anyone could throw the ball so far and wanted the ball as a souvenir. You ought to have seen 'Bon', the centre of admiration at Plymouth barracks after that throw.

The Referee, November 1914

Hospitality varied for early Australian tourists. Murdoch's men ran foul of the notorious autocrat Captain Henry Holden, secretary of Nottinghamshire. When the Australians played at Trent Bridge in 1882 the gallant Captain 'forgot' to organise any lunch for them, and when asked about it replied that amateurs found their own meals. The Captain went even further by telling the Australian captain that he, as Notts' secretary, decided how long the wicket should be rolled between innings – it had nothing to do with either the team captains or the umpires. The next day some rude comments on Holden were discovered chalked on the door of the Australians' hotel in Nottingham. Holden openly accused the Australian manager of writing the remarks. It was later discovered that the comments had been the work of one of the hangers-on who followed the Australians.

'Give Me Arthur': A biography of Arthur Shrewsbury, Wynne-Thomas

The inhospitality of English weather has been a ritual Australian complaint, though nobody has taken this beef as far as 1893 tourist Arthur Coningham while playing at Blackpool.

Arthur Coningham was fielding in the country. It was a cold, raw day and the Australians were fielding in their sweaters. The batting not being too brilliant or lively, the outfielders had little to do and the idea evidently struck Coningham that he would like to get warm. So he gathered some bits of sticks and grass, piled them up, and then asked one of the spectators for a match. Having obtained this he set fire to the little pile of grass and commenced to warm his hands. It amused a section of the spectators who applauded him, and one wag suggested that he go inside and get a couple of hot potatoes to put in his pockets.

The Quest for Bowlers, Turner

Most, like Reg Duff in 1902, content themselves with milder protests.

Reggie Duff found a picture of 'Old Sol' and pasted it inside his hat. Someone saw him staring into it and asked, 'What are you looking at, Reg?'

'I'm having a look at the sun,' he said. 'I have not seen it for a month.'

Sydney Sun, 28 May 1930

You never know whom you might meet in England.

Public men and celebrities often come to our dressing-room to be introduced. Sometimes the situations are comical. Upon one occasion the present prime minister of England, when he was First Lord of the Treasury, came in, and while shaking hands with some of our team the wearing apparel was very scanty. One gave his right hand to Mr Balfour whilst he held his trousers up with his left. Another had one leg in his trousers and the other out. Others were drying themselves after a bath without even that much covering.

Nearly all the waiters in England are foreigners. Many are in the country for the purpose of learning the language. Well-connected people of Germany and elsewhere take positions in leading hotels without salary

solely for the object of acquiring the accent and pro-
nunciation of the better-class people. I never, however,
met any who refused a tip. So little do some understand
the language that we have often played tricks upon
them. We would look at the menu card and order possum soup, roast bustard on kangaroo tails, emu wings
with lizard sauce or some other ridiculous dish. The
waiter would say, 'Yes, sir!' and hurry away. Later he
would return and explain, 'I am sorry, sir, there is no
more, it is just off.'

An Australian Cricketer on Tour, Laver

And there are always celebrities eager to entertain and
well-wishers generous with gifts. Warwick Armstrong's
men of 1921 carried all before them.

By now, the Australians' tour had become more like
a pageant, their games like social events. They were
watched by the King, the Prince of Wales, Prime
Minister Lloyd George, even members of the guard
accompanying Prince Hirohito on his first visit to
England. They were entertained by the Duke and
Duchess of Portland, the Duke of Newcastle, and Lord
Saville. Armstrong was plied with gifts: Lord Lons-
dale, entertaining the team at Cumberland's Lowther
Castle, presented him a huge box of cigars bearing the
Hohenzollern crest, a pre-war gift from the Kaiser him-
self. He could neither visit theatres without provoking
a chorus of 'For He's a Jolly Good Fellow' nor move in

public without a gaggle of schoolboy admirers forming round him. Even a visit to a boxing bout with Johnny Douglas' father was news. 'He was attired in evening dress and really looked more formidable than any of the heavyweights,' the *Evening News* reported. 'The popular Australian expressed the opinion that boxers earned their money far harder than cricketers.'

Some might have found such constant attention a strain; Armstrong was unembarrassed, perhaps unembarrassable. During a day's golf at Gleneagles a large crowd gathered to watch Armstrong tee off. It trickled a few inches. 'Even this catastrophe,' noted Oldfield, 'did not seem to worry him.' Armstrong could obey the forms. He was a self-effacing Australian at a dinner in Skinner's Hall hosted by Surrey's president Sir Jeremiah Coleman. 'Sir Jeremiah made some reference to "barracking" in Australia. I think that "yours truly" has gotten most of it (laughter).' He was a loyal Briton at the House of Commons with Lord Privy Seal Austen Chamberlain. 'We have come a long way to play this game and we hope you will find that we know how to play it. It is only a game after all. If we lose, we hope that we will take it in the same fine way that you Englishmen took it in Australia (cheers).' But of losing, Armstrong harboured no thoughts. His team were not merely beating opponents, but extirpating them, taking two days each to dispose of Northamptonshire by an innings and 484 runs (Armstrong claiming 6–21 from twenty overs) and Nottinghamshire by an innings and 517 runs (Macartney bludgeoning 345 in less than four hours). It was as though no-man's land had been relain over twenty-two yards, but patriotic antipodeans liked it that way. After the Australians had attended her final concert at Covent Garden, Nellie Melba wired Armstrong instructing him 'not to be beaten on any account'. In London for the Imperial Defence Conference, Billy Hughes reminded the team at Australia House that they were 'a very great advertisement for Australian trade and its development from a settlement to a colony to a Commonwealth with an equal voice in the Empire'.

The Big Ship, Haigh

In England in 1956, the team were entertained by the war heroes Douglas Bader and Leonard Cheshire; Lindsay Hassett and Ian Johnson performed a song called 'The Kangaroo Hop' with Winifred Atwell for a Cheshire Homes function. At the Lord Mayor's reception in May 1961, Ken Mackay, Bill Lawry and Frank Misson were thrilled to encounter the horror icon Boris Karloff. 'Can I get you a drink?' asked the former Frankenstein. 'A pint of blood, perhaps.'

There were frequent gifts, ranging from semi-official perquisites (the 1953 team received a Roger David blazer, two pairs of Grip U cricket trousers, a bat and a Philips shelf radio) to anonymous jests (Keith Miller was always in receipt of hair nets to tame his flowing locks). An unknown admirer, in fact, apparently under-wrote Norm O'Neill's only English Test hundred.

On the eve of the Fifth Test at the Oval in 1961, O'Neill received a 'lucky' coin whose owner hoped that its fortune would rub off. 'I don't put a lot of faith in superstition,' he recalls. 'But I didn't think it would do any harm so I just dropped it into my fob pocket.' O'Neill felt for the coin instinctively when, at 19, he was dropped at second slip. The luck continued for another hundred runs. He recalls, 'Everything went right. The ball went where I wanted it to, my feet were moving. When I got out, I took off my batting trousers and watched the cricket for a while. Then I thought, 'Oh, reckon I'll go and get that coin.' I couldn't find it anywhere. And there was no address on the letter so I couldn't write back.'

The Summer Game, Haigh

The exalted company, as a young Richie Benaud found out at a party in Nottingham, meant you had to be a little careful.

I had made 3 that day, knocked over by Alec Bedser. Hassett was drinking a scotch. I was having orange juice. Hassett turned to me and said, 'Why are you drinking that stuff? Have a scotch.' I told him I couldn't do that because there was a Test Match on. He again told me I should drink something harder, so I asked him to let me try his scotch. I tasted it and said to him I didn't know how he could drink the stuff because it had no taste.

Hassett turned to the bartender and said, 'Give Mr Benaud a double scotch. He thinks this one is a bit tasteless.' I had eleven doubles and a treble and, when I got back to the hotel, the bed dumped me on the floor. I had a rugged night.

I got up the next morning to go to the Duke of Portland's place. I walked onto the bus and sat down next to the driver so I could quickly ask him to stop if I wasn't feeling exactly 100 per cent. Just then I heard a voice from the back of the bus say, 'Good morning, Richie.' It was The Don sitting next to Lady Bradman. So I sat on that bus for 18 miles with my teeth clenched. It was the most agonising trip I've ever gone through.

Howzat! Sixteen Australian cricketers talk,
Butler

Test cricket also offers Australians one of their few chances of meeting royalty – sometimes, when the stern Bill Woodfull was captain, nervously.

A schoolmaster by profession, he exercised a dominie's discipline and kept them in their dressing-room pretty sharply when they were not on the field, while it is said that they were so sharply grounded in the 'not for publication' rule that one day when the King was speaking to a nervous youngster who had just been presented to him, the lad in his embarrassment began to reply with the words, 'Well, sir, not for publication . . .'

Cricket My Destiny, Hammond

Royalty, in fact, were not nearly so intimidating.

At Sandringham Palace, Bill Woodfull's 1930 team turned up to be greeted by King George V and Queen Mary. It was the Sunday rest day of the match against Cambridge University. 'Two men walked towards our party,' Clarrie told me. 'At first they were too far away to recognise. Soon we could identify one of the men. It was the king. As soon as he saw us he changed direction and walked briskly to our group. Our escort introduced Bill Woodfull and we stood to attention like palace guards as the two chatted casually. Then we were introduced. The king was fascinated by slow bowling and he asked Clarrie to explain the Bosey. Grimmett demonstrated with an orange. Nobody could find a cricket ball when it was most needed, but the well-spun orange gripped and turned on the sun-drenched Sandringham turf.'

Clarrie Grimmett: The Bradman of spin,
Mallett

Others enjoy the moment – like Wally Grout who, during the pulsating Lord's Ridge Test of 1961, greeted the Duke of Edinburgh with a black eye.

'Look after that eye,' said the Duke. 'I suggest you put some steak on it.' Wally, who I have never known to be stuck for a word, came back with, 'We eat all our steak, sir.'

Slasher Opens Up, Mackay

Ashley Mallett also enjoyed the company of high society in England.

He bought a deerstalker hat, tweed jacket and hooked meerschaum pipe and at boring receptions, where most of the team were huddled together to exclude earbashers, Mallett would declare, 'Hellow, Mallee's the name' in a murderous Oxford accent. 'From the antipodes, ackchewally, small property in the west, 30 000 acres . . .' The team fell about.

Greg Chappell: Cricket's incomparable artist, McGregor

His *faux pas* during the Lord's Test of 1968 was a classic.

I distinctly remember talking among a group of fellow players when I saw from a distance of about 10 yards the figure of a rather elegant-looking woman approaching. My short-sightedness had never really embarrassed me before, but I really couldn't make out who the woman was and called out, 'I say, my dear, will you not join us here?' By now you will have realised that it was none other than Queen Elizabeth.

Rowdy, Mallett

Dennis Lillee, however, challenged Mallett's *faux pas* when, following the celebrations after victory at Lord's four years later, Ian Chappell's team visited Buckingham Palace.

He went along very quietly that afternoon, with no-one taking much notice what he was drinking. When we got to the palace we had to line up in two groups. I had to introduce the Queen to the players while Ray Steele did the same for the Duke. Everything went well until we got to John Gleeson. I said, 'Your Majesty, this is John Gleeson.' Gleeson said, 'How do you do, ma'am,' in the correct manner. Next in line was Lillee. 'Your Majesty, this is Dennis Lillee,' I said. 'G'day,' said Dennis.

This was rather embarrassing and I didn't know whether to laugh, cry or run out of the room. I'm sure the Queen didn't know what to do either, and the situation didn't improve when we moved on to Rod Marsh, the next in line, who found it hard to keep a straight face. When the royal couple moved off I went over to Steele and said, 'You wouldn't want to know what Dennis said to the Queen.' Ray gritted his teeth, 'I suppose it was g'day, exactly the same as he said to the Duke.'

Chappelli: Ian Chappell's life story, Chappell

Rodney Hogg in 1981 didn't even have the excuse of alcohol.

The royal couple moved across to the English team and we daren't whisper a word. When they were opposite Rod Hogg and myself, Hoggy nudged me and tried to attract my attention. After several attempts at ignoring him I finally gave in and asked what the problem was. He simply pointed towards the Queen and said in a voice that could have been heard at Buckingham Palace, 'Jeez, Henry, she hasn't got bad legs for an old sheila, has she?' I nearly fainted.

Henry: The Geoff Lawson story, Lawson

In 1989, though, it was the Duke of Edinburgh who got in first when meeting Terry Alderman, Merv Hughes and Geoff Lawson.

Merv, Clem [Alderman] and I were standing together chatting away as usual when the Duke came up, shook hands with Clem, got to Merv and looked across at me. 'So that's why you chaps bowl so well,' he said. We all looked at each other wondering what he was talking about. 'You never shave,' he explained. Following a long tradition, we don't shave during a Test and by now were looking fairly untidy, though Merv would look untidy in a dinner suit.

Diary of the Ashes 1989, Lawson

**It isn't hard to get lost in England, as Charlie McLeod
demonstrated during The Oval Test of 1905.**

Clem tells the story of how, during a Test match in
England, Charlie came down to breakfast at the hotel
at a quarter past eleven and seeing the room empty
of guests said to the waiter, 'Am I first down?' 'Yes,'
replied the waiter, 'first down to lunch!' In that case
Charlie, minus a breakfast, landed at the ground just
in time. But on another occasion he entered a bus to
go to the Surrey Oval, and after reaching the terminus
and seeing no signs to denote there was a cricket match
in the vicinity he said to the driver, 'Where is the Surrey Cricket Ground?' 'Oh, that's miles away,' was the
reply. 'You've taken the wrong bus.' 'Lightning' listened
to a set of directions that made him wonder if he would
ever see his companions again, but this he did manage
to do in time to be abused roundly and later fined a
fiver – his third fine for late arrivals. Poor Charlie was
always in trouble and in his opinion it was always due
to his abominable luck!

Not Test Cricket, Monfries

**You can even get lost inside the grounds, like Ken
Mackay and John Rutherford at Lord's.**

We walked proudly down the steps from the dressing-
room, the complete cricketers, determined to do
something worthy of this famous ground if only we
could get onto it. Not knowing the route through the

Long Room we wandered long corridors poking our heads through any door that suggested an exit. We finally stumbled through a door and found ourselves facing the oval all right but about thirty yards upfield from the players' gate. If those venerable members at Lord's thought we were playing a frivolous schoolboys' joke on their revered ground, I assure them it was all done in innocence. We negotiated the fence and strode as unconcernedly as possible to the wicket.

Slasher Opens Up, Mackay

When Keith Miller was captaining Australia, as he did against Yorkshire in 1953, disorientation was almost guaranteed, as cricket writer Basil Easterbrook recalled.

The match started on a Saturday. That evening Miller organised a party. 'Right, boys, enjoy yourselves.' Monday morning dawned lovely and bright. Easterbrook was on the point of leaving for the match when the manageress informed him that both Mr Miller and Mr Lindwall were still in their rooms. Easterbrook hurried there. Miller and Lindwall were throwing clothes on; the alarm had not rung, the rest of the team were already on their way to the match and there wasn't a great deal of time left. Grindleford, where the Australians were staying, was a picturesque, Swiss-style village overlooking a valley; there was no question of cabs.

In 1953 a Yorkshire match was almost like a Sixth

Test. Bramall Lane would be packed. With the Australians fielding, Miller would be expected to lead the side out and nobody had yet kept Bramall Lane waiting. Then Easterbrook recalled that a local funeral parlour had a black limousine. The funeral parlour was willing; the limousine was procured. By the time it arrived at the ground there were only a few minutes before the start of play and the 30 000 crowd were expectantly looking at their watches. Miller jumped out of the limo and shouted to Easterbrook, 'Pay the cab, Bas, and collect it from Davies!' He rushed inside the pavilion and changed just in time to lead the Australians out.

The fare came to £2 but George Davies [manager] refused to entertain the claim. He suggested that Easterbrook write to the Australian Cricket Board. Though £2 was a fair bit of money in 1953, Easterbrook reluctantly decided to forget the whole thing. Almost twenty years later the 1972 Australians were playing at Old Trafford. There was rain and, as is Easterbrook's habit, he was quietly reading a book. Lindwall came up to him and thrust £5 into his pocket. 'That's for Grindleford, Bas.'

Keith Miller: A cricketing biography, Bose

Air travel replaced the gracious days of the 1960s sea journeys, but that doesn't suit everyone. Greg Chappell gave a vivid account of leaving Adelaide bound for England in 1972, with Ashley Mallett as companion.

According to Greg, Rowdy [Mallett] had in his pocket a diary which he soon produced in the airport lounge to note that at 7.25 he 'arrived at airport'. The moment they fastened their seat belts on board the plane, says Greg, Rowdy went through the usual routine. He stopped an air hostess and ordered a double scotch as soon as the bar opened; then he reached into his bag and fossicked around until he came out with a cigarette, which he placed between already trembling lips, matches at the ready for the instant the 'no smoking' light went out; then instead of sitting back in his seat with a customary firm grip on the arm rests he dived into his bag. Greg couldn't help noticing him pull out his diary and make a second entry: '7.45, taxied to leave for Sydney, from where we will go to England.' Back went the diary into the bag. Soon the aircraft was off the ground and again Rowdy plunged into his ghastly bag. Out came the diary and in went the third message: '7.49, plane took off for Sydney on way to England.'

Greg thought, that's terrific, Rowd, you're really doing well. Off went the 'no smoking' light and the cigarette was lit in such a hurry that he dropped his matches into the open bag and set fire to some of the newspapers. Rowdy had stamped that out when the stiff scotch arrived. In the process of receiving that godsend he spilt most of it on himself. As Greg reported to the team later, 'The nerves really had a grip on Rowd then. Next thing he was back into his bag, fossicking round for some time without coming up for air. I wasn't game to ask him what he was looking for, but after a while he became very agitated. Then he emerged with a grim look on his face, a pen in his hand and a corner of a charred newspaper, whereupon he wrote the following words: '8.09, lost diary.'

You'll Keep, Marsh

Travel round England has normally been by the more conventional means of train or coach. Australian teams of the 1970s, however, were indulged with cars: as Greg Chappell discovered, a Jaguar XJ12 brought out the testosterone in Jeff Thomson.

Greg dozed in the front seat until after about half an hour he heard Thommo ask, 'What do you reckon I should do?' 'About what?' asked Greg. 'That blue light flashing in the rear-vision mirror,' said Thommo. 'How long had it been there?' 'Oh, about twenty minutes.' Then he had better slow down and let it catch up. Thomson moved into the second lane and a police Range Rover pulled them over in pouring rain.

Police: 'Do you know the speed limit on the motor-way is 70 mph?'

Thommo: 'Yeah.'

Police: 'Do you realise that I've been following you for the past 15 minutes at 120 mph and couldn't gain on you?'

Thommo: 'Yeah, that'd be right.'

Police: 'Do you realise that when the road's wet if you hit the brakes you're aquaplaning, your wheels aren't actually touching the surface of the road?'

Thommo: 'Yeah, I've done that three times already.'

Police: 'Bloody hell! I don't mind if you kill yourself but I've nearly killed myself twice trying to catch you.'

After identifying the culprits the police radioed base and relayed their instructions: our jurisdiction runs out five miles down the motorway, be a bit sensible and get going.

Greg Chappell: Cricket's incomparable artist,
McGregor

The days when Australian cricketers saw England as 'home' are now also long gone, and Paul Reiffel attests that their knowledge of England is rusty.

I particularly remember a long drive early in the tour from Taunton to Hove. Eventually everyone fell asleep except me. Suddenly we drive past Stonehenge. It was there in the window one minute, gone the next. I woke up a few of the guys and told them and they said, 'You're kidding? Stonehenge?' And Merv said, 'What's Stonehenge?' I said, 'You know, that thing that Chevy Chase knocked down in *European Vacation*.' To which Merv replied, 'Oh, *that* Stonehenge!'

Inside Out, Reiffel and Baum

Then again, so is their knowledge of cricket, as well-informed Steve Waugh found out on that same 1993 tour.

I decided to quiz Brendon Julian about the history of Australian cricket. It proved a topic he would be foolish to choose if ever he was a contestant on *Mastermind*. My first question was pretty simple. When I asked him who Stan McCabe was he replied, 'Isn't he the guy out of *Jake and the Fatman*?' End of quiz!

Ashes Diary, Waugh

The first English teams in Australia were always the centre of a social whirl, revealing hidden capabilities in players like George Lohmann in 1891–92.

At one stage a picnic was arranged, and George, who was always at everybody's service on social occasions, undertook responsibility for the luncheon. Provision was made for about thirty people, but about fifty turned up, and the possibility of the eatables running short loomed before us. But George got over the difficulty. How he did it I don't know, but the provisions for thirty did duty for fifty and no-one went on short commons. The ladies were all in love with George for the attentive care with which he saw that everybody had what they wanted.

Cricket Reminiscences and Personal Recollections,
Grace

Strangers in a strange land could find it a little
unsettling, like England's Dick Lilley ten years later.

Of course, the travelling in the remoter districts was
not so comfortable as that between the chief centres
such as from Adelaide to Melbourne, and Melbourne
to Sydney, and those discomforts were naturally
present which are inseparably associated with a trop-
ical climate. It was rather a novelty, for instance, the
first night we spent up country to find the beds cov-
ered with mosquito nets, but I was not sufficiently
versed in the use of these things to effectively pro-
tect myself, and when I awoke the next morning my
face was a pitiable sight. However, I was subsequently
given a very effective remedy by an old traveller. This
consisted merely of sprinkling a few drops of eucalyp-
tus on a handkerchief and hanging it over the head.
The smell of the drug was certainly not particularly
pleasant, but infinitely preferable to the attentions of
marauding mosquitoes.

Twenty-Four Years of Cricket, Lilley

Then there was the sense of being watched, as Frank
Foster found when in Melbourne a decade later. His
slower ball and its signal to his wicketkeeper Tiger
Smith fooled every Australian, save one.

I love trams and riding in them far better than motor
cars. One day in Australia I got into conversation with
the conductor of a tram I was riding in. He astounded

me with his knowledge of the game and I sat and sat, looked and looked until the man must have thought I was potty! My mouth was opened, my nostrils were distended, and I answered 'Yes' and 'No' just like a fool!

'You get off here,' he finally said, 'and I shall be watching you myself in an hour. So, take my advice and bowl that slow one a bit more often, and when you bowl it don't change your step!' Dear reader, as true as I sit here I fondly imagined that there was only one person who knew of my sign to Tiger Smith, and you may guess who *that* person was.

Cricketing Memories, Foster

The English team of 1920–21 found the fauna hard to get used to, particularly, Jack Hobbs recalled, when in quarantine at Fremantle.

One day when Parkin and some others were playing cards Howell brought into the hut a dead iguana, and it was deposited by someone in Parkin's cap, which was lying on the bed holding his money. We went off to the next hut and awaited developments. Like myself, Parkin was terrified of snakes. When he put his hand into his hat to pay out he saw what he took to be a snake. There was a terrific yell. Later on he was heard to swear that he would give a black eye to the fellow who had placed the reptile near him. It is not for me to say who that fellow was.

My Life Story, Hobbs

The terrain, recalled Walter Hammond in 1932–33, was of considerably less interest.

The journey from Perth to Adelaide, where we were due for our next fixture, is not much short of 2000 miles. To anyone who has never travelled 2000 miles by train, I give Mr Punch's advice to those about to marry: Don't. It is said that one of the members of the team wrote home during this train journey: 'Dear Father, this country is just hundreds and hundreds of miles of damn all, and then hundred of miles more of it.'

Cricket My Destiny, Hammond

Likewise the vegetation, recalled by Les Ames in 1936–37.

Through the customs they were ushered with alacrity – just a pause to give anxious officials their autographs – and into a posse of motorcars for the 12-mile journey to Perth. 'You see that tree,' Leslie Ames said to [Ken] Farnes, squinting in the great glare as they bumped along at 35 mph. 'Well, it's a gum tree and you won't see any other sort for five months.'

Summers in Winter, Meredith

But the 'natives' weren't so bad when you got to know thom, as Jim Swanton discovered ten years later . . .

The driver of a taxi regaled him with vivid descriptions of the manifold delights and attractions of Australia. He ended his recital with bluff words of welcome,

'Yeah, it's a great country. Remember it's yours as well as ours – and if you don't enjoy it here, it'll be your own ruddy fault.'

The Bedsers: Twinning triumphs, Hill

. . . also then Walter Hammond.

Typical of the Australian enjoyment of the Tests was the attitude of a Sydney policeman who gave us one of the best laughs of the tour. We were returning from the cricket ground to our hotel, through a crowded and dusty thoroughfare in that splendid city, and were about twenty yards from one of the major traffic crossings when a very pleasant young policeman spotted me in the leading car. How he did so I don't know, for he had his hands full with rivers of traffic rushing in at him from every direction. He walked forward, rested his white-gloved hand on the driver's window, and said smiling, 'Well, how did you go today?' We were feeling completely embarrassed, for traffic was piling up everywhere, but the guardian of the law was not at all dismayed. 'You boys like a winner for the races tomorrow?' he enquired. Not waiting for us to reply he fetched out of his trouser pocket an afternoon newspaper and insisted that we write down the names of the horses he would give us. Then he hummed and hawed over every horse and gave us his tip for every race. Finally he folded the paper, put it back judicially in his pocket and, with a big smile and a cheery 'I'll be seeing you!', strolled slowly back to his post.

Cricket My World, Hammond

Travel round Australia might now be by plane but, as 'Gus' Fraser recalled after a short trip from Adelaide to Port Pirie in 1990, it can still have its hazards.

The warning signs were there before we got aboard when Phil Tufnell, who is a bad flier, asked the pilot which way we were going. When the pilot said, 'Over there' and pointed to a mass of dark clouds where a thunderstorm already seemed in progress, Tuffers turned white and grabbed his St Christopher.

Everybody panicked once the flight started; what made it worse was the pilot asking for someone at the back of this tiny plane to move down the front and sit with him to improve the balance. Our heads were hitting the roof we were being bumped so much. Laurie Brown the physio was swigging at a bottle of Drambuie to calm his nerves, and Tuffers was sitting with his head buried in the back of the seat in front, sweat dripping off his hands with the fright of it all. Then, at our lowest point, everybody started laughing at the same time. It was as if we couldn't be any more scared; we suddenly realised there was nothing we could do, and broke out in nervous laughter. Whether or not we survived was out of our hands.

Fraser's Tour Diaries, Fraser

It was on that tour, too, that David Gower found how expensive flying could be.

Between the Tests, mercifully, we registered our opening first-class win of the tour against Queensland. That was the good news. The bad news was when two of our batsmen who were already out, David Gower and John Morris, left the ground to buzz the ground in a hired Tiger Moth. The press took the manager Peter Lush by surprise when they asked him about the prank, and when Peter came to the pavilion to ask David about it we found that he and Morris had returned to the airport to pose for press photographs in the cockpit, dressed up in Biggles outfits. In some newspapers in London next day the pictures shared the front page with coverage of the Gulf War! That let us down badly, I thought. Lush, Micky Stewart, Lamb and I decided to fine them both 1000 pounds.

The Autobiography, Gooch and Keating

6 | CRICKET FEVER

'Cricket as a passion is distinctly contagious,' wrote David Frith. At times of the contestation of the Ashes, in fact, cricket fever can be every bit as incurable as the common cold. It was a member of the sporting public who initiated the original obituary for English cricket, and female fans who burned the bail for sealing in the urn as a response. Since then, fans have ensured the Ashes' continued relevance, even when the cognoscenti have been inclined to dismiss them.

This chapter collects stories of public ardour sometimes as heartfelt as that among the participants. More recent developments are not so benign. Cricket is no longer a passion for many spectators; it is victory. Hostility is less bridled. Generosity is rarer. Cricket, it is often said, reflects the society that plays it. Sometimes this is not entirely a good thing.

The first Test series followed with equal fanaticism on both sides of the globe was England's trip to Australia in 1894–95 under the captaincy of Drewy Stoddart.

At peak times during the Test series business stood still – even at the Ballarat Stock Exchange where victory and defeat sent a London-born sharebroker soaring off into 'Rule Britannia' in a 'tenor voice of high register', soon to be challenged by some Australian brokers who raised the Southern Cross to flap alongside the British flag and lustily sang 'The Men of Australia'. Then a Cornishman leapt onto a chair and hollered, 'Look here, you! It's all very well you talking about Hingland and Horstralia, but where would you be without Cornwall, eh?' And they all burst into 'God Save the Queen'. Communications between the Melbourne Exchange and Ballarat were limited one afternoon to a wire which read, 'Nothing doing; cricket mad; Stoddart out.'

To be there was everything for there was no TV substitute, or even action close-ups in the newspapers. A Captain Lee, in command of *Arawatta*, even delayed her sailing from the Port of Melbourne during the Second Test match so that he could witness more of the cricket in person. Hunger for news of the Tests even spread to the maritime species. When the mail steamer *Arcadia* berthed at Adelaide, passengers raced to The Oval to watch the stirring Third Test, with many of the crew making do with updates as various launches came to and fro. When *Arcadia* sailed on the Saturday evening with Australia well-placed, she passed sister ship *Himalaya* out of Melbourne and flying the signal, 'How's The Cricket?' The score was flown in reply.

Stoddy's Mission: The first great Test series 1894–1895, Frith

After the First World War the whole of Australia seemed to be hanging on the 1920–21 Ashes series, as Jack Hobbs reported home.

In a country centre a wedding ceremony was being performed. Just as the question 'Will you?' etc. was about to be put, a telegraph messenger came in and handed a telegram to the bridegroom. He read it and handed it to the bride, who read it and handed it to the best man, and it went round the whole immediate group. 'Something's happened, the wedding's off,' whispered one of the onlookers. Nervously clutching the paper, the officiating minister said, 'Armstrong 100, Kellaway 80, total 3 for 300-odd!'

'Too much public attention is given to the Test match!' exclaimed a severe-looking gentleman on a tram car. 'It disorganises everything. We should keep our balance and not allow sport to sway us so much.' Presently a man jumped on the car and remarked, 'Armstrong has got his century.' 'Ah, I thought he would!' said the severe-looking gentleman.

The Big Ship, Haigh

Australian crowds were known for a mercurial temper, as Dick Lilley found when he caught Bert Hopkins at Sydney in 1902.

I caught the ball and also knocked the bails off, and when they saw Mr Hopkins leaving the wickets they immediately commenced to hurl uncomplimentary epithets at my offending head. They are very keen, and it was obvious that he was not stumped; but they failed to observe that he was given out by Argill and were under the impression that the decision had been given by Crockett for stumping. J.J. Kelly the Australian wicketkeeper thereupon went to the crowd and explained to them that Mr Hopkins had been caught at the wicket and that the decision was a perfectly correct one. They at once altered their demeanour and commenced shouting: 'Good old Lilley!'

Twenty-four Years of Cricket, Lilley

Sydney Barnes, too, as he bowled his heart out at Melbourne in 1912, here recalled by H.V. Hordern.

Australia won the toss, went in on a perfect wicket and promptly lost six of the best batsmen for 36 runs. Barnes at one period had four wickets for 4, and that after bowling for nearly an hour; his bowling on this occasion is generally conceded to be the finest ever done on a plumb wicket in Australia. The crowd gave him wonderful recognition, round after round of applause coming from all parts of the ground.

I happened to be the advanced guard of the tail end, and was batting with our wicketkeeper 'Sep' Carter – a very fine bat he was, too. Australia was in a desperate plight and we were doing our little best to pull the match round. Carter had a fine repertoire of strokes and in particular cut beautifully, whereas my shots were decidedly limited.

The late J.W.H.T. Douglas captaining the English side very naturally had a man deep on the boundary for Carter's cut, and brought him close up for me. There is not much in that surely to start a riot, but it did. Sending the man out and bringing him back took up a certain amount of time and during one of these periods a few hoodlums called out: 'Get on with the game!'

Barnes, evidently strung up to concert pitch, suddenly lost his temper, foolishly threw the ball on the ground, facing the crowd and, folding his arms, stood glaring at them. Then he got what he was looking for: they howled at him just as heartily as they had previously cheered, and I am sorry to say hooting came from every part of the ground.

As Barnes ran in to bowl, pandemonium broke loose. I stepped away from the wicket and sat on my bat, plainly asking the crowd to 'shut up' and behave. This happened three times and I sat so long the last time that the hooting abated and the game proceeded. These are absolute facts; and wasn't it all so very wrong and so very silly?

Googlies, Hordern

Crowd size and noise could be intimidating, as Cec Parkin found in 1920.

A crowd of fifty thousand sits in the terrific sunshine. To see a Test match Australians have been known to travel a thousand miles. Work is suspended in the afternoons and a contrast with the packed ground is the quietness of everywhere just outside. Sometimes when the heat is unbearable you will see thousands of spectators sitting in shirtsleeves, even without their waistcoats. Boys go round the field all day long selling ices and iced drinks and there is a great demand for 'tonsil varnish'. If you make a mistake, you have to go through it. I remember during the First Test match I somehow got fielding in the long-field. The crowd just behind me kept shouting, 'What's your name, cocky? Who said you could play cricket? It's a rumour.'

Parkin on Cricket, Parkin

But they were redeemed by shafts of wit . . .

Each time that Tate just missed bowling Ponsford he put his hand to his head and looked up into the sky. While he was doing this one wag in the crowd shouted, 'It's no good, Tate, He won't help you.'

Twenty-five Years Behind the Stumps,
Strudwick

After watching Sutcliffe fossicking around the wicket at intervals for a few hours, a Melbourne barracker bawled, 'Take it easy! Leave something for the footballers to play on next winter.'

Between Wickets, Robinson

After one ultra-short ball had whizzed over a batsman's head, a Sydney barracker called, 'Eh, Harold! That would have been a yorker if you'd bowled it from the other end.'

Between Wickets, Robinson

. . . and generosity, remembered Herbert Sutcliffe.

We played two matches at Brisbane, one against an Australian XI and the other immediately afterwards with Queensland. The fielding position was close to the scoring board and there, of course, I was in range of the famous scoreboard squad which used to control the barracking. For four days they hammered me unmercifully, but when the second game came along I was in favour with the barrackers having, evidently, passed through their fire with honours, chiefly, I believe, because I took and countered the comments of the squad. The final day's play ended and then, to my great surprise, the barrackers swarmed on to the ground to present me with a case of pipes – a gift which carried with it a tribute of which I am exceedingly proud.

For England and Yorkshire, Sutcliffe

They even took their fanaticism abroad, as Charlie Macartney learned on a visit to Europe with his wife in 1928.

One day while we were traversing the miles of art in the Vatican Museum intently gazing at the wonderful sculpture, tapestries, paintings and other works of art, I was touched on the shoulder by a man who introduced himself as from north Queensland and promptly asked me what I thought about the coming Test matches in Australia. I was speechless for a moment, as I cannot think of a place in the world where the mind is so devoid of any thoughts of cricket as the Vatican Museum. However, satisfying him that I had no idea which side would win, I heard him question the guide with the next breath as to why so many cats were kept in the Trajan Forum.

My Cricketing Days, Macartney

English supporters in Australia were few and far between in those days, but some emerged in Melbourne that 1928 summer when the tourists triumphed there.

Among the welcoming crowd was one jubilant Yorkshireman. He had tied a handkerchief to his walking stick and waved it like a flag. He said, 'I've come 200 miles to see this match and I don't care if I have to live on bread and water for the next three months.'

Herbert Sutcliffe: Cricket maestro, Hill

And they were also in Sydney, recalled Harold
Larwood.

I can recall that at Sydney in 1928 one lone fellow
sat there constantly calling out, 'I'm a Pommie and
I'm proud of it.' The crowd around him shouted
back, 'Shut your bloody mouth and watch the
cricket.'

The Larwood Story, Larwood and Perkins

Sydney, however, was generally regarded as the
preserve of Stephen Harold Gascoigne, the Balmain
rabbitoh who became an SCG legend for his wit on the
Hill as 'Yabba'. Among his mots were:

'Put Arthur on and don't waste time – poor Johnny
is wanted on the telephone.' (Encouraging the use of
Arthur Mailey to Johnny Douglas.)

'Stand up on yer legs. Here's the Governor-General!'
(When Charlie Macartney came in to bat.)

'Thank goodness he's not a flaming centipede.'
(When Maurice Tate, who took size thirteen boots,
took a long time to adjust them.)

'You can take the body away, Hanson.' (To Hanson
Carter, wicketkeeper and undertaker, after he had
caught Hobbs.)

'What about a clap for Captain Bligh?' (To Jardine
in 1932–33.)

'Mind your stays, old man.' (To Jardine in a mock
public-school accent.)

'Go Back to Africa, Pat O'Dea.' (To the Nawab of Pataudi, who represented England in 1932–33.)

'Put a penny in his meter, George, he's stopped registering.' (To umpire George Borwick, a gas-meter inspector, in response to a slow innings by the Nawab.)

'It's no use, George, you'll have to wait until playtime.' (In a schoolboy falsetto to umpire Borwick as he held his arm aloft for some time waiting for a sightscreen to be moved.)

The Cricketer, April 1984

Yabba had his imitators; age, as Wally Hammond's Englishmen found on the first post-war Ashes tour, was no bar.

While we were playing at the nets getting the shipboard stiffness out of our wrists and clearing our eyes for the Australian sunlight, there were plenty of comments for us gratis and not a little free advice. It is deflating to listen to Australian youth sizing you up!

'That Hammond's not half the size they said he was!' growled one disgusted youth watching me bat. 'I'm going home – I've had enough of this!' I was sorry to disappoint him, but I couldn't look any bigger.

'This Edrich don't look much – pretty weak off the back foot I'd guess,' declared another child of about four feet nothing. 'Get yer nose over the ball there – you won't never do nothing like that.'

And another, 'I don't like the look of this Yardley's

wrists, look weak to me. Lindwall will cut his bat out of his hands, won't he!'

Best of all was the eight-year-old with the huge cap who critically watched Wright bowling, clicked his tongue in despair, and said, 'I'd rap the pickets with that myself, Pommy; you'll never move Bradman with that stuff!' That is the hallmark of Australia – free speech.

Cricket My World, Hammond

The occasional fan put their money where their mouth was, as Colin McCool found in making his maiden Test century in Melbourne that 1946 summer.

Jack Wren, one of the wealthiest businessmen in Australia, watched that innings. He liked his cricket and he suffered fiercely when things went against Australia. Certainly things weren't too good that day, because when I went in we were 6–192 and in his anguish he turned to a friend and said, 'I'll give this fellow a pound for every run he makes.' Next day a cheque for £104 arrived at the dressing-room.

Cricket is a Game, McCool

Sometimes visitors were singled out for special treatment, like young Cambridge fast bowler John Warr in 1950.

When the boat carrying the English team berthed at the Sydney dock a wharfie yelled out as J.J. came down the gang-plank, 'Hey, Warr, you've got as much chance of taking a Test wicket on this tour as I have of pushing a pound of butter up a parrot's arse with a hot needle.'

Long Hops and Larrikins,
Chappell and Rigby

The wharfie might have been vindicated had
a countryman not taken a hand.

Ian Johnson gave an exhibition of sportsmanship that could not have occurred during the bitterness of pre-war battles. Given not out in the Fourth Test at Adelaide after a unanimous appeal for a catch behind off John Warr, Johnson nodded his head to the umpire and walked out. Johnson said Warr had not obtained a wicket throughout the Test series and thought he thoroughly deserved his wicket. Warr finished the tour with a bowling average of 1 for 261. Johnson's remark as he walked in was typical of the new way of thinking. He said, 'Warr worked hard enough to take 50 wickets and when he gets one it's taken away from him. Fancy walking out in a Test match when an umpire gives you not out. I must be crazy!' But, like his mates, Johnson was playing the game as a game.

Straight Hit, Miller and Whitington

Mind you, some Englishmen could stand up for
themselves.

I well remember Eric Hollies after some rather rough

treatment at the hands of the batsmen being asked, 'Don't they bury their dead in Birmingham?' Eric's reply, swift and to the point, went down very well. He said, 'No, we stuff them and mark them "Export Only".'

Playing to Win, Bailey

A regular question was, 'What do you think of our beer?' And, once we got to Sydney, as sure as night follows day the question was, 'What do you think of our bridge?' Naturally enough we started off by giving careful, polite answers – and indeed the beer wasn't bad. Some of us, however, found the constant repetition wearing, not least Fred Trueman. He decided to do a little research on the subject of the Sydney Harbour Bridge. One night when the regular question was popped Freddie had his answer ready. 'What do I think of your bridge? It was built in Yorkshire by a firm called Dorman Long – and it isn't paid for yet!'

Over to Me, Laker

And encouragement was not unknown. Colin Cowdrey, making twin centuries against South Australia in 1954–55, enjoyed one urger's efforts.

I received an unusual cable on leaving my hotel for the ground when I was 38 not out on my way to the second century. It was unsigned and said, 'SEE TWO KINGS THREE FOURTEEN.' A crank, I thought, and stuffed the paper away into a hip pocket. When sending my clothes to the dry cleaners a few days later I found the scrap of paper and opened it again. Suddenly it came to me, it was a quotation from the Old Testament, and further research found the prophetic words: 'And the Lord said to Elijah, do it the second time!' What a lovely message, but I never could reply to the kind sender.

Cricket Today, Cowdrey

And Alan Knott enjoyed others.

The Australians are very honest and forthright people and when a player is having a lean time they are not slow to inform him. Once when a catch flew past Colin Cowdrey at Melbourne there came the comment, 'Shake your head, Cowdrey, your eyeballs are stuck!' Then, when I was going through my loosening-up routine, a wag shouted, 'I'll buy you a pogo stick for Christmas!'

Stumper's View, Knott

In England crowds could be boisterous too, like that at Sheffield's Bramall Lane in June 1882.

Every dress was sombre and funereal, but the spectators were far from funereal in their manner. They were indeed the gayest, jolliest crowd I have ever seen. We had not been out in the field five minutes when each of us had a nickname, and by it we were known right through. Bonnor's tall form attracted special notice and he was called 'Jumbo', or 'Joombo', as the Yorkshiremen sound it. Everywhere Bonnor went in the field the cry 'Joombo' would ring in his ears. Alick Bannerman was nicknamed 'Little Joombo' and 'Quicklime', Horan 'Features', Palmer 'Ribs', Blackham 'Darkie', Spofforth 'Spider' and so on.

The Australasian, 5 August 1882

And they were also witty, as at Old Trafford in 1921 when Australia's Herbie Collins spent five hours over 40 runs.

Lionel Tennyson, a grandson of the poet, had replaced Johnny Douglas as England's captain. A.A. Thomson recalls, 'It was during Collins' Methuselah-like effort that a spectator in his agony called out to England's skipper, "Hey Tennyson, read him some of thy grandad's poems." And Parkin called back, "He has done. The beggar's been asleep for hours!"'

Great Characters from Cricket's Golden Age,
Mailes

English grounds had features that could be learned from, like the public address system at Swansea when Australia played Glamorgan in 1930.

I was leading the Australian side and the announcer came across to me at the fall of each wicket to discover the identity of the next batsman. When our eighth wicket fell I said, 'Wall is next, but you may as well announce Wall and Walker together. They won't take long out there.' As Wall walked onto the field the fellow announced, 'The next batsman is Mr Wall of South Australia, but Mr Richardson has asked me to announce Mr Wall and Mr Walker together as they won't take long.' Like true South Australians, Tim and Charlie did not let me down. Three balls were enough to dispose of the pair of them.

The Vic Richardson Story,
Richardson and Whitington

As Ernie McCormick found after bowling seventeen no-balls in his first two overs in England in 1938, English fans are generally more considerate of feelings . . .

The matter gave rise to a standing joke in the Australian team. If a member of the public greeted McCormick in the street he would walk straight on without a turn of the head. A colleague would explain to the bemused cricket lover that the shouts of no-ball had affected his hearing.

Cricket's Dawn that Died: The Australians in England, 1938,
Valentine

. . . than Australian ones.

He had a letter from his sister after that. The McCormicks all have a rich sense of humour. 'Come home,' she said, 'you are making a fool of yourself – and more-over the tradesmen won't call on us now.'

The Ashes Crown the Year, Fingleton

They could be surprisingly tolerant . . .
'I was bowling pretty quick and one got up a bit and hit a fellow called Berry in the head,' says Ernie. 'He wasn't too good and had to be carted to hospital for observation. The following day off most of the Aussies went to an air pageant held nearby. While we were there I was introduced to Berry's charming wife. I felt terrible about what had happened and apologised profusely, but I wasn't ready for the reply. "Oh, don't worry," she said. "I've been wanting to do that for years."'

The Wit of Cricket, Brayshaw

. . . and deferential.
Norman Yardley said that he had received a letter from an old lady who had heard on the radio that Lindwall had two long-legs, one short leg and a square leg. 'Tell me, Mr Yardley,' she had asked him, 'what kind of creatures are these Australian cricketers? No wonder England can't win.'

Flying Stumps, Lindwall

They also understood their priorities, as Robert Menzies explained of his 1953 visit to England.
When Sir Anthony Eden cabled us about a conference

in January I replied, 'No. What about June? Isn't there anybody on your staff who reads cricket fixtures?' Eden's reply was, 'Point taken. Conference confirmed for day after Lord's Test.'

The Cricketer, October 1980

English crowds, too, can lay claim to winning a Test for their country, at The Oval in 1968. Derek Underwood explains that he was only able to take his match-winning 7–50 thanks to the crowd's hard work.

Somebody has since told me that the first drops of rain fell at exactly 1.27 p.m. Within ten minutes the rain was torrential. After half an hour most of the grass had disappeared under an inch of water. Another thirty minutes and the sun was shining brilliantly, but there seemed no chance of the match starting again. I remember gazing down at the scene and thinking, 'That's it. We'll never get out there again.' I can still picture the sight of Colin [Cowdrey] going out to the middle, his trousers pulled high over his boots, urging ground staff in their work. Soon the outfield was dotted with volunteers mopping up the water. Gradually the water drained away, the patches of green began to grow larger and link up again. The large hand on the Vauxhall Lane stand clock showed just past twenty to five when Snow went off his run once more.

Beating the Bat, Underwood

As Ian Chappell recalls of The Oval Test of 1972,
not everyone in an English crowd supports the
home side.

With only four runs required to win, a group of West
Indian supporters who had yelled loyally for Australia
the whole six days moved down to the boundary, and
I will never forget the biggest of the group picking up
the boundary flag, waving it round his head and calling
out, 'We are the greatest.' Such are the liaisons of international cricket!

Tigers Among the Lions, Chappell

Nor was every Australian solidly behind the weak
national team that was thumped 5–1 in 1978–79,
deprived of Chappell's great team by Kerry Packer.

In the course of the over a voice boomed out from
The Hill, 'Put on the other channel!' With its obvious
reference to World Series Cricket it was a not-too-
subtle complaint about the slow scoring, and one
with which most of the spectators would have been in
sympathy.

From the Outer, Meyer

These days the public isn't so well informed, as
Philippe and Frances Edmonds found in Australia.

'Mr DeFreitas!' shouted one precocious, if polite, ten-
year-old with a spiky, lavatory-brush crew cut. 'Mr
DeFreitas, please sign this for my autistic sister!' 'I'll set

my wife on you,' threatened Philippe-Henri, suddenly tired of his quota of requests.

'You're Emburey, aren't you?' asked one real afficionado, incomprehensibly offering Phil a copy of Allan Border's book for signature. 'Edmonds,' corrected Phil. 'Yes,' nodded the fan knowledgeably, 'John Edmonds.' In deference to the fellow's patently encyclopaedic knowledge of the game and its exponents, Phil signed the book 'Don Bradman'.

Cricket XXXX Cricket, Edmonds

Or, as Phil Tufnell learned, as polite.

The academy had been fun when it started, and among the thousands of words of abuse I'd received my personal favourite was, 'Tufnell, lend me your brain. I'm building an idiot.' By now, though, much of the humour had long since gone out of it.

What Now? Tufnell

Mind you, English fans aren't exemplars either, as Ian Healy discovered.

From there we headed back to our hotel where I soon found myself involved in an argument with an Englishman who annoyed me when he muttered, 'You guys think you're pretty good but you've only beaten England.' 'You're right,' I responded. 'They are soft and don't care enough for their country. You're probably the same.' I learned soon after that this bloke's wife had immediately rushed off and complained to the concierge desk, who contacted team manager Ian McDonald and, we were soon to discover, the police. 'Macca' insisted I go back and apologise, which I did. Back downstairs we saw a policeman, and Helen jokingly said to him, 'Here he is, officer, take him away.' Which was very funny, except that he was there to see me!

Hands and Heals, Healy

Sometimes there remains a glimmer of humour, recalled Mark Taylor . . .

Right from our arrival at Heathrow I had been reminded of the unrelenting pressure I was under. At the immigration I handed over my passport. 'Oh, Mark Taylor, eh?' said the bloke behind the desk. 'The Australian captain?' I agreed. 'Ahhh . . . but for how long?' he asked.

Time to Declare, Taylor

. . . but more often not, recalled Steve Waugh.

I decided to wander into the happening part of town, Leicester Square, to check out the buskers on the streets and catch a movie. While waiting in the queue to see *The Fifth Element* I was confronted by six drunken louts. They of course reminded me of the current situation in the Test series and the Texaco Trophy scoreline. Not content with that they began to angle for some kind of confrontation. The cretin who headed this 'brain-dead cast' eventually said, 'Hey, you know what you Aussies are going to win this summer?' To which I replied with great expectation, 'What?' The answer was in keeping with his intellect, '$%^&*? all, you Aussie bastard.'

1997 Ashes Diary, Waugh

7 | LUCK AND FATE

Many games start with a toss, but in no other pursuit is it so meaningful as cricket. Not only does the fall of the coin determine the order in which the match takes place and the conditions they will experience, but it is almost an act of propitiation to the cricket gods, acknowledging up front the role of luck and fate in the proceedings. Luck and fate have both exerted a gravitational pull on the Ashes since their origins. To deal with the randomness of chance, cricketers are apt to fall back on superstition. Great players are no less susceptible, and have harboured all manner of predispositions, from Fred Spofforth with his dread of cross-eyed women to Norm O'Neill's taste in lemon socks. No player, though, has been able to do without good fortune – and no-one would really want to.

In the annals of superstition, nobody had a stranger
one than Fred Spofforth.

There is truth in the statement of the Hon. R.H. Lyttelton that Spoff used to study night after night how to get
English batsmen out. He and W.L. Murdoch as a rule
chummed together, and Billy used to say, 'Spoff has got
a new plan today and says it will come all right provided he does not meet a cross-eyed woman.'

If the plan didn't come off Spoff would say, 'Well
you know, I met a cross-eyed woman and what could
I do after that?'

The Australasian, 2 October 1897

And nobody had a more devout one than Pelham
Warner en route to Australia for the Ashes of
1903–04.

He took his position very seriously and asked Bishop
Welldon, who was on the same ship on the way to Australia, the following question, 'Bishop, is it wrong to
pray to beat the Australians?'

Replied the bishop, 'My dear Warner, anything
that tends to the prestige of England is worth praying
for.'

Said Plum, 'I'll pray every night and morning and on
the field.'

Gods or Flannelled Fools,
Whitington and Miller

Warwick Armstrong's all-conquering 1921
Australians needed little supernatural support,
but took precautions.

During the early part of the tour, a rubber kangaroo
which could be inflated was presented to Warwick
Armstrong by Walter Brearley, England's fast bowler
of some years before, as a mascot for the team. At the
beginning of a match it was blown up and placed in
a prominent position in the dressing-room, and at the
conclusion of the match was deflated and packed away
in readiness for the next occasion. Later on we acquired
a horseshoe which was gaily attired in green and gold
ribbons and also hung in a prominent place next to the
kangaroo. Jack Gregory's cricket bag was generally the
receptacle for these mascots after the games. I have read
and heard that these two mascots were missing from
the dressing-room while the two matches we lost were
being played.

My Cricketing Days, Macartney

Bill Woodfull's 1930 Australians received a noisier
talisman.

They had an uproarious reception at Victoria Station,
and some of us attended the performances at the Col-
iseum and the Hippodrome where the Aussies were
guests and had tremendous receptions. At the former
place of entertainment, Tom Webster, the famous car-
toonist, presented the team with a wire-haired terrier as

a mascot, announcing in his speech that it had instructions 'to bite anybody who got Jack Hobbs out in the first over'.

My Life Story, Hobbs

Everything hinged on Bradman at Adelaide Oval in 1937 with Australia trailing 1–2, and Englishman Walter Robins granted him a crucial reprieve early in his match-winning 212, from the bowling of captain Gubby Allen.

Bradman came in, all grim face and big green cap and broad bat and carefully took his guard. Gubby bowled him three quiet ones of perfect length and Don stolidly met them with the dead bat. Then – as it seemed – the ball slipped from the hand, bounced short on the leg, and Don made a rather hesitant hook. The ball flew uppishly, Robbie failed to get all his hand to it, and it went past him for three runs. At the end of the over, Robbie, feeling disappointed and ashamed of himself, said as he crossed over, 'Terribly sorry, Gubby – I ought to have had him.' To which Gubby replied, 'Oh that's all right, but you've probably just cost us the rubber!'

Cricketing Days, Edrich

And at Lord's in 1948, Sid Barnes also got a much-needed slice of luck, from England's keeper Godfrey Evans.

Australia was all out for 350. Their first wicket fell at

3, when Sid Barnes was dismissed for a duck. Around this juncture Sid was having a bad time with the bat, and when he batted in the second innings he was very uncomfortable. If ever a man looked set for a pair he did. Like most keepers, I often chat to the batsmen during lulls in the play. 'Good luck, Sid,' I said. 'Hope you don't bag 'em.'

'I've never felt so out of form, Godfrey,' Sid answered glumly. 'I hardly know which end of the bat to hold.' He scraped around for about 20 minutes, still very uncomfortable, and then Jim Laker was put on at the pavilion end. Down came a half volley. Sid went out to drive and the ball beat the bat. I saw a stumping chance – but the ball turned so much that it beat me as well and went for four byes. The crowd groaned but Sid smiled as he turned to me. 'Thanks, Godfrey,' he said. 'That's the first bit of luck I've had in the last month. I hope I can take advantage of it.' He did – with 141 runs. His luck had changed.

Behind the Stumps, Evans

Peter May knew the value of luck.

As Peter left his coat in the Skinners' Hall cloakroom before a dinner for the 1956 Australians the hat-check girl passed him ticket 13. He handed it back saying, 'Not that one, ma'am, if you don't mind – not in a year when the Australians are here.'

Between Wickets, Robinson

So did May's rival Richie Benaud. After winning
the Ashes series of 1958–59, he lamented his luck
at the toss.

At the end of the series I said to Sir Donald Bradman,
who gave me the coin before the Brisbane Test, 'This is
not much good – I haven't won a toss with it.'

He just looked at me and replied, 'No, and you
haven't lost a Test with it, either.'

I've still got the coin and it still doesn't come down
the right way. But I suppose the time to start complaining is when we lose a series.

Way of Cricket, Benaud

Sometimes you need all the help you can get. When
bowling to the Rev. David Sheppard at Sydney in
1963, Alan Davidson called on heavenly guidance
through batsman/lay preacher Brian Booth.

In Sydney's Third Test I beat David with three consecutive outswingers. I scratched my head and walked past
Brian Booth on my way to my bowling mark saying to
him, 'Didn't you say a prayer for me last night?' Booth
replied, 'You've got to do a bit yourself you know.' I put
up my hands and offered a silent prayer. The next ball
Sheppard snicked and was caught at the wicket. Booth
laughed and said, 'See, it pays off if you do it yourself.
I hope that convinces all you other blokes, too.'

Fifteen Paces, Davidson

Usually the help comes in more prosaic forms, as it did in the next Test for Norm O'Neill after a run of outs.

On the first morning of the game I went down to the Adelaide Oval to leave some tickets for my wife. Gwen had just arrived and had a small brown parcel in her hand. She gave it to me and said, 'Darl, I remember your mother used to take care of a pair of lemon socks for you as they are supposed to give you luck. So I've bought you a new pair in the hope they will do the same trick.' I went straight back to the dressing-room and just like that day ten years before put on the lemon socks under a pair of ordinary cricket socks. Not long afterwards I was batting. I got through a slow start and went on to play one of the finest innings of my career. I scored exactly 100, my first century at home against England.

Ins and Outs, O'Neill

On the end of a string of dropped catches in 1972, Keith Stackpole gained a reputation as a lucky batsman – a reputation he didn't agree with.

In the Fourth Test I was at the bowler's end when the umpire David Constant said, 'Do you know what? You are the luckiest batsman I have ever seen.' I said, 'You see me snick them, but at least I snick them. You look at the Englishmen. You look at Luckhurst. How many times does he play and miss? They don't even get bat on ball. Does that make me a better player than them or what?' After that, whenever Luckhurst played and missed I looked across at Constant who had a grin on his face. At the end of the Test I said, 'See what I mean?' He agreed I was being maligned.

Not Just For Openers,
Stackpole and Trengove

And it's true that no great performance is without good fortune. Dickie Bird recalls that Geoff Boycott's triumphant return to Tests in 1977 – 442 runs at 147 – might have ended in his comeback game at Trent Bridge.

When he was 20, Boycott got an outside edge to a delivery from Jeff Thomson and the ball went straight in, and straight out of, Rick McCosker's hands at third slip. Greg Chappell standing next to McCosker went down on his knees in frustration. 'Oh no,' he said. At the end of the over Chappell walked past and I said, 'That could cost you the series.' And he replied, 'You're right.'

Not Out, Bird

Not even the most confident players are without their foibles, like Dean Jones.

When he is feeling fairly confident he will have a hand-kerchief hanging over the top of his trousers on the left-hand side. If he is feeling even more confident he will have part of one of the sashes that he uses to tie up his thigh pad hanging over the top of his trousers, too. Then if he also drags his bat behind him when he walks to the wicket you can be sure he is ready to take on the world.

Strike Bowler, McDermott and Derriman

When good fortune is around, too, you don't mess with it. When England's Bob Taylor and Geoff Miller turned round the Adelaide Test of 1979, David Gower and Ian Botham did their duty.

Goose [Bob Willis] and Hendo [Mike Hendrick] banned me and Both from watching for superstitious reasons because we weren't watching at the start just before lunch. So Both and I sat at the back of the dressing-room all afternoon signing millions of autograph sheets and playing 'Hangman'. Towards the end Both popped out to have a look at the partnership – and Dusty's out at once!

Anyone for Cricket? Gower and Taylor

The same voodoo kept Allan Border in a shower at Lord's ten years later as Australia chased on the last day.

I stayed in a fair while because I thought, 'I won't go back in the room until we get a bit closer; while I'm here nobody's getting out.' When I finally dried off and went back into the room Terry Alderman and the blokes ordered me back into the shower. 'Don't change a winning situation,' Terry shouted. When I couldn't stand the water any longer I had a shave. Finally they let me back into the room when we needed ten to win.

Ashes Glory: Allan Border's own story,
Border

8 | MATTERS OF CHOICE

Beachcomber's classic definition of 'bombshell' as 'the exclusion of a cricketer from a team' was rooted in fact. Nothing is quite so calculated to cause umbrage and indignation as a selection or exclusion apparently undeserved or misguided. Cricket fans can usually explain to themselves why they did not go further in the playing of the game, but all cricket fans fancy themselves as selectors.

Mike Brearley once said that selectors were like modern families – only noticed when there was blame to apportion. It's almost true, but not quite, for selectors are surely noticed by those they favour, who bless them for their wisdom and insight. This chapter looks at selection from all sides: the pickers, the picked and the picky.

Selection for one's country, recalled Bert Oldfield, is historically a great moment.

We were at our evening meal when Charlie Kellaway, who lived nearby in Glebe Point, a suburb of Sydney, called and told the good news. My mother, whose face was wreathed in smiles, rushed back into the dining-room and the members of the family wondered what it was all about. After a while she came over and kissed me and loudly whispered, 'How wonderful, Bertie, you've been picked for the First Test!' I was so excited I could not finish my meal. I saw myself wearing the much-coveted green cap bearing the Australian coat of arms and walking out onto the field in the select company of such celebrities as Noble, Armstrong, Macartney, Kellaway, Bardsley, Cotter, Ransford and others whose skill had won for them international fame.

Behind the Wicket, Oldfield

And for Michael Slater it still is.

Not long after arriving at the NSWCA office on 2 April [1993] I was buzzed by Bob Radford. 'Come into my office, young fella,' he barked down the intercom line. I knew that a media release was sent out a couple of hours before the official announcement of the Test side so my mind was racing when I sat down in Bob's office. I could see that he had the press release, and I thought I could read the name Slater upside down. Bob started going on with all this stuff that I wasn't that interested in hearing, then suddenly he said, 'You're in. You're in the fucking squad. Ring whoever you need to then we're going to lunch.'

Slats: The Michael Slater story, Slater and Apter

Sometimes it's not so great, as when the 1890 Australians found themselves a wicketkeeper heavy.

Monday morning saw most of the team about town together, and then it was discovered that Kenny Burn had, to use his own words, 'never kept wickets in his life'. The mistake was the result of a curious misconception. Blackham had seen in print that 'Burn' had stumped men in Tasmania, but that Burn was Kenny's brother and quite an inferior player. However, the team was consoled by the reflection that the Tasmanian has the reputation of being a fine batsman, a fair bowler and a good field. Extraordinarily heavy work will fall on Blackham's shoulders, or should I say his hands, but like the keen cricketer he is, he looks forward cheerfully to the task.

The Australasian, 26 April 1890

And sometimes it can be quite scary, as Mike Whitney found when called up for the Fifth Test at Old Trafford in 1981 while playing as a Gloucestershire reserve.

Fred Bennett the manager had just rung. I was to get off the field and speak to him. I was to report to Old Trafford immediately.

I was elated to have been considered, but when Geoff Lawson had broken down, Hoggy the same, Carl Rackemann also injured, Thommo had gone home and Len Pascoe was recovering from a knee injury, I really was the only one available.

I made the trip up to Old Trafford and was met by Fred Bennett. Upon arriving at the dressing-room we were joined by Kim Hughes. He congratulated me and told me what he wanted me to do tomorrow – bowl line and length.

I said, 'What do you mean?'

He said, 'Haven't they told you? You're playing in the Test tomorrow!'

I couldn't believe it, having played just seven first-class games and a few John Player League games. It didn't hit me until the third day of the Test. Another thing that was amazing was that Ray Bright had moved out of his room so I was going to room with Dennis Lillee.

They gave me my cap and jumper and we left for the ground. It was a great thrill to walk onto the ground in the company of Marsh, Lillee and company. After Lillee and Alderman had bowled about 15 overs, Kim Hughes said this was it. I did all the stretches and limbering up for the cameras. Waved to my mum in Australia. Kim said, 'Bowl line and length and don't be nervous.' I really hadn't time to be nervous. I bowled my first ball and Chris Tavaré played it out to square leg, and down came the rain! All that exercising for one ball! Peter Philpott came over and said, 'That was a great ball.'

Wisden Cricket Monthly, January 1982

As the time for selection of a touring team nears, pulses always quicken.

On the eve of the announcement of the party to tour England in 1953, Alan Davidson was fielding in a Sheffield Shield match and heard a bellow from the bowels of the SCG's Sheridan Stand, 'Hey Davidson! You can pack your bags.'

Davidson's ears pricked. 'You beauty,' he thought. 'I've been picked.'

'Yep,' continued the anonymous orator. 'You can pack your bags for a boat trip!'

'Gee, he means it,' Davidson thought. 'I'm going to England.'

'Yeah, you can pack your bags for a boat trip,' the voice advised. 'To Manly!'

Two days later, however, the telephone rang at Davidson's Strathfield flat. It was his aunt from Epping: he'd been picked. There was silence at both ends of the line for a time, and Davidson replaced the receiver shaking. 'A dream come true,' he says.

For every dream come true was an ambition thwarted. When that Ashes team was read out in the Australian dressing-room after the Fifth Test against

South Africa on 12 February 1953, teenager Ron Archer's pleasure at selection was muted by knowing that it had been at the expense of 36-year-old Geff Noblet. 'Geff was a much more experienced player than me. A much better bowler, too. The sort of guy they said'd do well in England. I happened to be next to him when they announced the team: I was picked and he wasn't. I could tell he was really disappointed because it was his last chance to go, but I can also remember how gracious he was congratulating me. It was a great lesson.'

The Summer Game, Haigh

Some selectors don't fill one with confidence, like Jack Ryder when he saw off the 1964 Australians . . .
When the Board held a farewell dinner for the team in Melbourne, Jack Ryder greeted South Australian leg-spinner Rex Sellers as Ray and Novocastrian medium-pacer Graeme Corling as nothing at all. 'I know someone who didn't vote for us,' thought Sellers.

The Summer Game, Haigh

. . . or Sir Leonard Hutton, as Graham Gooch recalled on his Test debut in 1975.
At breakfast in the hotel dining-room Sir Len Hutton stopped to have a word with me. He seemed a kindly man, but a dry one. 'Good luck,' he said.

'Er, tell me young man, have you ever played against the Australians before?' I thought he was making fun of me. 'Yes, sir,' I said. 'You're one of the selectors who picked me after I scored 75 against them for MCC at Lord's last week.'

The Autobiography, Gooch and Keating

Other selections puzzle players, and in January 1987 it was uncapped Mark Taylor's turn.

The day before the announcement I was up in Newcastle playing against Tasmania. Someone from Channel Nine came up and said, 'Look, if you get into the Australian team would you mind coming for an interview on the *Today* show?'

We were back in Sydney the next morning and I get a phone call at five past six saying, 'This is the *Today* show. You're in the Test team. Can you come in?' So I raced to the shower and I'm thinking about all the things I should say on TV, but I got another phone call about fifteen minutes later, 'Mark, is there a P. Taylor who plays for New South Wales?' I said, 'Yes, there's Peter our off-spinner.' 'Has he played this year?' I said, 'Well, he played the last game against Tassie.' They asked, 'Could it be him that's picked?' And I said, 'It quite possibly could be.' Then they said, 'Will you still come in?' 'No,' I said. 'I'm not coming in.'

Extra Cover, Egan

One man's gain, after all, is another man's loss, and
for Mark Waugh in January 1991 that man was
his twin brother Steve.

'Congratulations,' he said. 'You're in.' Finally I asked,
'Who's out?' Steve replied, 'Me. But I'm just another
player.' We sat there stunned for about three minutes.
Obviously I'd rather have taken someone else's place,
but I thought my turn could come in a Test if I kept
scoring runs. Of all the wickets in the world to make
your debut on you'd have to pick Adelaide. I'd played
two previous first-class innings there and got 70-odd
and 172. I roomed with Merv Hughes and if I had any
tension he relieved it and I had a good night's sleep
before the Test. Merv is a great fun sort of fellow.

The Bedside Book of Cricket Centuries, Smith

Sometimes, too, you don't know what you've got till
it's gone, like Bob Simpson in England in 1993.

Simmo was hitting fly balls, calling out a player's name
and usually thumping the ball well away from him. Up
goes the ball. 'Deano,' shouts Simmo. Nobody moves.
Up goes the ball again. 'Deano.' And again it plops to
the ground. Simmo is looking a bit annoyed when Merv
shouts, 'He's not here, Simmo. You didn't pick him . . .'
Old habits die hard.

Deano: My call, Jones

9 | THE VERBAL GAME

The sound bite sounds like an infatuation of our own media-saturated age, but it is no stranger to the Ashes. You could have no more succinct a mission statement than Fred Spofforth's at The Oval in 1882 when Australia set out to defend 85 in the fourth innings. He said, 'This thing can de done.' Mind you, its survival owes something to the fact that the thing could be done after all.

Some remarks are justly famous. Fifty years after Spofforth threw down the gauntlet to his team-mates, Bill Woodfull threw down the gauntlet at his Bodyline opponents when he said, 'There are two teams out there. One is trying to play cricket.' Others are forgotten or lost, a victim of our permanent present, and they are the emphasis of these aphorisms, gripes, tributes, sneers, patriotic assertions and eternal verities vouchsafed by players, pundits, fans and friends in the heat and afterglow of Ashes cricket.

COMPLIMENTS

'All his life he was facing the next ball.' *A.A. Thomson of W.G. Grace.*

'Victor Trumper had the greatest charm and two strokes for every ball.' *C.B. Fry.*

'Please, Wilfred, give me some peace.' *Trumper to Wilfred Rhodes.*

'Yon booy could feald a cannon baal.' *A Yorkshireman admiring the cover fielding of Syd Gregory.*

'There is no-one like Clem to let you see when you are bowling rubbish.' *Hugh Trumble of Clem Hill.*

'Some batsmen use their bats like a shovel. This man uses it like a pen.' *Australian Alick Bannerman on Englishman Kenneth Hutchings.*

'Stay as long as you are making runs.' *Brisbane auction firm to employee Roger Hartigan while he was making a Test century on debut in Adelaide in 1908.*

'The most graceful of the efficient and the most efficient of the graceful.' *Ian Peebles on Frank Woolley.*

'A snick by Jack Hobbs is a sort of disturbance of cosmic orderliness.' *Neville Cardus.*

'The sound of his bat somehow puts me in mind of vintage port.' *A.A. Milne on Jack Hobbs.*

'Is Richardson human?' *Headline to a* Sydney Morning Herald *leader in December 1928 after a virtuoso display of cover fielding by Vic Richardson.*

'This kid'll get a hundred.' *Maurice Tate, after Archie Jackson had glanced his first ball in Test cricket for 4; he made 164.*

'Well fielded, cock.' *Farmer White's ritual encourgement.*

'Maurice Tate did not merely play cricket; he lived in it.' *John Arlott.*

'Such a giant of the game seemed always to dwarf the rest of the team, and the moment he faced up to bowling that had held difficulties for other batsmen that bowling appeared to lose its venom.' *Len Hutton on Wally Hammond.*

'My feet feel tired when I think of him.' *Joe Hardstaff on Donald Bradman.*

'Bradman probably sits up in the middle of the night and roars with laughter at such feeble attempts to get him out.' *Arthur Mailey.*

'They were two beautiful balls – good enough to have beaten me if I'd been a hundred.' *Don Bradman on his last two balls in Test cricket, from Eric Hollies.*

'I want England to win – but directly I saw Harvey's masterly yet carefree batting I wanted him to get his hundred.' *Jack Hobbs on Neil Harvey.*

'I am never quite sure what he is going to do next and I don't think he knows himself until he is about to do it.' *Len Hutton on Keith Miller.*

'He seemed to attack from all directions.' *Don Bradman on Bill O'Reilly.*

'It was a battered old piece of willow but in Denis's hands it was like a Stradivarius in the hands of Yehudi Menuhin.' *Colin Cowdrey on Denis Compton.*

'You only have to see him play one shot to see his class.' *Keith Miller on Peter May.*

'I've never felt so glad in my life as when I saw who was coming in.' *Peter May recalling the sight of Cyril Washbrook coming in to bat with England 3–17 at Headingley, 1956.*

'He doesn't need to.' *Ron Archer, asked if Frank Tyson swung the ball.*

'When I watch Ken Barrington at the crease – and I have had the opportunity for many, many, many hours! – my thoughts are that I only wish I could have been as good a cricketer.' *Bill Lawry.*

'You must have an awful job to keep pace with these fellows, Patsy. The speed of it would be too much for me.' *Robert Menzies to scorer Patsy Hendren after twenty scoreless minutes at Lord's in 1956.*

'In public relations to benefit the game, Benaud was so far ahead of predecessors that race-glasses would have been needed to see who was at the head of the others.' *Ray Robinson on Richie Benaud.*

'Keep it up, youse blokes – you're doin' real suave.' *Dennis Lillee to Bill Lawry and Keith Stackpole at an intermission in a partnership, Adelaide 1971.*

'He's got a degree in people, hasn't he?' *Rodney Hogg on Mike Brearley.*

'Hope you don't drop this.' *Card accompanying a bottle of champagne sent by Alan Knott when Rod Marsh broke his world wicketkeeping record at Headingley, 1981.*

'Ian Botham would make a great Aussie.' *Jeff Thomson.*

'Of course Shane Warne doesn't sleep with sheep. He could sleep with whoever he likes.' *Paul Burnham of the Barmy Army defending songs involving Shane Warne's exploits with sheep.*

'Merv Hughes.' *Steve Waugh, asked his favourite animal.*

CONDEMNATIONS

'My God! Look what they've sent me!' *Captain Archie MacLaren on England's team for the 1902 Old Trafford Test.*

'It is disillusioning to one of my youthful loyalties to realise that the majestic MacLaren was an extremely stupid, prejudiced and pig-headed man.' *George Lyttelton on Archie MacLaren.*

'You know, Fender, there is no man in England whose bowling I would rather bat against than yours; and there is no batsman in England I would rather bowl against either.' *Johnny Douglas bolsters the confidence of team-mate Percy Fender en route to Australia.*

'From Douglas's captaincy no idea ever emerged.' *C.B. Fry's assessment.*

'Johnny [Douglas] used to bowl them in then chuck the ball to me to bowl them out.' *Cec Parkin.*

'That fellow Parkin is very sure of himself, I must say.' *Lord Hawke.*

'Compared to Verity his bowling was like a glass of fizz with a cup of cat's piss.' *Leonard Crawley comparing Wilfred Rhodes to Hedley Verity.*

'The only question that remained in one's mind about his fielding was the continual doubt as to which end he was throwing at.' *Jim Laker on his young team-mate Ted Dexter in Australia, 1958–59.*

'The only fellow I've met who fell in love with himself at a young age and has remained faithful ever since.' *Dennis Lillee on Geoff Boycott.*

'There's only one head bigger than Greig's – and that's Birkenhead.' *Fred Trueman.*

'If this letter reaches you the Post Office thinks more of you than I do.' *The contents of an envelope addressed to 'Mike Denness, Cricketer' in 1974–75.*

'Don't tell me we have to put up with him for another minute.' *Doug Walters when Mike Denness came in to bat at Sydney, 1975.*

'You make Denness look like Don Bradman.' *Melbourne barracker to Mike Brearley.*

'The most overrated player I've seen.' *Harold Larwood on Ian Botham.*

'England have only three major problems. They can't bat, they can't bowl and they can't field.' *Martin Johnson of* The Independent *just before the Brisbane Test of 1986, which England won.*

'The other advantage England has got when Phil Tufnell is bowling is that he isn't fielding.' *Ian Chappell during the Fifth Test, Perth 1991.*

'Do that again and you're on the next plane home, son.'
Allan Border to Craig McDermott at Taunton, 1993.

'The mincing run-up resembles someone in high heels and a panty girdle chasing after a bus.' *Writer Martin Johnson on Merv Hughes.*

MODESTY

'If I ever bowl a maiden over, it's not my fault.' *Arthur Mailey.*

'I wish I was as accurate as they think.' *Tim Wall after receiving letters of complaint from English fans for breaking Herbert Sutcliffe's thumb during the Ashes of 1930.*

'I'm only setting these records up for Hutton to break them.' *Sutcliffe looks forward to the rise of his protégé, Len Hutton.*

'One does not go seeking records. They just happen.' *Donald Bradman.*

'There's runs to be had out there – if only a man had legs.' *Bradman after being dismissed for 234 in the Sydney Test of 1947.*

'Well, at last I'm in the record book with the little chap.' *Sid Barnes, dismissed for the same score in the same Test.*

'When you get old three things happen. You can't remember other people's names . . . and I can't remember the other two.' *Ernie McCormick.*

'Yes, your majesty, and unless my batting improves it will be my last.' *Ian Craig, when the Queen commented that the Ashes tour of 1953 was his first.*

'I'm glad I wasn't up here when I was down there.' *Lindsay Hassett the commentator recalls Lindsay Hassett the batsman.*

'Well, I haven't brought a Harlequin cap.' *Peter May when asked by an Australian pressman if he was the toughest England captain since Jardine.*

'I didn't do it, Trevor – it must have hit something.' *Ray Lindwall after bowling Trevor Bailey for a pair with what appeared to be an unplayable leg-cutter.*

'I think a little roast duckling would be appropriate.' *Bailey placing his restaurant order.*

'No good hitting me there, mate! Nothing to damage!' *Derek Randall after taking one on the head from Dennis Lillee in the Centenary Test, 1977.*

'I was forced to play too many shots.' *Chris Tavaré, explaining how he'd lost a game of snooker to a team-mate.*

'I am a born pessimist.' *Bob Willis.*

'I am 32. I reckon I could play for England until I am at least 33!' *David Gower in 1989.*

'I dunno, mate. I've buggered up five hundreds myself, you know. Why don't you try to do it with a six?' *Steve Waugh responding to Ian Healy's request for advice about batting in the nineties, Trent Bridge 1993.*

'I still have the butterflies but now they are flying in formation.' *Mark Taylor after ending a run of poor form with a century at Edgbaston, 1997.*

'Mike said that he'd read Wilbur Smith when he was eight. That's why he went to Cambridge and I didn't.' *Graeme Hick compares himself to his captain Mike Atherton.*

CONFIDENCE

'The damned sweat got me out. One of these days I'll make a thousand.' *Jack Lyons after being dismissed for 134 at Sydney in 1892.*

'I will cheat fair.' *Sydney-born, Somerset-bred Sammy Woods volunteering to umpire a game between Australia and Somerset.*

'Ah luv a dog fight.' *Herbert Sutcliffe.*

'Umpire, you've created a record in no-balling me – and you needn't be worried any other umpire will ever equal it.' *Clarrie Grimmett, appalled to be called for overstepping.*

'Come on, youse! Straight up the centre – no short passes – boots and all!' *The football-inspired battle cry of Bill Woodfull's 1930 Australians.*

'Somebody's got to have a crack at this fella.' *Vic Richardson before going out to face Larwood for the first time.*

'It may be for years or it may be forever.' *Stan McCabe about to do the same.*

'He'd hit it clean over the bakery I expect.' *Ernie Toshack asked by a Surrey member how Bradman would respond to being bowled a bread roll.*

'I have a go at 'em anyway.' *Neil Harvey when Len Hutton told him he played and missed too often.*

'Yes, if you don't mind him being killed.' *Peter May asked by Ian Johnson if it would be all right if a close-in fielder came even closer.*

'There is no sitting duck like a scared duck.'
Ray Lindwall.

'To bowl quick is to revel in the glad animal action; to thrill in physical prowess and to enjoy a certain sneaking feeling of superiority over the other mortals who play the game. No batsman likes quick bowling and this knowledge gives one a sense of omnipotence.'
Frank Tyson.

'At the crease my attitude to three bouncers has been that, if I'm playing well enough, three bouncers an over should be worth twelve runs to me.'
Ian Chappell.

'Didn't you go to the team meeting? They would have told you you can't bowl on middle-and-leg to me.' *Dean Jones to Gus Fraser, after hitting him through mid-wicket for 4 at Trent Bridge in 1989.*

'I think you're a great bloke, Phil, and you're really bowling well.' *Greg Matthews to Phil Tufnell in Perth in 1991.*

'Three days and a result is better than five days of boring stuff.' *Steve Waugh unconcerned to be winning Tests in three days.*

'It's like in *Dumb and Dumber* when the girl says, "You've got a one in a million chance of sleeping with me" and Jim Carrey says, "So you're saying I've got a chance," I live by that.' *Michael Slater weighs up his chances of an international recall.*

'I wouldn't nick it.' *Adam Gilchrist asked if he would walk if he nicked a ball with Australia needing two runs to win the Ashes with one wicket in hand.*

CHAGRIN

'Nobody is so soon forgotten as a successful cricketer.' *Ranjitsinhji*

'It takes a long time to be recognised in big cricket and just as long to be dropped from it.' *J.A. Dixon of Nottinghamshire.*

'Who are the MCC and what are they doing in Australia?' *Winchester headmaster Montague Rendall when England's Rockley Wilson sought leave to tour Australia in 1920–21.*

'Frank, they'll get a thousand.' *Stan McCabe to umpire Frank Chester after bowling the first over in the Oval Test of 1938: England made 7–903.*

'Where's the groundsman's hut? If I had a gun with me, I'd shoot him.' *Bill O'Reilly in conversation with the same umpire in the same Test.*

'You woke up in the night time and your arm was still going round.' *Chuck Fleetwood-Smith's recollection.*

'It is amazing how the public steadfastly refuse to attend the third day of a match when so often the last day produces the best and most exciting cricket.' *Frank Woolley.*

'There goes the old man's axe through the radio.' *Sam Loxton after being dismissed at Headingley in 1948 essaying a huge swipe on 93.*

'The bowlers seem a little different. Not quite as quick as the new ball bowlers a few years ago.' *Len Hutton asked about changes to the game since his retirement.*

'Sorry about that, but you've a day's rest tomorrow.' *Brian Statham talking to his feet after a thirty-over spell.*

'It's like standing in the middle of a darts match.' *Jim Laker to Neil Harvey while batting against Ian Meckiff and Gordon Rorke in 1958–59.*

'I'm the last of the straight-arm bowlers.' *Ray Lindwall when he was recalled during that 1958–59 series.*

'Dear Mum, today I received a half volley. In the nets.' *David Lloyd writing home from MCC's 1974–75 tour of Australia.*

'I don't really like being the New Dennis Lillee. There's no substitute for bowling fast and being able to make the good players jump.' *Dennis Lillee.*

'The older I get the better cricketer I seem to become.' *Jim Laker.*

'They said to me at The Oval, come and see our new bowling machine. Bowling machine? I said. I used to be the bowling machine.' *Alec Bedser.*

'Sometimes it takes him a fortnight to put on his socks.' *England's coach Mickey Stewart on the very mellow Devon Malcolm.*

'The way I play my cricket is intense – that's the way people think you are off the field, but I think if you asked any of my mates what I'm like it'd be a lot different to what you see out there.' *Steve Waugh feeling misjudged.*

'Concentration is sometimes mistaken for grumpiness.' *Michael Atherton.*

'Do you wake up in the middle of the night thinking you might have dropped the Ashes? I have got Herschelle Gibbs' phone number here if you want some counselling.' *Phil Tufnell baits Shane Warne for dropping Kevin Pietersen in the 2005 Ashes decider.*

'I don't owe Shane anything. I have dropped six catches and nobody bought me a beer.' *Kevin Pietersen asked if he had bought Warne a beer in gratitude.*

THE ENGLISH WAY

'International cricket matches are not only cricket matches. They tend to excite as well as to promote a kindly feeling between nations which take part in them.' *Bishop Welldon.*

'We all admired and liked the Australians of those days. But, by Jove, we did like beating them!' *C.B. Fry.*

'Good heavens, they've asked me to captain England.' *Hon. Lionel Tennyson receiving the telegram at his London club, 1921.*

'Next to representing England in a Test match at home, it is the highest ambition of every cricketer to be selected to go on tour to Australia.' *Lord Hawke.*

'Dammit, we've done 'em!' *George Geary after hitting the winning runs in the 1928–29 Ashes series.*

'By, and it were gawin'.' *Eddie Paynter on the 6 with which he won the Ashes in 1933.*

'It's the Ashes! It's the Ashes!' *Commentator Brian Johnston as Denis Compton swept the winning runs in the Oval Test of 1953.*

'The aim of English Test cricket is, in fact, mainly to beat Australia.' *Jim Laker.*

'I have on occasions taken a quite unreasonable dislike to the Australians.' *Ted Dexter.*

'One is always a little nervous watching England bat.' *Peter May.*

Journalist: 'Do you feel that the selectors and yourself have been vindicated by the result?'
Mike Gatting: 'I don't think the press are vindictive. They can write what they want.' *Gatting after winning the 1986–87 Ashes.*

'You play your first for love and the rest for money.' *Senior England player to Mike Atherton during the 1989 Ashes.*

'We're a soft touch in this country.' *Brian Close.*

'Our cricket is too gentle – all of it.' *Alec Stewart.*

THE AUSTRALIAN WAY

'Unconsciously, and perhaps without any suspicion on their part that such is the case, the Australians have seriously aggravated the symptoms of a commercial spirit in cricket.' *Lillywhite's Cricketers' Annual 1883.*

'The Australian climate is a great aid to bowling and fielding. Its warmth and mildness prevent the rheumatic affections that so often attack the arms and shoulders of our players, and the Australians consequently retain their suppleness of limb and activity of youth longer than their English cousins.' *A.G. Steel.*

'Watch an Australian bowler: he is always doing something to the ball with his fingers, and never bowls a ball down unless he has some object in view.' *A.O. Jones.*

'We are going to see certain things in the Australian game which are not to their detriment but which are not in our game. We are up against a lot of things which we don't do but which other people do.' *Percy Fender.*

'The Australian plays cricket to win: he has usually left it to Mr Warner to make Empire-binding speeches.' *Neville Cardus.*

'Australians will always fight for those 22 yards. Lord's and its tradition belong to Australia just as much as to England.' *Prime Minister John Curtin in 1945.*

'Australians will not tolerate class distinctions in sport.' *Jack Fingleton.*

'To play first-class cricket is a goal, and to reach the Australian XI is probably a higher honour than to go to England in the strict practical sense. But for many reasons it is a tour of England upon which most youngsters set their hearts.' *Don Bradman.*

'I admire the Australians' approach to the game; they have the utmost ability for producing that little extra, or instilling into the opposition an inferiority complex that can have, and has had, a crushing effect. Australians have no inhibitions.' *Len Hutton.*

'Equally, the Australians throughout cricket history have been quick to strike back even from a position of apparently imminent defeat.' *John Arlott.*

'It is said that the hardest-headed Australian has a quasi-religious respect for Lord's and feels an extra urge to succeed there.' *John Arlott.*

'When appealing the Australians make a statement; we ask a question.' *Vic Marks.*

'They are all pricks.' *Allan Border asked at Hove in 1993 why he was not talking to English reporters.*

ADVICE

'Keep your left shoulder up and say your prayers.' *A.N. Hornby to his protégé Archie MacLaren.*

'You must persuade that Bosanquet of yours to practise, practise, practise those funny "googlies" of his till he is automatically certain of his length. That leg-break of his which breaks from the off might win a Test match.' *C.B. Fry to Pelham Warner before MCC's 1903–04 tour of Australia.*

'When I play back and miss the ball I like to see it hit Wilson.' *Rockley Wilson, England vice-captain of 1920–21, a staunch advocate of getting behind the line.*

'I want no more of that fourth-form behaviour.' *Douglas Jardine to his exuberant colleague Walter Robins.*

'Listen carefully, Tiger. I want you, above all, not to get hit.' *Bill Woodfull to Bill O'Reilly before he went out to bat in the Bodyline series.*

'A happy frame of mind is half the battle.' *Denis Compton.*

'In a Test season, centuries do the talking.' *Bill O'Reilly to Arthur Morris, who'd just surrendered his wicket carelessly for 68.*

'Why don't you read your own book?' *Spectator to Clarrie Grimmett, author of* Tricking the Batsmen, *on a rare day he was collared.*

'Hit the ball along the ground.' *Don Bradman's advice to Neil Harvey in 1948 when the young man complained about being caught too often.*

'Remember, laad, one day we'll have a fasst bowler, and ah hope that day is nae too far off.' *Len Hutton after a series of bouncers from Ray Lindwall.*

'I'd send home for another bowler.' *Len Hutton to Denis Compton who had asked him for advice in 1950.*

'Now now, children! No naughty words!' *Keith Miller when rival captains Len Hutton and Ian Johnson became locked in an argument about bowlers' footmarks in 1954–55.*

'Ian, you'll have to curb your swearing if you're going to captain Australia.' *Bob Parish, manager of the 1968 Australians, to Ian Chappell.*

'Hey Lawry! Give Gleeson a bowl – his grandmother lives in Geelong!' *Brisbane barracker to Bill Lawry when he had Victorians Alan Connolly and Bob Cowper bowling at opposite ends in a Test.*

'I don't really sledge batsmen. If I beat his outside edge and say, "You're a shit batsman" and then the next ball he hits me for six, who's the prat?' *Phil Tufnell.*

'My diet is still pizza, chips, toasted cheese sandwiches and milkshakes. I have the occasional six-week burst where I stick to fruit and cereal: it bloody kills me.' *Shane Warne on his secrets of success.*

'Shane Warne's idea of a balanced diet is a cheeseburger in each hand.' *Ian Healy.*

'I never saw a fitter, stronger or healthier cricketer become a worse cricketer.' *Graham Gooch.*

WISDOM
'Find out where the ball is, go there, hit it.' *Ranjitsinhji's three principles of batsmanship.*

'If the batsman thinks it's spinnin', it's spinnin'.'
Wilfred Rhodes.

'Cricket would be a better game if the papers didn't
publish the averages.' *Jack Hobbs.*

'Unless you get to the top where the plums are, it is a
bare living, and when your cricket days are over you
have to find a new career.' *Jack Hobbs counsels against
a professional cricket career.*

'Remember, the bowler can only deliver one ball at a
time.' *Herbert Sutcliffe.*

'The mentality of the medium-pace bowler as a general rule does not rate up to that of the more subtle
type of bowler. With very few exceptions the great spin
bowlers of cricket were personalities and men of character – not always pleasant but invariably interesting.'
Arthur Mailey.

'It is wise not to be too rude about autobiographies;
you never know who has written them!' *Neville
Cardus.*

'An ounce of luck is worth a ton of skill, son.' *Alan
Kippax.*

'When you see a cricket coach, run off as fast as you can.' *Bill O'Reilly.*

'Test cricket is not a light-hearted business, especially that between England and Australia.' *Donald Bradman.*

'To me the best preparation for batting, bowling and fielding was batting, bowling and fielding.' *Peter May.*

'I can't think of any player who has been put off his game by verbal abuse.' *Mark Taylor.*

'This is like dying and going to heaven.' *Boris Karloff looking down from the balcony at Lord's.*

BIBLIOGRAPHY

Allen, David Rayvern, *Arlott: The authorised biography*, HarperCollins, London, 1994

Allen, Peter, *The Invincibles*, ABC Books, Sydney, 1998

Amiss, Dennis and Michael Carey, *In Search of Runs*, Readers' Union, Newton Abbot, 1977

Anonymous, *The 'Sporting English?'* Macquarie Head Press, Sydney, 1933

Arlott, John, (Ed.), *Cricket: The great ones*, Pelham, London, 1967

Arlott, John, *Jack Hobbs*, Penguin, London, 1981

Atherton, Michael, *Opening Up*, Hodder & Stoughton, London, 2002

Bailey, Trevor, *Playing to Win*, Hutchinson, London, 1954

Bannister, Jack, (Ed.), *The Innings of My Life*, Headline, London, 1993

Barker, Ralph, *Innings of a Lifetime*, Collins, London, 1982

Bedser, Alec and Eric Bedser, *Our Cricket Story*, Evans Brothers, London, 1951

Bedser, Alec and Eric Bedser, *Following On*, Evans Brothers, London, 1954

Beecher, Eric, (Ed.), *Cricket Close-up*, Newspress, Melbourne, 1978

Benaud, Richie, *Way of Cricket*, Hodder & Stoughton, London, 1960

Benaud, Richie, *A Tale of Two Tests*, Hodder & Stoughton, London, 1962

Benaud, Richie, *Willow Patterns*, Hodder & Stoughton, London, 1969

Bird, Dickie, *Not Out*, Arthur Baker Limited, London, 1978

Boon, David, *Under the Southern Cross*, Harper Sports, Sydney, 1996

Border, Allan, *Allan Border: An autobiography*, Methuen, Sydney, 1986

Border, Allan, *Ashes Glory: Allan Border's own story*, Swan Publishing, Byron Bay, 1989

Border, Allan, *Beyond Ten Thousand: My life story*, Swan Publishing, Nedlands, 1993

Bose, Mihir, *Keith Miller: A cricketing biography*, Allen & Unwin, London, 1979

Botham, Ian, *The Incredible Tests*, Pelham, London, 1982

Bowes, Bill, *Express Deliveries*, The Sportsman's Book Club, London, 1958

Boycott, Geoffrey, *Put to the Test*, Arthur Barker, London, 1979

Brayshaw, Ian, *The Wit of Cricket*, The Currawong Press, Sydney, 1981

Brearley, Mike, *The Ashes Retained*, Hodder & Stoughton, London, 1979

Brearley, Mike, *Phoenix from the Ashes*, Hodder & Stoughton, London, 1982

Brodribb, Gerald, *Maurice Tate*, London Magazine Editions, London, 1976

Brown, Freddie, *Cricket Musketeer*, Nicholas Kaye, London, 1954

Brown, Lionel H., *Victor Trumper and the 1902 Australians*, Secker & Warburg, London, 1981

Buchanan, Handasyde, (Ed.), *Great Cricket Matches*, Eyre & Spottiswoode, London, 1962

Butler, Keith, *Howzat! Sixteen Australian cricketers talk*, Collins, Sydney, 1979

Callaghan, John, *Boycott: A cricket legend*, Pelham, London, 1982

Catton, J.A.H., *Wickets and Goals: Stories of play*, Chapman & Hall, London, 1926

Chappell, Greg, *The 100th Summer*, Garry Sparke, Melbourne, 1977

Chappell, Ian, *Tigers Among the Lions*, Investigator Press, Leabrook, 1972

Chappell, Ian, *Chappelli: Ian Chappell's life story*, Hutchinson, Melbourne, 1976

Chappell, Ian and Ashley Mallett, *Chappelli Speaks Out*, Allen & Unwin, Sydney, 2005

Chappell, Ian and Paul Rigby, *Long Hops and Larrikins*, Lansdowne, Sydney, 1983

Chester, Frank, *How's That?* Hutchinson, London, 1956

Close, Brian, *I Don't Bruise Easily*, Futura, London, 1978

Cowdrey, Colin, *Cricket Today*, Arthur Barker, London, 1961

Cowdrey, Colin, *MCC*, Hodder & Stoughton, London, 1976

Darling, D.K., *Test Tussles On and Off the Field*, published by the author, Hobart, 1970

Davidson, Alan, *Fifteen Paces*, Souvenir Press, London, 1963

Denness, Mike, *I Declare*, Arthur Barker, London, 1977

Derriman, Phil, *Bodyline*, Fontana, Sydney, 1984

de Vitre, Fedrun, *Willow Tales: The lighter side of Indian cricket*, Marine Sports, Bombay, 1993

Dexter, Ted, *Ted Dexter's Cricket Book*, Arthur Barker, London, 1963

Docker, E.W., *Bradman and the Bodyline Series*, Angus & Robertson, Sydney, 1978; Methuen, London, 2002

Bibliography

Douglas, Christopher, *Douglas Jardine: Spartan cricketer*, Allen & Unwin, London, 1984

Edmonds, Frances, *Cricket XXXX Cricket*, Pan, London, 1987

Edrich, Bill, *Cricketing Days*, Stanley Paul, London, 1950

Egan, Jack, *Extra Cover*, Pan Books, Sydney, 1989

Evans, Godfrey, *Behind the Stumps*, Hodder & Stoughton, London, 1951

Evans, Godfrey, *The Gloves Are Off*, Hodder & Stoughton, London, 1960

Ferguson, W.H., *Mr Cricket*, Nicholas Kaye, London, 1957

Fingleton, Jack, *Masters of Cricket from Trumper to May*, Heinemann, London, 1958

Fingleton, Jack, *Four Chukkas to Australia*, Heinemann, Melbourne, 1959

Fingleton, J.H., *Cricket Crisis*, Cassell, Melbourne, 1946

Fingleton, J.H., *Brightly Fades the Don*, Collins, Sydney, 1949

Fingleton, J.H., *Brown and Company: The tour in Australia*, Collins, London, 1951

Fingleton, J.H., *The Ashes Crown the Year*, Collins, Sydney, 1954

Fletcher, Duncan, *The Ashes Regained*, Simon & Schuster, London, 2005

Foot, David, *Walter Hammond: The reasons why*, Robson Books, London, 1996

Foster, Frank R., *Cricketing Memories*, London Publishing Co., London, 1930

Francis, Tony, *The Zen of Cricket*, Stanley Paul, London, 1992

Fraser, Angus, *Fraser's Tour Diaries*, Headline, London, 1998

Frith, David, *My Dear Victorious Stod: A biography of A.E. Stoddart*, published by the author, Guildford, 1970

Frith, David, *The Fast Men*, Richard Smart Publishing, Sydney, 1975

Frith, David, *Thommo*, Angus & Robertson, Sydney, 1980

Frith, David, *The Slow Men*, Richard Smart Publishing, Sydney, 1984

Frith, David, *Stoddy's Mission: The first great Test series 1894–1895*, Richard Smart Publishing, Sydney, 1995

Frith, David, *Bodyline Autopsy*, ABC Books, Sydney, 2002

Frith, David, *The Battle for the Ashes 2005*, ABC Books, Sydney, 2005

Fry, C.B., *Life Worth Living*, Eyre & Spottiswoode, London, 1947

Gately, Mark, *Waugh Declared*, Ironbark, Sydney, 1992

Giffen, George, *With Bat and Ball*, Ward, Lock and Co., Melbourne, 1898

Gilchrist, Adam, *Walking to Victory*, Macmillan, Sydney, 2003

Goldman, Arthur, *Cricket Capers*, Afrikaanse Pers-Boekhandel, Johannesburg, 1964

Gooch, Graham and Frank Keating, *The Autobiography*, Collins Willow, London, 1995

Gordon, Sir Home, *Background of Cricket*, Arthur Barker, London, 1939

Gordon, Sir Home with Lord Hawke and Lord Harris, *The Memorial Biography of Dr. W.G. Grace*, published by Sir Home Gordon, London, 1919

Gough, Darren, *Dazzler*, Michael Joseph, London, 2001

Gower, David and David Norrie, *The Autobiography*, Collins Willow, London, 1992

Gower, David and Bob Taylor, *Anyone for Cricket?* Stanley Paul, London, 1979

Bibliography

Grace, W.G., *Cricket Reminiscences and Personal Recollections*, James Bowden, London, 1899

Greig, Tony, *My Story*, Stanley Paul, London, 1980

Grout, Wally, *My Country's Keeper*, Pelham Books, London, 1965

Growden, Greg, *A Wayward Genius*, ABC Books, Sydney, 1991

Haigh, Gideon, *The Cricket War*, Text Publishing, Melbourne, 1993

Haigh, Gideon, *The Border Years*, Text Publishing, Melbourne, 1994

Haigh, Gideon, *One Summer, Every Summer: An Ashes journal*, Text Publishing, Melbourne, 1995

Haigh, Gideon, *The Summer Game*, Text Publishing, Melbourne, 1997

Haigh, Gideon, *The Big Ship*, Text Publishing, Melbourne, 2000

Haigh, Gideon, *Game for Anything*, Black Inc., Melbourne 2004

Hammond, Walter R., *Cricket My Destiny*, Stanley Paul, London, 1946

Hammond, Walter R., *Cricket My World*, Stanley Paul, London, 1948

Hammond, Walter R., *Cricketers' School*, Stanley Paul, London, 1950

Harvey, Neil, *My World of Cricket*, Hodder & Stoughton, London, 1963

Hawke, Neil, *Bowled Over*, Rigby, Sydney, 1982

Healy, Ian, *Hands and Heals*, Harper Sports, Sydney, 2000

Hill, Alan, *Hedley Verity: Portrait of a cricketer*, Mainstream, London, 1986

Hill, Alan, *Herbert Sutcliffe: Cricket maestro*, Simon & Schuster, London, 1991

Hill, Alan, *Bill Edrich*, Mainstream, London, 1995

Hill, Alan, *Peter May: The authorised biography*, Andre Deutsch, London, 1996

Hill, Alan, *The Bedsers: Twinning triumphs*, Mainstream, London, 2001

Hobbs, Jack, *My Cricket Memories*, Heinemann, London, 1924

Hobbs, Jack, *My Life Story*, Hambledon, London, 1980

Hookes, David and Alan Shiell, *Hookesy*, ABC Books, Sydney, 1993

Hordern, H.V., *Googlies*, Angus & Robertson, Sydney, 1932

Howat, Gerald, *Len Hutton*, Mandarin, London, 1990

Hutton, Len, *Cricket is My Life*, Hutchinson, London, 1956

Hutton, Len and Alex Bannister, *Fifty Years in Cricket*, Stanley Paul, London, 1984

Iredale, Frank, *Thirty-three Years of Cricket*, Beatty, Richardson, London, 1920

Jaggard, Ed, *Garth: The story of Graham McKenzie*, Fremantle Arts Centre Press, Fremantle, 1993

James, C.L.R., *Beyond a Boundary*, Stanley Paul, London, 1963

Jardine, Douglas, *In Quest of the Ashes*, Hutchinson, London, 1933

Jessop, Gilbert, *A Cricketer's Log*, Hodder & Stoughton, London, 1922

Johnson, Ian, *Cricket at the Crossroads*, Cassell, London, 1957

Jones, Dean, *Deano: My call*, Swan Publishing, Nedlands, 1994

Keane, Patrick, *Merv Hughes: The full story*, Harper Sports, Melbourne, 1995

Bibliography

Knott, Alan, *Stumper's View*, Stanley Paul, London, 1972

Knott, Alan, *It's Knott Cricket*, Methuen, London, 1985

Laker, Jim, *Spinning Around the World*, Frederick Muller, London, 1957

Laker, Jim, *Over to Me*, Frederick Muller, London, 1960

Lamb, Allan and Peter Smith, *Lamb's Tales*, Queen Anne Press, London, 1985

Larwood, Harold and Kevin Perkins, *The Larwood Story*, Bonpara, Sydney, 1982

Laver, Frank, *An Australian Cricketer on Tour*, George Bell, London, 1905

Lawry, Bill, *Run Digger*, Souvenir Press, London, 1966

Lawson, Geoff, *Diary of the Ashes 1989*, Angus & Robertson, Sydney, 1990

Lawson, Geoff, *Henry: The Geoff Lawson story*, Ironbark, Sydney, 1993

Lemmon, David, *Johnny Won't Hit Today*, Allen & Unwin, London, 1983

Lilley, A.A., *Twenty-four Years of Cricket*, Mills & Boon, London, 1914

Lindwall, Ray, *Flying Stumps*, Arrow Books, Great Britain, 1957

Lloyd, David, *G'day Ya Pommie B. . . . . . ! and Other Cricketing Memories*, Weidenfeld & Nicolson, London, 1992

Lloyd, David, *The Autobiography*, Collins Willow, London, 2000

Macartney, C.G., *My Cricketing Days*, William Heinemann, London, 1930

McCool, Colin, *Cricket is a Game*, Stanley Paul, London, 1961

McDermott, Craig and Phil Derriman, *Strike Bowler*, ABC Books, Sydney, 1992

McGilvray, Alan, *The Game is Not the Same ...* ABC Books, Sydney, 1986

McGilvray, Alan, *The Game Goes On*, ABC Books, Sydney, 1987

McGilvray, Alan, *The Captains of the Game*, ABC Books, Sydney, 1992

McGrath, Glenn, *Pacemaker*, Macmillan, Sydney, 1999

McGregor, Adrian, *Greg Chappell: Cricket's incomparable artist*, UQP, Brisbane, 1990

McHarg, Jack, *Stan McCabe: The man and his cricket*, Collins, Sydney, 1987

McHarg, Jack, *Bill O'Reilly: A cricketing life*, Millennium, Sydney, 1990

McHarg, Jack, *Arthur Morris: An elegant genius*, ABC Books, Sydney, 1995

Mackay, Ken, *Slasher Opens Up*, Pelham Books, London, 1964

Mackay, Ken, *The Quest for the Ashes*, Pelham Books, London, 1967

Mailes, Jeremy, *Great Characters from Cricket's Golden Age*, Robson, London, 2000

Mailey, Arthur, *10 for 66 and All That*, Shakespeare Head, London, 1958

Mallett, Ashley, *Rowdy*, Lynton, Blackwood, 1973

Mallett, Ashley, *Clarrie Grimmett: The Bradman of spin*, UQP, Brisbane, 1993

Marsh, Rod, *You'll Keep*, Hutchinson, Melbourne, 1975

Marsh, Rod, *The Gloves of Irony*, Lansdowne Press, Sydney, 1982

Mason, Ronald, *Warwick Armstrong's Australians*, Epworth Press, London, 1971

May, Peter, *A Game Enjoyed*, Stanley Paul, London, 1985

Meredith, Anthony, *Summers in Winter*, The Kingswood Press, London, 1990

Meyer, John, *From the Outer*, published by the author, Wembley, 1979

Miller, Keith, *Cricket Crossfire*, Oldbourne Press, London, 1956

Miller, Keith, *Cricket from the Grandstand*, Oldbourne Press, London, 1959

Miller, Keith and R.S. Whitington, *Catch!* Latimer House, London, 1951

Miller, Keith and R.S. Whitington, *Straight Hit*, Latimer House, London, 1952

Miller, Keith and R.S. Whitington, *Gods or Flannelled Fools?* Macdonald, London, 1954

Monfries, J. Elliott, *Not Test Cricket*, Gillingham, Adelaide, 1950

Mosey, Don, *Boycott*, Methuen, London, 1985

Mosey, Don, *Laker*, Queen Anne Press, London, 1989

Moyes, A.G., *A Century of Cricketers*, Angus & Robertson, Sydney, 1950

Moyes, A.G., ('Johnnie'), *Australian Bowlers*, Angus & Robertson, Sydney, 1953

Moyes, A.G. ('Johnnie'), *The Changing Face of Cricket*, Angus & Robertson, Sydney, 1963

Murphy, Patrick, (Ed.), *Declarations*, Ringpress, London, 1989

Noble, M.A., *The Game's the Thing*, Cassell, London, 1926

Oldfield, W.A., *Behind the Wicket*, Hutchinson, London, 1938

Oldfield, W.A., *The Rattle of the Stumps*, George Newnes, London, 1954

O'Neill, Norman, *Ins and Outs*, Pelham Books, London, 1964

O'Reilly, Bill, *'Tiger'*, Collins, Sydney, 1985

O'Reilly, W.J., *Cricket Conquest*, Werner Laurie, London, 1949

Page, Michael, *Bradman: A biography*, Macmillan, Melbourne, 1988

Parkin, Cec, *Parkin on Cricket*, Hodder & Stoughton, London, 1925

Pawson, Tony, *Runs and Catches*, Faber, London, 1980

Peebles, Ian, *Talking of Cricket*, Museum Press, London, 1953

Peebles, Ian, *Batter's Castle*, Pavilion, London, 1986

Philpott, Peter, *A Spinner's Yarn*, ABC Books, Sydney, 1990

Ponting, Ricky, *Ashes Diary 2005*, Harper Sports, Sydney, 2005

Pullin, A.W., *Alfred Shaw: Cricketer*, Cassell, London, 1902

Randall, Derek, *The Sun Has Got His Hat On*, Collins Willow, London, 1984

Ranjitsinhji, K.S., *With Stoddart's Team in Australia*, James Bowden, London, 1898

Ray, Mark, *Border and Beyond*, ABC Books, Sydney, 1995

Redpath, Ian, *Always Reddy*, Garry Sparke, Melbourne, 1976

Reese, Daniel, *Was it all Cricket?* Allen & Unwin, London, 1948

Reiffel, Paul and Greg Baum, *Inside Out*, Harper Sports, Sydney, 1998

Richardson, V.Y. and R.S. Whitington, *The Vic Richardson Story*, Rigby, Adelaide, 1967

Ringwood, John, *Ray Lindwall: Cricket legend*, Kangaroo Press, Kenthurst, 1995

Robinson, Ray, *Between Wickets*, Collins, London, 1949

Robinson, Ray, *From the Boundary*, Collins, Sydney, 1950

Robinson, Ray, *Green Sprigs*, Collins, London, 1955

Bibliography

Robinson, Ray, *Cricket's Fun*, Building Publishing Company, Chippendale, 1970

Robinson, Ray, *The Wildest Tests*, Cassell, Sydney, 1979

Robinson, Ray, *On Top Down Under*, Cassell, Sydney, 1981

Rosenwater, Irving, *Sir Donald Bradman: A biography*, B.T. Batsford, London, 1978

Ross, Alan, *Ranji*, Collins, London, 1983

Russell, Jack, *Unleashed*, Collins Willow, London, 1997

Sharpham, Peter, *Victor Trumper*, Hodder & Stoughton, Sydney, 1985

Sheppard, Rev. David, *Parson's Pitch*, Hodder & Stoughton, London, 1964

Simpson, Bob, *Captain's Story*, Stanley Paul, London, 1966

Slater, Michael and Jeff Apter, *Slats: The Michael Slater story*, Random House, Sydney, 2005

Smith, E.J., *'Tiger' Smith of Warwickshire and England*, Lutterworth Press, Guildford, 1981

Smith, Rick and Ron Williams, *W.G. Down Under: Grace in Australia 1873–74 and 1891–92*, Apple Books, Launceston, 1994

Smith, Terry, *The Bedside Book of Cricket Centuries*, Angus & Robertson, Sydney, 1991

Snow, John, *Cricket Rebel*, Hamlyn, London, 1975

Stackpole, Keith and Alan Trengove, *Not Just for Openers*, Stockwell Press, Melbourne, 1974

Stewart, Alec, *A Captain's Diary*, Collins Willow, London, 1999

Strudwick, Herbert, *Twenty-five Years Behind the Stumps*, Hutchinson, London, 1958

Sutcliffe, Herbert, *For England and Yorkshire*, Edwards Arnold, London, 1935

Swanton, E.W., (Ed.), *Barclay's World of Cricket*, Collins, London, 1980

Synge, Allen, *Sins of Omission*, Pelham, London, 1990

Taylor, Mark, *A Captain's Year*, Ironbark, Sydney, 1998

Taylor, Mark, *Time to Declare*, Ironbark, Sydney, 1999

Travers, Ben, *94 Declared*, Elm Tree Books, London, 1981

Trelford, Donald, *Len Hutton Remembered*, Witherby, London, 1992

Trueman, Fred, *Fast Fury*, Stanley Paul, London, 1961

Trueman, Fred, *Ball of Fire*, Dent, London, 1976

Trumble, Robert, *The Golden Age of Cricket: A memorial book of Hugh Trumble*, published by the author, Melbourne, 1968

Tufnell, Phil, *What Now?* Collins Willow, London, 1999

Turner, C.T.B., *The Quest for Bowlers*, Cornstalk Publishing Company, Sydney, 1926

Tyson, Frank, *Test of Nerves*, Macmillan, Sydney, 1975

Tyson, Frank, *The Centenary Test*, Australian Cricket Board, Melbourne, 1977

Underwood, Derek, *Beating the Bat*, Stanley Paul, London, 1975

Valentine, Barry, *Cricket's Dawn that Died: The Australians in England, 1938*, Breedon Books, Derby, 1991

Vaughan, Michael, *A Year in the Sun*, Coronet, London, 2003

Walters, Doug, *The Doug Walters Story*, Rigby, Adelaide, 1981

Walters, Doug, *One for the Road*, Swan Publishing, Sydney, 1988

Warne, Shane, *My Own Story*, Swan Publishing, Sydney, 1997

Bibliography

Warne, Shane, *My Autobiography*, Hodder & Stoughton, London, 2001

Warner, P.F., *How We Recovered the Ashes*, Chapman & Hall, London, 1904

Warner, P.F., *Cricket Between Two Wars*, Sporting Handbooks, London, 1946

Warner, P.F., *Long Innings: The autobiography of Sir Pelham Warner*, Harrap, London, 1951

Waugh, Steve, *Ashes Diary*, Pan Macmillan, Sydney, 1993

Waugh, Steve, *South African Tour Diary*, Pan Macmillan, Sydney, 1994

Waugh, Steve, *1997 Ashes Diary*, Harper Sports, Sydney, 1997

Waugh, Steve, *Never Say Die*, Harper Sports, Sydney, 2003

Wellham, Dirk, *Solid Knocks and Second Thoughts*, Reed, Sydney, 1988

Whitington, R.S., *Fours Galore*, Cassell, Melbourne, 1969

Whitington, R.S., *Captains Outrageous? Cricket in the seventies*, Hutchinson, Melbourne, 1972

Whitington, R.S. and Keith Miller, *Gods or Flannelled Fools*, Macdonald, London, 1954

Wild, Roland, *Ranjitsinhji*, Rich & Cowan, London, 1934

Williams, Charles, *Bradman: An Australian hero*, Little Brown, London, 1996

Writer, Larry, *Winning: Face to face with Australian sporting legends*, Ironbark, Sydney, 1990

Wynne-Thomas, Peter, *'Give Me Arthur': A biography of Arthur Shrewsbury*, Arthur Barker, London, 1985

Yardley, Norman, *Cricket Campaigns*, Stanley Paul, London, 1950

ACKNOWLEDGEMENTS

If you can't be playing cricket, reading about it is not a bad way to spend your days. It's incumbent on me, therefore, to thank Richard Smart for coming up with the idea from which this book germinated and for his able editorial assistance. David Frith's contribution of the foreword continues a valued friendship begun when he published an unsolicited story of mine sixteen years ago: his prodigious knowledge and unflagging industry still provide me with an inspiriting example. Where my own resources fell short, I was able to rely on the good offices of David Studham at the Melbourne Cricket Library, with its happy society of volunteers. For much of the time, in fact, the library was officially in storage, awaiting its move into the refurbished stadium. Yet it never seemed to bother David how many boxes we needed to move in order that I have the right book: he is a prince among men.

I'd like to acknowledge my debt, principally, to the works of the following writers (in alphabetical order): David Allen, Peter Allen, Dennis Amiss and Michael Carey, Jeff Apter, John Arlott, Michael Atherton, Trevor Bailey,

Acknowledgements

Alex Bannister, Jack Bannister, Ralph Barker, Greg Baum, Alec and Eric Bedser, Eric Beecher, Richie Benaud, Dickie Bird, David Boon, Allan Border, Mihir Bose, Ian Botham, Bill Bowes, Geoffrey Boycott, Ian Brayshaw, Mike Brearley, Gerald Brodribb, Freddie Brown, Lionel H. Brown, Handasyde Buchanan, Keith Butler, John Callaghan, Neville Cardus, J.A.H Catton, Greg Chappell, Ian Chappell, Frank Chester, Brian Close, Colin Cowdrey, D.K. Darling, Alan Davidson, Mike Denness, Phil Derriman, Ted Dexter, E.W. Docker, Christopher Douglas, Frances Edmonds, Bill Edrich, Jack Egan, Godfrey Evans, W.H. Ferguson, Jack Fingleton, Duncan Fletcher, David Foot, Frank R. Foster, Tony Francis, Angus Fraser, David Frith, C.B. Fry, Mark Gateley, George Giffen, Adam Gilchrist, Arthur Goldman, Graham Gooch, Sir Home Gordon, Darren Gough, David Gower, W.G. Grace, Tony Greig, Wally Grout, Greg Growden, Walter Hammond, Lord Harris, Neil Harvey, Lord Hawke, Neil Hawke, Ian Healy, Alan Hill, Jack Hobbs, David Hookes, H.W. Hordern, Gerald Howat, Len Hutton, Frank Iredale, Garth Jaggard, C.L.R. James, Douglas Jardine, Gilbert Jessop, Ian Johnson, Dean Jones, Patrick Keane, Frank Keating, Alan Knott, Jim Laker, Alan Lamb, Harold Larwood, Frank Laver, Bill Lawry, Geoff Lawson, David Lemmon, A.A. Lilley, Ray Lindwall, David Lloyd, Charlie Macartney, Colin McCool, Craig McDermott, Alan McGilvray, Glenn McGrath, Adrian McGregor, Jack McHarg, Ken Mackay, Jeremy Mailes, Arthur Mailey, Ashley Mallett, Rod Marsh, Ronald

Mason, Peter May, Anthony Meredith, John Meyer, Keith Miller, J. Elliott Monfries, Don Mosey, A.G. Moyes, Patrick Murphy, Monty Noble, David Norrie, Bert Oldfield, Norm O'Neill, Bill O'Reilly, Michael Page, Cec Parkin, Tony Pawson, Ian Peebles, Kevin Perkins, Peter Philpott, Ricky Ponting, A.W. Pullin, Derek Randall, Ranjitsinhji, Mark Ray, Ian Redpath, Daniel Reese, Paul Reiffel, Vic Richardson, Paul Rigby, John Ringwood, Ray Robinson, Irving Rosenwater, Alan Ross, Jack Russell, Peter Sharpham, Rev. David Sheppard, Alan Shiell, Bob Simpson, Michael Slater, E.J. Smith, Peter Smith, Rick Smith, Terry Smith, John Snow, Keith Stackpole, Alec Stewart, Herbert Strudwick, Herbert Sutcliffe, E.W. Swanton, Allen Synge, Bob Taylor, Mark Taylor, Ben Travers, Donald Trelford, Alan Trengove, Fred Trueman, Robert Trumble, Phil Tufnell, C.T.B. Turner, Frank Tyson, Derek Underwood, Barry Valentine, Michael Vaughan, Fedrun de Vitre, Doug Walters, Shane Warne, P.F. Warner, Steve Waugh, Dirk Wellham, R.S. Whitington, Roland Wild, Charles Williams, Ron Williams, Larry Writer, Peter Wynne-Thomas and Norman Yardley.

The Australasian, *The Bulletin*, *Cricket of Today*, *The Cricketer*, *Cricketer International*, *Inside Edge*, *The Referee*, *Sporting Life*, *The Sporting Times*, *Sydney Sun*, *Wisden Cricket Monthly*, *Wisden Cricketers' Almanack* are also cited.

Gideon Haigh

Acknowledgements

I offer particular thanks to the following agents, copyright owners, estates, publishers, writers and various individuals, either for granting permission for extracts to be used, or for their valuable, much appreciated and patient assistance contacting copyright owners:

ABC Books (Sophie Higgins), Gary Allen, Allen & Unwin (Troy Henderson), Michaela Andreyev, Apple Books (Rick Smith), Eric Beecher, Richie Benaud, Mihir Bose, Mike Brearley, Carolyn Butler (for Alan McGilvray), Ronald Cardwell, Ian Chappell, Philip Derriman, Madonna Duffy (UQP), Jack Egan, John Fordham, Angus Fraser, Fremantle Arts Centre Press (Clive Newman), David Frith, Malcolm Gemmell (for Jack Fingleton), Greg Growden, Gideon Haigh, HarperCollins Australia and UK (Annette Renshaw and Laura Scott), Ros Heal, WACA, Alan Hill, Hodder & Stoughton UK (Jamie Cowen), Ed Jaggard, Geoff Lawson, Adrian McGregor, Jack McHarg, Mainstream Publishing (Bill Campbell), Ashley Mallet, Rod Marsh, Jim Maxwell, Methuen UK (Naomi Tummons), Marie Miller (for Keith Miller), Michael Page, Roger Page, Pan Macmillan Australia (Roxarne Burns), Penguin Books Australia and UK (Angela Crocombe and Rachel Atkinson), Kevin Perkins, Random House Australia (Nerrilee Weir), Jilly Robinson (for Ray Robinson), Robson Books (Jeremy Robson), Rosenberg Publishing (David Rosenberg), John Ross, Simon and Schuster Australia (Camilla Dorsch), Swan Sport (Austin Robertson), Norm Tasker, Donald Trelford, Steve Waugh, Niels Weise, PFD Theatre Department (for Ben Travers), Larry Writer, Peter Wynne-Thomas.

Full publishing details about all titles featured in the book can be found in the bibliography. Please direct any extract enquiries to me by email: rsppublish@primus online.com.au.

Finally, working on this book from the other side of the publishing oval has not only been a pleasure but also very instructive. And for that I thank Penguin Books' Claire de Medici, a fine example of the professionalism found in the flourishing Australian book publishing industry.

Richard Smart

The Penguin Book of Australian Sporting Anecdotes

Edited by
Richard Smart

Australians are sport-obsessed. We love to watch or play, to talk and read about, even to put our hard-earned money on, the 'game' and the players. Fans travel great distances to witness their favourite team in action. Families and friends are united or divided by their allegiance to particular competitors or codes.

In *The Penguin Book of Australian Sporting Anecdotes*, eight of Australia's greatest sports writers offer insights into ten of our favourite sports.

Jim Webster – Athletics, Golf, Swimming
Jim Martin – AFL
Grantlee Kieza – Boxing
Philip Derriman & David Frith – Cricket
Bill Whittaker – Horse racing
Alan Clarkson – Rugby league, Tennis
Greg Growden – Rugby union

All Out for One:
and Other Cricket Anecdotes

by
Ken Piesse

Tall tales and true from the game's biggest names –
Bradman, Gilchrist, Harvey, Miller, Ponting, Warne . . .

Awesome records
Billy Bowden's boots in the fridge
Centuries in the dark
Double hat-tricks
the **E**rrol Flynn of cricket
a **F**ourteen-ball over
Gems from Nugget
Hassett's billygoat
the **I**nvincibles
Jamaica, Tangles Walker and glass of rum
the **K**arachi crawl
Lessons from the Don
Merv Hughes in the Science lab
Net sessions from Hell
One-Test wonders
Ponting's wise grandma
Quips (classic)
Rescues from drowning
Sledging with a smile
Toothbrushing with Foster's
Underarms
Veivers' 90 overs in one innings
when **W**augh was a ring-in
Xavier Tras
Yankees
Zany occurrences on and off the field

You'll find all these and more in this highly entertaining,
alphabetical collection by renowned cricket writer Ken Piesse.